NATIONALISM AND IRONY

NATIONALISM AND IRONY

BURKE, SCOTT, CARLYLE

YOON SUN LEE

OXFORD
UNIVERSITY PRESS

2004

OXFORD

UNIVERSITY PRESS

Auckland Bangkok Buenos Aires Cape Town Chennai
Dar es Salaam Delhi Hong Kong Istanbul Karachi Kolkata
Kuala Lumpur Madrid Melbourne Mexico City Mumbai Nairobi
Sao Paulo Shanghai Taipei Tokyo Toronto

Copyright © 2004 by Oxford University Press, Inc.

Published by Oxford University Press, Inc.
198 Madison Avenue, New York, New York, 10016

www.oup.com

Library of Congress Cataloging-in-Publication Data
Lee, Yoon Sun
Nationalism and irony : Burke, Scott, Carlyle / Yoon Sun Lee
p. cm.
Includes bibliographical references and index.
ISBN 0-19-516235-8
1. English prose literature—19th century—History and criticism.
2. Literature and history—Great Britain—History. 3. English prose literature—
18th Century—History and criticism. 4. Burke, Edmund, 1729–1797—Knowledge—History.
5. Scott, Walter, Sir, 1771–1832—Knowledge—History 6. Carlyle, Thomas, 1795–1881—
Knowledge—History. 7. Burke, Edmund, 1729–1797—Political and social views.
8. Scott, Walter, Sir, 1771–1832—Political and social views. 9. Carlyle, Thomas, 1795–1881—
Political and social views. 10. Nationalism—Great Britain. 11. Nationalism in literature.
12. Irony in literature. I. Title.
PR778.H57N38 2004
828'.80809358—dc22   2003054452

1 3 5 7 9 8 6 4 2

Printed in the United States of America
on acid-free paper

For my parents

Acknowledgments

It is with the deepest pleasure that I tally my long, though far from complete, list of acknowledgments. Since this book began as a dissertation at Yale University, I wish to thank my friends and teachers there: particularly, my advisors, David Bromwich, who taught me to feel a proper astonishment at Edmund Burke, and Sandy Welsh, from whom I learned everything I know about Scott. For me they continue to remain trusted and revered figures. My sincere thanks to David Marshall and Bill Jewett for reading the dissertation. Ian Duncan must be thanked in a separate sentence for the characteristic generosity with which he has read, encouraged, and inspired my work over many years. Ina Ferris has been, as anyone who knows her will guess, kindness itself. I am grateful to her for the warm encouragement and support that she has offered all along, and for her patient, scrupulous readings of my "crab-wise" chapters. John Farrell continues to provide friendship, advice, and the very best conversation. I am indebted to John Plotz for his friendship, contagious enthusiasm, and the generous zeal with which he has read my work at important moments. I owe much to the writing groups that have helped improve and push this project forward through close community and careful readings: in particular, Audrey Bilger and the group at the Claremont Colleges, and Maria Davidis, Suzy Anger, and the Harvard group. At Wellesley College, I have found not only institutional support in the form of several Faculty Research Awards and a junior sabbatical leave, but also the friendship and mentoring that helped turn this project into an actual book. I wish to thank all my colleagues in the English Department for years of patient reading, tolerant listening, robust encouragement, skeptical questioning, wise guidance, and for the inspiration of their example—Margery Sabin, Bill Cain, Kate Brogan, Alison Hickey, Kathryn Lynch, Susan Meyer, Jim Noggle, Tim Peltason, Lisa Rodensky, Larry Rosenwald, Vernon Shetley, Marilyn Sides, Terry Tyler, Frank Bidart, Margaret Cezair-Thompson. I also wish to thank Ann Rowland, Sonia Hofkosh, Maureen McLane, and other members of the Romantic Literature Seminar at Harvard's Humanities Center for the opportunity to present work related to this project. I am grateful to my editor at Oxford, Elissa Morris, for her patient and continuous support, and to the anonymous readers for the press, whose comments greatly helped my revision.

Finally, there is my indebtedness to my family: to my parents, for their love and high expectations, to Hesun Kim, for her thoughts and prayers; to Yu Jin Ko, for understanding me so well, for space, time, validity, and pleasure; to Ji Min and Ji Hoon, for joy.

Contents

NATIONALISM AND IRONY

I

Public Irony, Conservatism, and the British Nation

With "a smile of good-humoured complacency," Maria Edgeworth's tale, *Castle Rackrent* (1800), declares itself in favor of the impending Union that was, by joining Ireland to its neighbor, to form what we now know as the United Kingdom.[1] An exemplary loyalty to the new nation seems to be promised by its narrator, the ancient Irishman Thady Quirk, who has faithfully served nearly four generations of Anglo-Irish masters. But his extravagantly professed devotion notwithstanding, Thady Quirk seems quite aware of his independent identity and interests. He begins his "Memoirs of the Rackrent Family" thus:

> I think it my duty to say a few words, in the first place, concerning myself.—My real name is Thady Quirk, though in the family I have always been known by no other than *'honest Thady'*—afterwards . . . I remember to hear them calling me *'old Thady;'* and now I'm come to *'poor Thady'*—for I wear a long great coat, winter and summer, which is very handy, as I never put my arms in the sleeves (they are as good as new), though, come Holantide next, I've had it these seven years; it holds on by a single button round my neck, cloak fashion—to look at me, you would hardly think 'poor Thady' was the father of attorney Quirk; he is a high gentleman . . . but I wash my hands of his doings, and as I have lived so will I die, true and loyal to the family.[2]

This loyal servant's identity proves as mystifying and as riddled with contradictions as his discourse. He has always had the same name, he asserts, though it has changed.[3] And what is the basis of his present name? Neither land nor forebears, but apparently, in some fashion, his great-coat. The coat grounds and secures his identity. It signifies his poverty and his secret resourcefulness (the sleeves are "as good as new"). It conceals the alarming truth that Thady is the father of attorney Quirk, who has exploited his masters' weaknesses in order to purchase the Rackrent estate for himself. Thady could well be independent. Yet Thady's adherence to this costume publicly signifies his intention to remain where he is, socially as well as spatially. For its conservatism, Thady's decision to remain in his place would have been highly welcome to a state fighting a war with revolutionary France and suppressing rebellions at home. For its irony, Thady's declaration of dependence would have appealed to subjects who privately objected to the state's conduct on both fronts.

Through Thady's example we can glimpse the value, "winter and summer," of an equivocal, ironic form of allegiance to a larger "family." In a mock-serious footnote placed at the bottom of the page, Edgeworth suggests that Thady's cloak played an important role in Ireland's national past and that it may continue to do so in the future. Quoting from Edmund Spenser's *View of the State of Ireland* (1633), she notes that while "'most nations of the world antiently used the mantle . . . [and] it seemeth that the mantle was a general habit to most nations,'" the mantle bears a particular significance in Ireland, where "'it is a fit house for an outlaw, a meet bed for a rebel, and an apt cloak for a thief.'"[4] At the same time the mantle seems to transcend nationality, according to Spenser, and also to signify Ireland's particular case as a nation frustratingly difficult for the English to colonize. By referring to the Irish mantle not as a harmless covering but as a refuge for lawlessness, Spenser shows how Ireland cannot, within the limits of his colonial discourse, be recognized as a legitimate nation. In Edgeworth's footnote, the cloak's semantic shiftiness itself functions as a sign for the indeterminacy of nationhood: some nations such as Great Britain can be acknowledged while others such as Ireland cannot. The difference reflects only the contingent outcomes of political struggle. On another level, by quoting this passage about the mantle or habit, Edgeworth slyly puns on a crucial theme of the conservative discourse that Edmund Burke, another Irishman, had inaugurated a decade earlier. In his counterrevolutionary manifesto, *Reflections on the Revolution in France* (1790), Burke had used the metaphor of "habit" to defend proudly the irrational character of the British constitution and of prejudice attached to it. Burke argued that patriotic feelings were linked more to habit and acculturation than to reason. Yet perhaps remembering Ireland, he also punned on the other meanings of habit as fashion, covering, or external guise deliberately assumed. While Burke extols the way in which a common culture molds its members, the nation's deep shaping power also turns out to be something that can be doffed almost at will.[5] Thady's cloak thus deserves the attention Edgeworth gives it. It signifies Britain's desire to see itself as a natural object of loyalty, while, at the same time, suggesting all that is adventitious, artificial, and contentious about the nation and the civic feelings it demands. Like his cloak, Thady's loyal feelings can apparently be of a piece and yet shelter other tendencies not exactly conducive to British unity or stability.

In the period studied by this book, the half-century between 1790 and the mid-1840s, Britain placed a premium on the display of loyal feelings: on the civic emotions which were to keep the nation's parts in their places. These civic emotions were feelings held about the state, its symbols, traditions, history, and one's given place within it. The forces of derangement and disaffection were many. They included the practices of a long-established commercial society, inclined to view relationships, persons, and things as entities negotiable in the marketplace. To these habits were added new revolutionary doctrines that preached equality and the emptiness of artificial distinctions. Closer to home, radical denunciations of government as abusive imposture, as mere magic shows, tried to remove the awe that might have kept subjects where they had been placed.[6] To the social conservatives who still dominated British politics, to belong to the nation meant not so much to participate in a horizontal formation as to occupy a specific place within a larger, hierarchical whole: a place defined by geography as well as by social class and gender, a place not chosen by those who held it. Romantic nationalism's challenge was to assert the stern necessity of these differences while insisting on the unity and, at some level, the fraternity of the nation. Its mandate was to discover the ideas and emotions that could keep these parts in their subordinate places, in spite of the myths of equality, liberty, and uniform character offered explicitly or implicitly by British nationalism. One of Romantic nationalism's achievements, this book argues, was the rediscovery of irony's civic potential. Inheriting an earlier tradition of Tory satire, but reflecting the uneven economic development and cultural nationalism that had transformed Britain's peripheries in the eighteenth century, important non-English conservatives like Edmund Burke, Walter Scott, and Thomas Carlyle explored irony's capacious address.[7] Irony could acknowledge the anomalies of Britain's identity, structure, and relation to its own past. Most significantly, it could at this moment not only inflect the expression but also license the experience of particular types of feeling beneficial to the state. A nationalism allied with irony could speak to those left unmoved by ideologies that took for granted spontaneous, deep attachment to a whole that was unproblematically given.

As the following chapters of this study will show, Romantic Britain's ironic nationalism explored the correspondences between civic emotions and the discourse of theatrical experience, between patriotism and the marketplace, between conservatism and fetish-worship. It promoted a deliberate indifference to the contradictions between discourses that stressed fixed, incommensurable, native values and those that saw value as contingent and commensurable, a projection of subjective whim or fluctuating collective demand.[8] Irony both questioned and upheld the nation's claim to be an entity bequeathing itself to itself, a whole that necessarily gave meaning to its parts. Thus, ironic nationalism could capitalize on awareness of the contingencies that had formed the pseudounity of Great Britain out of groups with separate identities, interests, and histories.[9] More broadly, irony could be used to temper and to meet demands for individuals, classes, and cultural nations to subordinate themselves to a greater, hierarchically ordered whole. Irony also kept alive claims about the possibility of individual choice and agency, even as it disavowed them. In the public and private writings of conservatives like Burke, Scott, and Carlyle, irony often manifests itself through a disturbingly conspicuous social deference—a self-serving, self-conscious deference possessed of an indeterminate political meaning.[10] Acts of assent to national authorities could be performed so as to emphasize their radical contingency. To bow before a person or an image claiming to represent the nation could be done not so much out of a pure intuitive feeling, a sense of legitimacy, or an apprehension of truth, though elements of these might be present, but more from something less exalted: a mastery of convention and a politic sense of the unique pressures of the moment as they intersect with one's independent interests. Even as it publicly affirmed one's place within the national whole, such ironic deference could strongly suggest that no position was fixed, no identity was permanent or true.

Walter Scott gives us a curious illustration of such equivocal, self-cancelling deference in his account of another nation vital to Britain's self-definition, the nation that Burke called "gentis incunabula nostrae," the source of English manners: France. In 1815, finally under British sway, the French capital was occupied by British troops; its new monarch, Louis XVIII, could even possibly be compared, according to the *Quarterly Review*, to "a sovereign chosen in this country, like a Lord Mayor, by acclamation of the good citizens of London."[11] Paris thus becomes for the moment imaginable as a version of London, and in its streets the following pageant is enacted. In Scott's words:

> A man . . . was condemned to death, to whom it had been resolved to extend the royal pardon, and the king imagined . . . that he had nothing to do but issue one from his chancery. But no—that would have been to defraud the public of their share in the scene. So he was advised to go (by pure accident,) in the course of his evening drive, into some remote corner of the city, where he was to meet (also accidentally) with the municipality, who were to fall on their knees, and beg mercy for this delinquent, which the king was then to grant with characteristic grace and bounty, and all the bystanders were to shout *Vive le Roi*.[12]

The focal point of Scott's verbal irony is found within his parentheses; the course of the king's drive reflects not "pure accident" but careful scheming. The crowd's actions are likewise choreographed, at least in anticipation. But a much larger irony pervades this scene: while the king naively imagines that he has the power to act, the actual agent who directs this scene is never named. The ominous excessiveness of the municipality's deference seems to signify this critical vagueness. While the behavior of the actors is only pseudo-accidental, the cynicism of the passage points toward a genuine contingency in the location of power. For the duration of one imagined scene, by popular demand, the monarch officially represents the nation.[13] But the very eagerness with which the crowd takes up its theatrical role hints that the petitioners may in fact confer authority rather than merely recognizing it. By theatricalizing their sentimental celebration of the king, these citizens transform the nature of their self-submission. Indeed, the mob's power could hardly be more strikingly displayed than in this scene of whimsical deference. The scene's irony gestures toward the conditions under which Romantic conservatism in Britain, too, had to make its appeals for patriotic feeling. Irony could reveal and legitimate the connections between incompatible knowledges, contradictory feelings, and competing interests. This study explores the different ways in which the conjunction of patriotic fervor with irony opened the way for Romantic subjects to see their own nationalism as both nature and disguise, habit and fashion, and their nation as both manufactured artifact and transcendental reality. Romantic Britain could thus conceive of itself less as a perfect unity than as a tense, tactful convergence of opposing tendencies—as a frangible, imperfect, and heterogeneous whole held together by a web of convention.

The Ground of Nationalism

While patriotic sentiments obviously have a much longer history, the beginnings of modern nationalism are generally traced to the decades following the French Revolution. In its simplest definition as a modern ideology, nationalism is, in Ernest Gellner's words, the "political principle, which holds that the political and national unit should be congruent."[14] More recently, it has been defined as "collective action designed to render the boundaries of the nation congruent with those of its governance unit."[15] In recent theoretical discussions, and perhaps even from the moment it emerged as a recognizable ideology, nationalism has stimulated in its observers, if not always in its practitioners, a critical self-examination of modernity. Especially if modernity is understood broadly as a movement toward rationalized, contractual relations between individuals and institutions, nationalism raises troubling questions about how far or how deep such a trend can go. For every so-called civic nationalism that defines national belonging in legal and political, participatory terms, there seems to be an "ethnic" form of nationalism asserting that "[t]he national bond is subconscious and emotional rather than conscious and rational," based on "the sense of shared blood."[16] The jury still seems to be out on whether such "ethnonationalism" is a meaningless atavistic reflex or whether it proceeds with an ominous dialectical necessity from the very nature of the capitalist marketplace, offering in compensation for impoverished human relationships and eroded communities "new and immensely richer sources of identity," in one theorist's words—so rich, in fact, as sometimes to inspire self-sacrifice, genocide, or both.[17]

Perhaps because of its equivocal relationship to modernity, nationalism has also provided scholars with a place from which to examine anew the intersections of fiction, consciousness, and politics. In his influential essay, "DissemiNation," for example, Homi Bhabha considers how "the nation speaks its disjunctive narrative" through a double discourse; it constructs itself through a "pedagogical" discourse that derives a continuous identity from a past origin, but also through a "performative" strategy that endlessly pursues the attempt to signify the nation "as contemporaneity."[18] Through the study of nationalism, phrases such as "the invention of tradition" and "imagined communities" have become commonplace in the discussion of history and literature.[19] While not all its observers agree with Benedict Anderson in seeing nations as fabricated but not for that reason "false," nationalism has proved fascinating to many for the way that it seems to offer a unique stance in which skepticism and credulity can coexist productively. Nationalism's adherents seem to be capable of believing in national myths and celebrating supposed national traditions, even while suspecting them to be false in one case and of recent vintage in the other. One commentator suggests that perhaps the very sense of colluding with the state in producing and living by the fictions of nationalism can lend a community further solidarity.[20] In this way, some theorists of nationalism, including Benedict Anderson and Terry Eagleton, have themselves been pointing the way toward the concept of irony, though the term has not always been invoked.[21] It should be remarked that this view represents something of a departure from what has been called the "orthodox theory of nationalism," which stresses singleminded, deep, and potentially violent emotional attachment to the idea of a national community.[22]

In the particular context of Romantic Britain, traditionally thought of as extending from 1789 to around 1832 (though the boundaries of the period are constantly being questioned and redefined), nationalism has been viewed along more orthodox lines. Numerous important studies have argued that British Romantic nationalism relies primarily on "biologizing" ideas of citizenship and nationality, making these appear to be part of a "natural" order, and depicting the nation as an organic entity deeply rooted in instinctive emotional relationships between people and the land.[23] With increasing frequency, Edmund Burke is cited as one of the first and most influential figures to have articulated this vision of the British nation. Burkean Romantic nationalism has been criticized for turning its back on the modernizing forces of industrial capital that in fact sustained the British nation, presenting instead an archaic vision of the nation as, in one critic's words, "a patriarchal tribe, motivated by an instinctual love of kin that spreads out into loyalty for the national kind."[24] Marilyn Butler and others have shown how this counterrevolutionary nationalism depended on the zealous promotion (and policing) of domesticity and family life in the 1790s.[25] More recently, there has developed another fruitful line of enquiry into cultural nationalism or nationalism devoted to establishing a separate cultural identity rather than political autonomy. Focusing on the cultural nationalism of Scotland, Ireland, and Wales, Katie Trumpener has argued that writers from this colonized "Celtic periphery," even more so than English writers, stressed the organic quality of their own nations, trying to reinvest their lands with the distinctive characters, voices, and histories that had been overlooked or even systematically eradicated by Enlightenment "improvers" and capitalists.[26] To defy the imperializing policies and discourses that occupied, exploited, and maligned their lands and tried to erase local differences in the name of modernization, Celtic writers presented their national communities and feelings as rooted in nature.[27] Thus, the naturalizing impulse of Romantic nationalism, condemned when exercised in the service of imperial domination, is vindicated here by seeing it as an act of colonial resistance. Nevertheless, Trumpener's theoretical model of Romantic nationalism still assumes the primacy of what the literary theorist Mikhail Bakhtin has described as the genre of the "idyll": the depiction of a "small but secure and stable little world of the family, where nothing is foreign, or accidental or incomprehensible," a world that is "organic[ally] . . . graft[ed] . . . to a familiar territory."[28]

But besides the strident emphasis on family, home, and attachment to the land, there are other voices within the rich mixture of British Romantic nationalism—sometimes within the very same texts and even, in the case of Edmund Burke, within the confines of one sentence. Burke and the writers who most closely follow him often explore the ironic production of feeling as a necessary supplement to and sometimes even substitute for spontaneous emotion. Burke, of course, celebrates the quasi spontaneity of second nature, and the ways in which a cultural collectivity generates traditions, habits, and structures of feeling. But Burke and others like him also reveal how emotions, particularly those expected from subalterns, may require not only the insensible interposition of cultural agency but also an active struggle to renounce one's own agency and to suspend one's disbelief. This is particularly the case when emotions of veneration are involved. Carlyle, for instance, memorably finds his most powerful feelings elicited not by the figure of the father, but by his empty clothes: "[t]he Hat . . . Coat-arm . . . the Breeches . . . Waistcoat," the purely conventional signifiers of patriarchal authority, gathered together by chance in an old-clothes stall.[29] Strong sentiment may as easily be felt for an object of momentary contrivance as for something supposedly given by nature. Toward the land as well, an awareness of contrivance seems capable of adding piquancy to emotional claims of attachment. Maria Edgeworth gives us two suggestive anecdotes, added to the 1810 edition of *Castle Rackrent*, that hint at quite a different way of viewing the physical basis of the nation. In Ireland "some years ago," Edgeworth remarks, two landowners were disputing the boundaries of their properties. "[A]n old tenant of Mr. M's cut a *sod* [from his master's land] and inserted it in a spot prepared for its reception [in the disputed territory]. . . . The old man who was to give his evidence as to the property, stood upon the inserted sod when the *viewers* came and swore that the ground he *then stood upon* belonged to his landlord."[30] In another anecdote, the Duke of Sussex, visiting an Irish seminary in Rome, is invited to make good his Irish title and his connection to that country by standing on a shovelful of dirt brought from Ireland.[31] Apparently intended to illustrate a colonial joke about Irish shrewdness, these anecdotes bear in fascinating ways on the nature of nationalist claims about identity and loyalty and the ground of such feelings. In both these cases, the truth of the asserted connection to the land rests on the literal detachment of the piece of ground, its risibly stark manipulation or relocation. It seems as though the land has to be cut off, crudely delimited in some fashion before it can be sworn to be one's own. But is the part being used in good faith to represent the whole? It seems likelier that an ironic as well as a literal detachment is being performed, in which the fragment is facetiously substituted for the whole. While it is obviously true in a literal sense that the peasant and the peer stand on and swear by "Irish ground," this truth is undeniably equivocal. It forces us to rethink our assumptions about what "the ground" of a nation, its extent, and its provenance need to be. The equivocation, moreover, stems directly from the nature of the situation: these claims are not being made within the idyllic context of the family but within a context of legal and political wrangling over the power to possess and to represent the land. Finally, Edgeworth's anecdotes provide an allegory of a broader type of irony. If we take the ground in these stories as a metaphor for certainty, Edgeworth suggests that the avowal of attachment to one's land rests on a perilously (or ludicrously) narrow grounding of truth: true here and now, perhaps, but not for all time.

Edgeworth's anecdotes, however suggestive, are themselves a slender basis on which to rest any assertion about British Romantic nationalism. But several recent historical studies also point the way toward seeing British patriotism in this period as more pragmatic than dogmatic. Nationalism may have functioned as a way of acting and talking used to frame an event, to make things happen as well as to understand what has happened.[32] Given the anomalous semi-independence of Scotland and Ireland within the British nation, and the agitations of social groups for various kinds of social and political reform, the project of uniting Britons into one imagined community had to tactfully accommodate diverse interests. Linda Colley and Marilyn Morris, among others, have shown how unifying symbols were forged and creatively revised in order to create a common British identity.[33] But nationalist ideas were also strategically manipulated by distinct groups and classes in order to further their own separate interests. Such groups could claim to participate in a common British identity in order to demand (somewhat inconsistently) to be recognized and treated as different.[34] For some conservatives, the awareness of these complex webs of interests within which nationalist discourse functioned could lead to anxiety about whether patriotic avowals were merely performances. Could they be less than sincere? Could the king's health and the country's unity be celebrated ironically? The counterrevolutionary *Anti-Jacobin* (1797–98), for example, complained that "Half-indications of something which is never thoroughly explained" are "the very soul of Reforming Societies, from the Whigs . . . to the United Irishmen."[35] Winks, hints, arch looks, and odd gestures suggested the presence of irony. A patriotic Liverpool printer writing to John Reeves, organizer of the loyalist Association for the Preservation of Liberty and Property, warns more explicitly:

> I think it necessary for the Friends of the King to keep an eye upon his Enemies. They are subtle and designing. . . . They know themselves weak in number, and therefore act by strategem on all occasions.—They are the first in all mixed companies to drink the "King and Constitution," but it is easy to discover by their *looks* and *motions* to each other, that they do it in derision only.[36]

In a classic if somewhat clumsy case of verbal irony, these false patriots appear to mean the opposite of what they say in public.

Non-English conservatives like Burke, Scott, and Carlyle redefined Romantic nationalism broadly and inventively so as to make a place within rather than outside it for these and other types of irony. Even as they spoke of instinctual attachments, feelings, and actions, their representations of the British nation were far from idyllic or sentimental. Like the Irishmen in Edgeworth's anecdotes and like Edgeworth herself, these writers understood that the act of avowing deep attachment to land or community could be something quite other than a spontaneous expression of a natural sense of belonging, even if it was capable of producing such feelings in the end. Rather, such an avowal was a political act performed in a situation configured by law, power, and competing interests. Unlike Reeves's printer, they did not try to distinguish irony from legitimate patriotism. This is not to say that they openly celebrated duplicity or insincerity; in fact, Burke's and Carlyle's reputations largely rested on the passion with which they attacked public hypocrisy. But instead of assuming that the coherence of a nation or of nationalism as a discourse rested on a static, internal homogeneity of elements, they saw national wholeness as an ideal invoked and sometimes achieved through numberless daring acts of equivocation.

Romantic Irony and the National Whole

To some modern theorists and to some Romantic observers, irony appears to exist in an unacknowledged but oddly intimate relationship to nationalism. But how does irony in situations like those described by Reeves's correspondent differ from simple political disaffection? Does irony just mark the outer limit of nationalism, the point at which nationalism ceases to be believed and starts to be regarded skeptically? Or can irony be seen as more closely involved, in its origins and structure, with the modern discourse of nationalism? This section argues that some particular explorations of irony were not merely contemporaneous with modern nationalism but in fact offered overlapping investigations of similar themes. One of its chief disseminators in Britain, Thomas Carlyle, developed the discourse of Romantic irony so that it could represent the anomalous subordination of some groups (the non-English, the working classes) to others within the national whole.

Irony has traditionally been regarded as a verbal or rhetorical device: saying one thing when you mean something else—complimenting someone, for instance, on a virtue which he pointedly does not possess.[37] Some have seen this type of verbal irony more broadly as what characterizes literary as opposed to ordinary use of language: even if it is not strictly allegorical, a poem carries more and other meanings than the sum of what its words literally mean.[38] More recent critics have been interested in the "trans-ideological" uses of verbal irony: how it can be used to subvert or to reinforce political ideas, and how, when it succeeds, irony attests to a discursive community's existence. Irony is still understood in this case as the transmission of unspoken meanings on the one hand and the collection of unvoiced intentions on the other.[39] But in the same historical moment that saw the rise of modern nationalism, the concept of irony was being explored and applied in other ways. Some European writers saw irony not just as a special case of communication but as a mentality that responded to the political contradictions of the moment, the bewildering succession of rulers, states, and ideologies on the historical stage of what Benjamin Constant called "our century."[40] Constant is one important example. He saw irony as the dominant cultural characteristic of modern commercial society in an age of revolution and nationalism. Derived from the discourse of the Scottish Enlightenment, his ideas converge neatly with the perspective of writers such as Scott. And theories of irony developed by German Romantics, including Friedrich Schlegel, make their way back to England at the hands of Thomas Carlyle, who, perhaps more than any other single figure, was responsible for introducing such ideas to the British reading public.

In his tract, *On the Spirit of Conquest and Usurpation and their Relation to European Civilization* (1814), Benjamin Constant focuses on the bizarre collusion of the French public with Napoleon's projects for imperial France. This collusion, he insists, is equivocal; it contains a private mockery that belies the approbation publicly expressed. Noting the "pretended sanctions, those monotonous congratulations" routinely offered for Napoleon's military victories, he labels them "a singular kind of artifice, which fools nobody! Contrived comedy, which impresses nobody. . . . Everyone thinks to regain through mockery the honour of independence and, satisfied with disavowing his actions by his words, is at ease in belying his words by his actions."[41] Here, irony consists not in a completed circuit of tacit communication but rather in a private disaffection stemming from the desire to see oneself as skeptical or independent. These private disavowals run parallel to each other rather than converging. "Everyone thinks to regain through mockery the honour of independence," but that independence fails to become collective, even as an illusion. The unvoiced dissent that Constant detects has to do with the particular, highly militaristic nationalism fostered by the Napoleonic regime. As Walter Scott remarks, "Through the abuse of this sentiment . . . Napoleon was enabled to consolidate his usurped government. . . . Did the people ask for bread?—he showed them a temple. Did they require of him the blood of their children?—he detailed to them a victory." Thus, according to Scott, Napoleon himself trained the French in a certain kind of irony, teaching them to become "indifferent to the distinction betwixt what is unreal and what is solid."[42] Constant views this indifference as the self-protective response of a society dominated by the exchange of commodities. Following the analysis of commercial society offered by Scottish Enlightenment writers such as Adam Ferguson, Constant argues that "the infinite and complex ramifications of commerce have placed the interest of societies beyond the frontiers of their own territory; the spirit of the age triumphs over the narrow and hostile spirit that men seek to dignify with the name of patriotism."[43] Transactions that are felt to matter occur between individuals or corporate entities that are independent of states. Narrow self-interest, somewhat paradoxically, leads to disregard for the narrow boundaries of nations. "Commerce has brought men together and has given them virtually identical customs and habits," a common nature that is peaceful, diffident, acquisitive, hedonistic, driven only by the "desire for pleasure."[44] "[A] great mass of human beings now exist that, despite the different names under which they live . . . are essentially homogeneous in nature."[45] The nation is merely a name; nation and empire alike are "abstract notions that have no reality"; "[i]ndividuals . . . detach themselves from a fatherland that they can nowhere see. Its entirety becomes a matter of indifference."[46] The call to national spirit becomes meaningless, an affront to what Constant calls "the spirit of the age" or "the age of commerce."[47] The globalized human nature that transcends national boundaries appears to be an ironic one, however, for Constant reiterates that public collusion with the state's demands symptomizes a deep private indifference:

"their enthusiasm contains a bizarre mixture of analysis and mockery. They seem, lacking much faith in their own convictions, to be trying . . . to stupefy themselves with acclamations and relieve themselves by raillery, and to anticipate the moment when the glory will be past."[48] The irony that marks the age here appears as a vertiginous self-dissociation from an act of political assent. It covertly anticipates the demise of nations even while it outwardly participates in nationalist enthusiasm. "Our century, that . . . opposes its irony to every real or feigned enthusiasm, could not content itself with a sterile glory," Constant argues.[49] But irony freely licenses the feigning of enthusiasm. Irony thus appears as a means by which the dubious whole of a nation is held together, at least in show.

German Romantic writers such as Friedrich Schlegel also treat irony as a sign of a collective dilemma, though at first glance a less explicitly political one. Romantic irony, as practiced and theorized by the Schlegels, Schleiermacher, and others in the *Athenaeum* (1798–1800), manifests, in Anne Mellor's definition, an "all-important consciousness of the limitations of human knowledge and of human language."[50] This type of irony is often linked by critics to a philosophical understanding of absolute reality as chaotic flux. Irony, it is claimed, manifests this insight through aesthetic forms, such as the fragment, that make no claim either to be self-identical or to represent a totality — claims that would be fallacious in light of the ceaseless becoming that is reality.[51] Thus, discussions of Romantic irony have tended to focus on the relations between consciousness, nature, language, and art, considered rather abstractly.[52] But in the *Athenaeum* and in Schlegel's *Critical Fragments*, which have been placed among its most important theoretical formulations, Romantic irony provides a code for exploring not only the abstract limitations of language or knowledge but also the very practical problem of conscious self-subordination to a larger whole. Romantic irony shows a concern for establishing the boundaries of the self that converges in some ways with Constant's diagnosis of modern nations.[53] In Schlegel's terse aphorisms, irony may explore the potential dilemma of feeling self-sufficient, unlimited, or superior to the whole that commands your subordination.[54] This discourse takes up a variety of detailed social and historical contexts not fully explored by its leading twentieth-century theorists. Romantic irony, in fact, seems to prove useful for the way in which it connects the banal to the sublime, the aesthetic to the political. It mediates in the sense described by Fredric Jameson as "a code . . . [that] can be used about two distinct phenomena."[55] Among numerous fragments that discuss national character (French, English, German), revolutions, gender difference, wit, friendship, and many other subjects, we find this typical reference in *Athenaeum* fragment 362 to irony as a way of simultaneously achieving and negating the banal goal of social acceptability: the "extraordinarily intelligent man" can only make himself acceptable to a group by exercising "the irony that might cause him to raise himself consciously outside his intelligence and, by renouncing it, offer himself up as one of nature's creatures to whatever use society may find for him."[56] Irony manifests itself here as an arch deference that can mitigate the envy of less intelligent peers. In many other fragments, too, irony carries with it the notion of equivocal self-resignation to a larger *social* whole as well as to a metaphysical whole.[57] This larger social whole possesses its own intentions and follows its own logic in assigning the subject a place and a function. But to be able to resign oneself consciously to a subordinate position implies a mastery or an "agility" that gainsays the justice and even the practicability of such subjection.[58] As Schlegel remarks, "one can only restrict oneself at those points and places where one possesses infinite power."[59] One can only view self-restriction in such a light by radically eliminating a social context composed of other minds, wishes, and powers. A discussion of "perfect practical genius" also notes that such a character "never makes a futile attempt to escape the recognized limitations of the moment, and yet always burns with a longing to augment himself still further."[60] As in *Athenaeum* fragment 362, irony proposes this paradox: that resigning oneself consciously to be merely a limited part of a greater whole indicates a capacity, and most likely a desire, to be something more than just a subordinate part. Irony declares a highly conditional dependence.

Irony's political implications emerge when the abstract concept of the part takes on a concrete character. Just as easily as an aesthetic or formal part, it may be a person, a nation or a subnation that is endowed with the consciousness of its own power and invited to use that power through self-restriction. Perhaps what is ultimately at stake in these fragments about irony is an idea of agency analogous to the one embodied in the "revolutionary democratic" idea of the nation: the belief that a nation comes about when "sovereign citizens" come together to determine their own laws and form of government.[61] The idea that sovereignty rightfully belonged to the citizen-parts of a nation was used to challenge the legitimacy of existing governments. Without declaring a revolutionary challenge to a social whole, Schlegel's assertion that "one can only restrict oneself at those points . . . where one possesses infinite power" recalls the logic of the general will. According to Rousseau, even if a dissenting individual is forced to accept the majority's will, that restriction, in fact, testifies to his power and freedom, since he too, whatever his subjective belief, is a part of the sovereign, self-determining nation. But the whole, in Romantic irony, is not secured by a fiction of itself per se; it is only held together by the tense, tacit self-resignation of its parts. This mode of unity differs also from that envisioned by eighteenth-century political economy, which had seen harmony emerging from the unregulated behavior of subjects in civil society.[62]

Thomas Carlyle, who begins to publish in the late 1820s, acknowledges throughout his career his intellectual indebtedness not only to the German idealist philosopher Fichte, whose ideas were critical to the development of modern nationalism, but also to the Schlegels, Novalis, and especially Jean-Paul Richter, the leading theorists and practitioners of Romantic irony. Carlyle starts his career translating, reviewing, and explaining these unfamiliar writers to the British reading public, and many of these early essays treat various aspects of Romantic irony that Carlyle will himself use in works like *Sartor Resartus* (1829–1831).[63] Reviewing Richter's novels, for example, Carlyle notes with feigned shock and genuine admiration how the author deliberately shatters the aesthetic illusion he has created: Richter's novels are "interlaced with epigrammatic breaks, vehement bursts, or sardonic turns, interjections, quips, puns, and even oaths!"[64] In these essays, we can see Carlyle treating Romantic irony as an experiment in stretching conventional ideas of wholeness. Richter's novels clearly fail to satisfy classical standards of aesthetic unity; however, they put into play new types of wholeness.[65] Taking his insight further, Carlyle formulates the workings of Romantic irony in ways distinctly applicable to the British nation. For example, he observes of Richter's novels: "it is rare that any one of them leaves on us the impression of a perfect, homogeneous, indivisible whole. . . . Richter's works do not always bear sufficient marks of having been in *fusion*; yet neither are they merely *riveted* together . . . they have been *welded*."[66] By moving from the Coleridgean metaphor of *fusion* to that of *riveting* and then the compromise third term of *welding*, Carlyle envisions a new manufactured rather than organic kind of wholeness: an intentional pseudosynthesis in which the seams remain partially visible. His choice of metaphors draws attention to the industrial capitalism that linked Britain's increasingly hostile social classes together—the material basis that Romantic nationalism is often charged with concealing beneath its idyllic visions. Taken together with his attention to the fragmented condition of Germany (in his essay, "The State of German Literature" and elsewhere), Carlyle's discussion of Richter's Romantic irony provides a language capable of representing the British nation as something other than "a perfect, homogeneous, indivisible whole."[67]

Romantic irony constructs potential bridges between political and aesthetic entities in ways rich in implications for the discourse of nationalism. It permits Schlegel, for instance, to articulate a highly qualified endorsement of a political ideal in the guise of a literary one:

> Many works that are praised for the beauty of their coherence have less unity than a motley heap of ideas simply animated by the ghost of a spirit and aiming at a single purpose. What really holds the latter together is that free and equal fellowship in which, so the wise men assure us, the citizens of the perfect state will live at some future date.[68]

There is a self-conscious wit in the comparison between the parts of a literary work and the citizens of a state. Schlegel seems to adopt an ironic deference toward "the wise men," who see this unity just around the corner, and their credulous believers. However, he seems to do this in order to draw skepticism away from the very ideal of "free and equal fellowship" that is being upheld by these same wise men. This mock-deference draws irony away from the analogy between the perfect political state and the perfect aesthetic creation. Their conjunction seems merely to evidence a continuity that was there all along: both state and aesthetic creation imagine their antitheses as "motley heaps." As a kind of bracketing in time and attitude, irony lets Schlegel preserve this ideal unity in a state of temporary negation, awaiting a future when it can be believed and realized politically. Aesthetically, this free and equal fellowship might be achieved in the present; a skillfully composed novel, for example, could allow its parts to enjoy a simultaneous independence and solidarity. But where the polis is concerned, subordinate parts need to keep vital ideas like equality alive, even while appearing to disavow them.[69]

How Carlyle uses irony to limn the anomalous nature of the British nation becomes more apparent in his essay on the Scottish poet, Robert Burns, written for the *Edinburgh Review* in 1828. Standing in this essay for Scotland itself, Burns's life comes to illustrate ironic self-subordination to the greater whole of Anglo-Britain. But in a further twist, that larger whole remains complacently oblivious to the exercise of such irony and the infinite power that should thereby have been made manifest. Both Burns and Scotland possess a double nature in Carlyle's essay. On the one hand, both are self-contained and complete in themselves. Scotland is "our own stern Motherland . . . [a] venerable structure of social and moral Life, which Mind has through long ages been building up for us there."[70] Burns himself, the poet of Scotland, enjoys so rich an interiority that his subjective feelings overflow onto the outside world and transfigure it: "What warm, all-comprehending fellow-feeling . . . what generous exaggeration of the object loved! . . . The rough scenes of Scottish life, not seen by him in any Arcadian illusion, but in the rude contradiction . . . are still lovely to him."[71] Burns is not merely self-sufficient but powerfully creative; he is a force that overcomes even "rude contradiction" and writes Scotland's true laws in his songs: "if ever any Poet might have equalled himself with legislators on this ground, it was Burns."[72] But at the same time, both Burns and the Scotland he represents are oppressed and derided parts of a greater whole. From London, Scotland is considered simply "that obscure region" shrouded in "the fogs of darkness"; Carlyle has to plead under cover of irony that "man's heart . . . man's destiny, reveal themselves not only in capital cities and crowded saloons, but . . . in Mossgiel and Tarbolton, if we look well, as clearly as in Crockford's."[73] Coming from both a subordinate region and a subordinate class, Burns is doubly marginalized. Carlyle describes British culture (as opposed to "native" Scottish culture) in terms far removed from pastoral or georgic as "a boundless arsenal and magazine, filled with all the weapons and engines which man's skill has been able to devise," and remarks that Burns "stands on the outside of that storehouse, and feels that its gates must be stormed, or remain forever shut against him."[74] Like the Parisian mob to which Carlyle alludes, Burns wants to storm the Bastille of culture for "weapons" to turn against the class that dictates the larger nation's manners. In colonial fashion, the Edinburgh literati mimic the snobbery of the metropolis: "the Edinburgh learned of that period . . . seems to have looked at Burns . . . as at a highly curious *thing*."[75]

Burns himself never found sufficient satisfaction in the "irony that might cause him to raise himself consciously outside his intelligence and, by renouncing it, offer himself up as one of nature's creatures to whatever use society may find for him"—that strenuous indifference to self praised by Schlegel. Instead, in Carlyle's representation, Burns tends to exhibit a robust indifference to his patrons' claims and thus undercuts his own desire to achieve material independence. Unlike Burns, however, Carlyle's essay ends up deploying a masterfully ironic tact toward the ideal of a unified British nation. It suggests that particular differences are not so much resolved as veiled by the idea of Britishness. Carlyle's feelings about Scotland appear in his disparaging description of those Edinburgh Enlightenment figures—David Hume, the historian William Robertson, and Adam Smith, among others—who failed so signally to recognize Burns's value: "in this brilliant resuscitation," Carlyle writes, "there was nothing truly Scottish, nothing indigenous . . . Scotland, so full of writers, had no Scottish culture . . . our culture was almost exclusively French. . . . Never perhaps, was there a class of writers so clear and well-ordered, yet so totally destitute . . . of any patriotic affection."[76] Carlyle is indignant at eighteenth-century Scotland's cultural evisceration. In this context, the "patriotic affection" of writers like Hume would have meant an affection for a specifically "Scottish" culture distinct from England's. But Carlyle finds a way to disavow his indignation by turning to one area of "culture": the idea of literature as a concrete universal that reconciles particularity with universality. Disparaging the "attenuated cosmopolitanism" that distinguished eighteenth-century writers, Carlyle notes with somewhat muted satisfaction the "remarkable increase of nationality" that "British, particularly Scottish literature, has undergone."[77] Now, to be recognized as truly universal, Carlyle argues, "the thing written" must bear a "mark of place." Men and literary texts are now seen as unrepresentative of the species without a national postmark, as it were, or stamp of local origin. But whether that mark can be specifically Scottish, whether that place can be Scotland and still be recognized as universal, or whether only English particularity can arise to such a status, are questions that Carlyle leaves unresolved, suggested only by his edginess of tone. Without disavowing the possibility that "Britain" may be a counterfeit marker in wide circulation, Carlyle declares Burns to be a "true British poet," and on the ground of this equivocal, ironic example he asserts the nation's unity.[78] Carlyle will go on in his career to become this nation's public conscience, addressing it as "a teacher and a prophet . . . [with] a special message to deliver to the present age," in James Anthony Froude's words.[79] But as we shall see, both in the substance of his message and in his manner of addressing this nation in important works like *Past and Present* (1843), irony will continue to play a constitutive role.

Framing a Free and Equal Fellowship

Despite his prominence, Sir Walter Scott elicits only a glancing reference in Carlyle's essay on Burns as an example of the apparent revival of nationality by "our chief literary men."[80] Nevertheless, Scott's influence hovers over this essay and other works by Carlyle. In his review of J. G. Lockhart's biography and elsewhere, Carlyle uses Scott as an emblem of Romantic Britain: "the *kind* of worth which Scott manifested was fitted especially for the then temper of men. We have called it an age fallen into spiritual languor, destitute of belief, yet terrified at scepticism."[81] The cult of Scott-worship provides the semblance of a unified national culture, Carlyle asserts ironically:

> Hardly any literary reputation ever rose so high in our Island. . . .
> Walter Scott became . . . the favourite of Princes and of Peasants, and
> all intermediate men. . . . Solitary Ettrick saw itself populous: all
> paths were beaten with the feet and hoofs of an endless miscellany of
> pilgrims . . . male and female; peers, Socinian preachers. . . . there
> was no literary shrine ever so bepilgrimed.[82]

Scott inspires Carlyle to articulate a new model of national political unity, based on the fetishizing of literature, as the last chapter of this book will show. Carlyle celebrates Scott's contributions to the cause of British unity at the same time that he questions Scott's authenticity, his motives, his productions and what they represent. What is important here is not the psychological ambivalence of this response but rather its rhetorical capaciousness: the nation is affirmed, even as the question of authenticity is being raised, and in ways that eventually turn back to the idea of the nation.[83]

But it is precisely in this disarming function that we can locate Scott's value to British nationalism; his historical novels frame the nation, or one chosen part of it, through irony. He shows how the meaning of a national whole, even if it is experienced as an apparently natural feeling, stems from artificial and arbitrary constraints that are a matter of open knowledge. Sometimes patriotism is avowed under duress; at other times, it flaunts its alliance with self-interest. Scott's social communities, which even when small and marginal always represent a potential nation, seem to tremble with the imagination of alternative modes of being. Sometimes they actually break apart. Somewhere in the minds of the community's members there resides a vision of how their social life might be differently organized, of how the finely graded structure of rank, power, and social prestige that shapes their actions might be revised, or of how they themselves might come to occupy a different position within that whole. All this while, for the most part, they remain conservatively committed to the primacy of community and the need to preserve it unchanged. Social subalterns in particular—a crucial category in Scott's novels—show themselves to be accomplished ironists. These ironists, even more than his passive and law-abiding heroes, drive Scott's plots and lend a distinctive charge to the atmosphere of his historical novels. And these novels, as many of his contemporary readers were aware, formed Britain's national self-consciousness in the crucial decades of instability after the French wars.[84]

To suggest how Scott lays the groundwork of an ironic nationalism, I want to look briefly at a scene from Scott's first novel, *Waverley* (1814). *Waverley* uses the Jacobite rebellion of 1745 to tell a story about the relationship of Scotland and England. While many critics have seen the novel as chronicling the birth of a postideological Scotland, in which commerce would take the place of political or military exertion, I see *Waverley* as investigating with vivid irony the conditions, on the hither side of the 1707 Union, under which a politically semi-independent Scotland might exist within a larger Great Britain.[85] A famous set-piece in the novel alludes to one of those conditions: ironic collusion in a dramatic scene of willing self-subordination to a greater whole. In this scene, the young English protagonist, Waverley, touring the Highlands out of idle curiosity, is entertained at a full-scale tribal feast. The feast is put on for his benefit by the ambitious young chieftain, Fergus Mac-Ivor, who happens also to be a master of graceful, ironic self-debunking. As Waverley sits at the head of the "huge oaken table" next to Mac-Ivor, he looks down its length at the assembled feast and guests. The feast spills out through the doors into the far beyond, as all members of the clan, including children, beggars, and dogs, take a place if not at the table, then around or under it.

In the first place, Scott uses the figure of framing to suggest, paradoxically, an ironic instability of perspective.[86] The scene is viewed through Waverley's eyes, and its emphatic framing seems to reinforce the unchallenged supremacy of his English point of view. But it ultimately suggests to us what Waverley cannot see: for example, the fact that he is actually an object observed, himself framed by a rustic proscenium, rather than the sole observer of this scene. The table and the clan hierarchy arranged around it are described as a "long perspective" in the eyes of Waverley, trapped at its head in the position of honor:

> Even beyond this long perspective, Edward might see upon the
> green, to which a huge pair of folding doors opened, a multitude of
> Highlanders of a yet inferior description. . . . In the distance, and
> fluctuating round this extreme verge of the banquet, was a changeful
> group of women, ragged boys and girls, beggars, young and old
> . . . and curs of low degree; all of whom took some interest, more or
> less immediate, in the main action of the piece.[87]

What the English observer sees is literally framed by the "pair of folding
doors"; he cannot see what lies beyond it. Interestingly, the greater the distance from Waverley, the more lively, diverse, populous, and mobile the scene
appears to be. He sees a greater number of things even as he sees, presum-
ably, less clearly. What might lie beyond the frame? The framing, which is so
pronounced as to become a thematic as well as a formal element of the scene,
emphasizes an artificial coherence that is in part a function of Waverley's
point of view. That essentially aesthetic stance is lightly criticized by its articulation in the last sentence quoted above: "all of whom took some interest,
more or less immediate, in the main action of the piece." Using the language
of bourgeois London theater-going to describe how ragged children anticipate table scraps ironically points to the way in which Waverley mistakes the
nature of the scene and his own role within it. Taking his privileged position
at the table for granted, Waverley assumes that he has the power to observe
the scene without being affected by it. He fails to realize that he is a spectator only in his own eyes. As an important, though unwitting actor in the
"main piece," he is being avidly observed by the Highland audience and by
the reader as well. The England he represents believes itself to be seated at
ease in the audience; but Scott's framing suggests that it may be England itself that is partial, strange, and incomplete.[88]

The ironic framing of the scene in fact only anticipates another level of
artificial unity imposed on the scene: the apparently spontaneous, "unbounded" harmony is internally structured by a particular kind of logic in-
forming numerous acts of social calculation. After describing the guests present, Scott observes, "This hospitality, apparently unbounded, had yet its line
of economy."[89] Economy is what defines the places at the table. The seating
and the substance of the feast reaffirm an intricately graded hierarchy: the elegant food and drink at the head of the table gradually coarsen as they reach
downward through "elders . . . tacksmen . . . their sons, and nephews, and
foster-brethren; then the officers of the Chief's household, according to their
order; and . . . the tenants who actually cultivated the ground," ending with
"onions, cheese, and the fragments of the feast" for the motley group of
"women, ragged boys and girls, beggars . . . and curs of low degree" gathered outside. What appears to be a primitive display of abundance is in fact
structured by Mac-Ivor's precise calibrations of the minimal differences that

must be observed to satisfy the clansmens' own cherished sense of social distinction. There is also a broader exchange that upholds the scene; aside from the feudal dependence of clan on chieftain (Mac-Ivor urbanely complains to his visitor, "'These stout idle kinsmen of mine . . . account my estate as held in trust for their support; and I must find them beef and ale, while the rogues will do nothing for themselves'"[90]), Mac-Ivor needs his clan as symbolic capital. Their strength and number give him prestige and make his demand for a higher rank within the Jacobite enterprise plausible.

Economy defines the places at the table, but irony keeps everyone in his assigned position. There is yet another sense in which this scene is framed or constituted by the active collusion of its participants. After noting the rigid hierarchy of the feast, the narrator remarks:

> Nor did this inequality of distribution appear to give the least offence. Every one present understood that his taste was to be formed according to the rank which he held at table; and, consequently, the tacksmen and their dependents always professed the wine was too cold for their stomachs, and called, apparently out of choice, for the liquor which was assigned to them from economy.[91]

A less ironic or less imaginative observer would have portrayed the hierarchy of taste as unconscious; the lower orders would have been formed so as to really prefer coarser fare.[92] But quite strikingly, Scott refrains from portraying Mac-Ivor's dependents as having been conditioned in their tastes by their social rank: "[e]very one present *understood* that his taste *was to be* formed according to the rank which he held at table . . . and called, *apparently out of choice*, for the liquor which was assigned to them from economy." Taste could be less of an embodied bias "placed," in one theorist's words, "beyond the grasp of consciousness" than a tactical avowal made for interested reasons.[93] There is no "offence," it is true, and no grumbling. But the scene likewise refuses to show these social inferiors happily accepting the principle of inequality. If anything, these subalterns insist on professing their equality with their masters: we, too, are choosing our fare, having what we like.[94] An illusion of free and equal fellowship is painstakingly maintained. This illusion of having chosen is indeed all that they have in common, all being equally under the command of prescribed roles and straitened circumstances. Ironic self-restriction is what they can agree upon.

The ironic principle of this Highland feast lies in the appearance of "unbounded" harmonious unity that actually proceeds from an external constraint—the arbitrary visual framing of the scene—and from an internal constraint: the interested self-subordination of its parts, from upper tacksmen to the lowest beggars. The clan's collective irony manages both to evade and to acknowledge the necessity of the "economy" that assigns them their roles and relative positions within the whole. Here the regulation of a household is in question; and the household or clan is seen as archaic, almost Homeric. But in its thematics of hierarchy and collusion, and in the sly circumstances of its framing, the scene suggests semi-independent Scotland's situation within the modern national household formed by the 1707 Union. From the perspective of post-Union Scotland, Britain's apparent unity rested on an ironic self-restriction of the Scottish nation. The surviving Scottish institutions of law, religion, and education, the economic development enhanced by the Union, and the chance to participate in empire-building offered discrete and somewhat heterogeneous spheres of activity in which Scots could appear to choose other options besides political autonomy. Even the public sphere of post-Union Scotland was structured by an ironic tact. Until the mid-nineteenth century, Christopher Harvie has argued, politics and public life proceeded by means of "continual adjustments" between a "theoretically sovereign" England and an "informal, but complex and subtle, system of institutional consultation" between Westminster and the autonomous Scottish bodies that controlled the church, legal and educational systems.[95] While in reality, Scotland was run through a continuous ad hoc process of adjusting, arranging, and negotiating, the fiction of Westminster as the seat of national sovereignty was preserved.[96]

Waverley offers a more comprehensive figuring of Scotland's anomalous condition in the estate of Tully-Veolan, which Scott first describes in a chapter called "A Scottish Manor-House Sixty Years Since." Owned by the Baron Bradwardine, sacked by English troops during the rebellion, forfeited and then secretly repurchased and restored by Bradwardine's friends, the estate stands for the Scottish nation, even as its owner emerges as the incarnation of "old Scottish faith, hospitality, worth, and honour."[97] But in this happy ending, a distinct irony runs parallel to the sentiment. Everyone ostentatiously overlooks the changed legal and social basis of Bradwardine's tenure: he holds the estate not as feudal patriarch but as purchaser, on the basis of a fresh commercial transaction performed, moreover, by surrogates without his knowledge (Waverley buys the estate secretly, through his own agents, and gives it back to him).[98] The estate is an anachronistic imitation of itself, with new parts and pieces "selected in the same character with the old furniture."[99] Most importantly, the description places an exaggerated, even comic emphasis on the painstaking restoration of every trivial architectural detail to its proper place. The stone bears, emblems of Bradwardine's unrestored sovereignty, receive special sentimental attention: "not only the Bear who predominated over [the fountain's] basin, but all the other Bears whatsoever, were replaced on their several stations, and renewed or repaired with so much care, that they bore no tokens of the violence which had so lately descended upon them."[100] The rupture of history is conspicuously erased on the surface, as the estate flaunts its continuity. But as a result, the space is transformed: it becomes strangely public rather than domestic, the object of viewing rather than use. Tully-Veolan, earlier described as "monastic" in its stillness and absorption, becomes theatrical, according to Michael Fried's definition: animated by the "awareness of an audience, of being beheld."[101] The former Baron "gazed in silent wonder"; and visitors and former servants "attend[ing] in full costume," anticipate the gaze of others as openly as does the new portrait of Waverley and Mac-Ivor. A complex and subtle life appears to go on behind the scenes, while the public face of the novel's ending unites irony with nationalist sentimentality.

Scott's irony, then, as well as Scotland's, derives its sustenance and its occasion from visions of unified larger wholes. Rather than linking it with the figure of divided consciousness that has haunted discussions of Scotland since the late Victorian era, when the notion of the "Caledonian Antisyzygy" (or Scotland as a union of opposites) became popularized, I see Scott's irony as a political technique. With ironic tact, Scott promotes the fellowship of incompatible things and unequal entities as though such fellowship were spontaneous rather than calculated, free rather than forced, exuberantly irrational rather than coldly logical—while showing us the logic, the calculation, and the humiliation that have to be disavowed.[102]

Double-Edged Deference

By now Edmund Burke's importance in molding Romantic nationalism is a critical commonplace: Burke is often agreed to have held the British nation together against the destabilizing forces of revolution through a strategic blending of political repression and theatrical emotion. Burke's recent ubiquity in discussions of British nationalism comes about in part as a result of critical interest in sensibility, theatricality, and gender politics.[103] But the significance of Burke's irony has often been underestimated. The irony that undeniably pales when Burke is placed alongside Wordsworth and Coleridge becomes strongly visible when he is read as a crucial source of Scott's and Carlyle's ironic conservatism. Throughout his career, Burke uses a tactic that also distinguishes Scott's novels and Carlyle's essays: the irony whereby an individual subject, a humble and deferential part, shows how it *could suddenly—but does not fully—* become the pivot for a disenchanted view of the whole it purports to serve. Burke's irony inscribes a covert moral drama between the lines, as it were, of nationalist sentiment. What sets Burke apart from other English conservatives is the marked volatility of his deference for Britain's national institutions—a puzzling, inscrutable tone of defiance that Scott and Carlyle and many other conservatives will try to adopt with varying degrees of skill.[104] Sometimes only an unsettling rhetorical flicker, such defiance emerges openly when Burke surveys England's colonies: "all the miseries of Ireland have originated," he writes, "in what has produced all the miseries of India, a servile patience under oppression."[105] But the incongruous tone of dissent is strongest in Burke's most apparently servile protestations of loyalty. Especially in his counterrevolutionary writings, Burke utters orthodox sentiments with the air of one announcing a heresy and vice versa. He shows himself a master, above all, of equivocal deference—of assent that points to its own limits and conditions. Sometimes he performs an about-face on one word, as when he writes in 1792, "There are *few* things I wish more . . . than that the established Churches should be continued on a firm foundation in both Kingdoms"—the kingdoms, he means, of Britain and Ireland. He continues thus:

> When I say few, I mean to be exact: for some things, assuredly, I have much nearer my heart, namely the emancipation of that Great body of my original Countrymen, whom, a Jackanapes in Lawn Sleeves, calls Fools and Knaves. I can never persuade myself, that any thing in our thirty-nine articles . . . is worth making these millions of People Slaves, to secure its teaching at the publick Expence.[106]

Burke begins with a conventionally genteel, throwaway expression of support: "There are few things I wish more." He appears to be affirming his support for a key national institution (what Burke presents in his counterrevolutionary works as *the* national institution). But in this banal formula of good-will, Burke finds a startling route of escape. Through his literal interpretation of the word "few," Burke finds a way not so much to combine as to rivet opposing positions together: a sturdy loyalty to Britain's alliance of church and state, and a determination to view this alliance as a "vile" political oppression perpetrated by "Jackanapes in lawn sleeves" and on the benches of Parliament.[107]

The immediate matter at hand concerns Burke's support for the emancipation of Ireland's Roman Catholics from the harsh civil and political penalties legally imposed on them after the Glorious Revolution—an event which Burke reminds us was in Ireland "not a revolution but a conquest, which is not to say a great deal in its favour."[108] Without going so far as to make Ireland the explanatory key to all his actions, we can see Burke's deference as a way of reminding both himself and others of the imperfect state of the British union, even as he was defending it with increasing stridency against the contamination of so-called revolutionary principles.[109] Britain's much-vaunted liberty was not enjoyed by all. Indeed, Burke remarks in his "Letter to Sir Hercules Langrishe" (1792) that the Anglo-Irish Protestant ruling class "considered themselves . . . a sort of colonial garrison, to keep the natives in subjection to the other state of Great Britain."[110] In his speeches and correspondence about the Irish situation in the 1790s, when political fractures in Ireland culminated in the formation of a self-described "Protestant ascendancy," Burke both performs and portrays ironic self-subordination as a model of resistance.[111] He plays, however, a dangerous game. Excessive deference, particularly toward the clergy, was so much at the heart of the Protestant argument against granting political rights to Ireland's Roman Catholics that it could become a kind of shorthand for a whole position; Southey, for example, notes as a commonplace how "credulous Irish peasants were prone to the superstitions peddled by Catholic priests."[112] This was used as a major argument against granting the franchise to Catholics or even of removing the discriminatory legislation that denied them basic civil rights; it was also easily expanded into a widely credited pseudotruth about the nature of Irish Catholics.

Burke's view of this prejudiced belief that Irishmen's "Bodies and Souls were at the entire disposal of their Priests" can be seen in his letters to his son, Richard, who was the Catholic Committee's agent in 1792. Referring to the Protestant Ascendancy "Zealots" as "miserable Creatures . . . [who] have been fed with this stuff as their Nurse's pap," Burke declares the truth as one "who know[s] the Catholics of Ireland much better than these Gentlemen":

> The Fact is as I state it. A Catholic goes to confession . . . when he does it, he does it by a Table, which any Man can buy for sixpence— and he is well apprised that if he performs the common Conditions which he knew as well as his Parish Minister . . . he must have his absolution whether the Priest will or not. . . . It is so of all the Sacraments and other ritual Observances . . . there is no Penitent in Ireland who would not laugh his Priest to scorn, if sitting in the Confession Box . . . he was to say a word to him on this topic, or of the Election, or any other political topic whatsoever.[113]

To an outsider, the sacrament of confession seems to turn on the absolute power of the priest. But Burke insists that the transaction turns on a voluntary, somewhat equivocal deference. Going beyond the sacramental dimension of the act, which he interprets as the subordination of personal intention to traditional forms, Burke's Irish penitent views absolution as a right whose knowledge comes to him through "a Table, which any Man can buy for sixpence." The ritual does not occur as an exchange, but the open accessibility of what it offers in the present day is both likened to and grounded on the openness and modernity of the marketplace. Moreover, the superior's authority is fragile indeed: if he oversteps his bounds, or even makes a mistake, the penitent is ready "to laugh his Priest to scorn," knowing the rules "as well as his Parish Minister." Yet it is definitely not a transaction between equals that Burke describes. The appearance of the institution's authority is preserved through a conditional form of collective tact.

Particularly in recent Romantic studies, Burke has often been treated as a figure of rhetorical and political power so great that even his implicit endorsement of certain attitudes was sufficient to establish them as national dogma. Claudia Johnson has recently argued that Burke's *Reflections on the Revolution in France* "actually incited, and as a momentous national duty, . . . susceptibility to pathos."[114] Burke's capacity to command the feelings and thoughts of the English nation is rarely questioned. But in his own time, Burke's cultural identity was seen as suspect. His talents, particularly for showy, splendid oratory, were always recognized but in ways that usually reflected suspicion about the depth of his Englishness, the sincerity of his feelings, and the extent of his loyalty to the nation.[115] Burke was often ethnicized, portrayed in political caricatures (he was almost always in them, as a prominent public figure) as an outsider, in full Jesuit attire with papal accoutrements, sometimes even holding the whiskey bottle of which John Wilkes said his oratory "stank."[116] And not only his suspected religious sympathies but also his tendency to apply a double-edged deference to political situations linked him with Ireland. In particular, Ireland's shadow or "underground gentry," descended from Catholic landowners dispossessed in the seventeenth century, were identified with a tradition of highly equivocal deference to new colonial rulers.[117] Living as tenants on the land now owned by Protestants, these Catholic middlemen continued to enjoy a crypto-aristocratic status that called into question the legitimacy of the new landowners' claims. Edmund Burke's family belonged to precisely this middleman class, which seems to have perfected the art of paying ironic deference to its masters while hinting at its own social superiority.[118] An anonymous anti-Catholic pamphlet complained that "[e]ven though they seemingly show a great respect and submission to the English yet we must remember that all this is but forced . . . a feigned obedience and, therefore, but an unwilling subjection."[119] In a pseudo-ethnographic study published in 1804, Robert Bell claims, "[i]gnorant and obscure as they were, many families among them used to trace their pedigrees back to a very remote period; they knew the rank and estates which their ancestors once held in the country. . . . These families could ascertain every spot of ground which was said to have belonged to their forefathers and of which they looked on the modern possessors as so many usurpers."[120] Outward deference to the land's "modern possessors" only emphasizes the lingering influence of earlier social formations that had been brutally extirpated. Their deference is practiced so that it appears to be, as a contemporary observer noted, "only from the teeth outwards."[121] It calls up a buried history and gives the lie to the self-idealizing British nation of which Ireland became an official part in 1800. Through acts of semi-respectful submission, these Irish subjects made it hard to know where to draw the lines between consent and force, between disguise and nature—distinctions on which rulers and uneasy Protestant landlords might like to rely.[122]

Like the Romantic British nation that he also celebrated, Burke's deference was less a perfect, homogeneous whole than an amalgam of assent and defiance. Far from simply reaffirming the nation's authority, Burke's performances implicitly contest that authority through intimations of a higher knowledge at odds with his claims. His self-subordination contains within it the ironic knowledge that it was both free and unfree. Even more clearly than Scott's fictional clansmen did, Burke "understood that his taste was to be formed" by his position as the Whig aristocracy's intellectual factotum. The landed aristocracy was the British national institution which, even more than the established church, Burke publicly cherished as the material and the spiritual basis of the nation's unity. But only a few years after notoriously glamorizing the aristocracy in the *Reflections*, Burke remarks of a great representative of the English Whig aristocracy, "I have strained every nerve to keep the Duke of Bedford in that situation, which alone makes him my superior."[123] Ostensibly defending his right to a small pension at the end of his career, Burke's *Letter to a Noble Lord* (1796) memorably portrays the Duke of Bedford, who had spoken against it, as a monstrous social solecism: a fatuous young man possessed of spectacular wealth that violates the rules of social justice, an equally disproportionate influence that affronts common sense, and a self-destructive propensity for radical politics. But Bedford's weak inanity is important chiefly as it gives occasion for Burke's keenest irony. Burke's political career with the Rockingham Whigs had been spent defending the aristocracy as the national institution of paramount importance. Burke now exhibits this career as an ironic self-subordination on a nearly Socratic scale to what is essentially a fetish of his own making: a nation pictured as a harmonious order, crowned by the likes of Bedford. It is appropriate that the *Letter to a Noble Lord* should feature a gruesome fantasy of dismemberment. Burke memorably imagines Bedford's great estates being carved up in imagination by French revolutionaries like the pictured cow in the butcher-shop window, divided by dotted lines into various cuts of meat. Not that Burke wished such a fate for Britain; but the brief indulgence in this grotesquerie allows him to point out, with equal pain and pleasure, that there is nothing inherently indivisible about the nation or the great estates that buttress its social order. Through Burke's irony, as we shall see, Romantic nationalism acquired much-needed ideological flexibility, capaciousness of tone, and the freedom to explore rather than to hide the incoherence of some cherished official ideas about political unity, authority, and allegiance.

Public Sphere and Public Fetish

Some of the fractures within conservatism lay not far from the surface. While the political position of conservatism revolved around the defense of social hierarchy, as recent studies have shown, the arguments used to accomplish this defense were not always compatible and sometimes even mutually contradictory.[124] Inequality was presented by orthodox Anglican conservatives like Thomas Nowell, as the handiwork of God:

> When men consider themselves placed in their several subordinate stations, not by mere chance, or by any compact or agreement of their own framing, but by the will of Him who is the fountain of government . . . when they consider that all authority, dominion, and power, are his prerogative, and derived from him to those, whom his Providence has delegated to be his representatives upon earth; chearful duty, and willing obedience, will be the natural result of such reflections.[125]

Yet hierarchy was also defended on the grounds of economic necessity by Adam Ferguson, Adam Smith, among others, and even by Burke himself, reluctantly and angrily, as that which turns "the great wheel of circulation," the manufacture and retail of luxury commodities. Burke complains that "no consideration, except the necessity of submitting to the yoke of luxury, and the despotism of fancy, which in their own imperious way will distribute the surplus product of the soil, can justify the toleration" of Britain's social inequalities, citing "the innumerable servile, degrading . . . unwholesome and pestiferous occupations, to which by the social oeconomy so many wretches are inevitably doomed."[126] Social hierarchy was thus seen as both eternal and self-consuming; it was defended as both essential and inconsequential. It counted for nothing: rank bore no relation to individual or to collective, secular or eternal happiness.[127] While other discourses such as Christian political economy undertook to combine these types of conservative arguments, the irony exercised by Burke and his most important followers pointed out the discrepancies between such arguments, attitudes, and schemes of value even while bridging them.

Walter Scott and Thomas Carlyle were by no means the only British writers who explored the territory opened up by Burke's ironized deference. Even the authors of anti-Jacobin novels such as Charlotte Smith could include conservative shibboleths alongside more radical criticisms of social inequality and injustice.[128] Throughout her novels Maria Edgeworth, too, performs brilliant, sometimes even surreal parodies of conservative themes; in one scene in *Belinda* (1801), for example, a multitude of actual swine being raced by an aristocrat against a flock of French turkeys functions as a distraction that saves a pair of duelling, cross-dressed females from an angry crowd.[129] My study, however, gives most of its attention to one particular line of Burkean writers for several reasons. Burke, Scott, and Carlyle are linked not only by their gender, their non-English origins, and the cultural authority they enjoyed — factors which sometimes reinforce and sometimes undercut each other—but also by a particularly complex relationship to the institutions of literature and the public sphere.[130] These writers frequently forge alliances, sometimes uncouth ones, between disparate genres and kinds of writing—a strategy that both assumes and enhances their cultural authority. A work like Burke's *Reflections*, written in the form of a letter to a French correspondent, presents itself as a nonce genre, a puzzling blend of political and legal oratory, pamphlet-style invective, travel-writing, and the supposedly instantaneous inscription of sentiment associated with Richardson's epistolary novels.[131] Drawing on Spenserian romance, Shakespeare's history plays, polite history, antiquarian erudition and the novel, to name only a few sources from which he draws representational conventions, Scott's first novel, *Waverley*, offers as its public emblem the "white shield" of a "maiden knight"; despite its allusion to Burke's notorious defense of chivalry, the sign defies the reader to identify it.[132] And in *Past and Present*, for example, Carlyle constructs a powerful critique of Britain in 1843 by exploiting the affinities between literary reviewing, prophecy, political economy, satire, and antiquarianism. Through such defamiliarizing conflations, generic conventions come to appear even more arbitrary in their features, if not in their applications, rather than taking on a natural-seeming character. Most interestingly, when we attend to this particular genealogy, the distinction between fiction and nonfiction becomes less important than local maneuvers of tone, address, allusion, notation, and other conventions of discourse that travel between genres. I have chosen to bring out the generic diversity of these writers' productions because it suggests something about their views of Britain's public sphere and literature's role within it. Though they recognize the power of literature as an institution to shape social order, they do not value literature as a powerful means of making certain representations of the private sphere appear natural. The Waverley Novels turn away from the detailed imitation of everyday temporality and domesticity that Scott himself claimed to be the distinguishing feature of modern fiction. Instead, Scott sometimes comments directly on the conventions of novelistic representation, as in *The Fortunes of Nigel* (1822). Claiming that "I myself choose to present to my dearest reader the picture of my hero's mind . . . in the form of a speech," Scott tries to justify his decision to use stagey soliloquy rather than the discreet omniscience of free indirect discourse by entering into a long discussion of what must be "received as a conventional medium of communication betwixt the poet and the audience."[133] Though this is not invariably Scott's practice, he does often insist on how the reading of a novel resembles a public transaction made through the currency of convention. It is not like an invisible infiltration of the reader's subjectivity. Nor do Burke, Scott, and Carlyle seem to regard the public sphere as the domain of reason or intellectual enquiry.[134] Rather than representing the circulation of natural feelings in the private sphere or the exclusive use of critical reason in the public sphere, Burke, Scott, and Carlyle

share a concern with the public display of emotion toward the nation's favored symbols and tropes: a display that is sometimes theatrical, often necessarily ironic, and never disinterested.[135] Of the public sphere and the expressions that belong there, they would agree with Burke that "it is a thing to be
settled by convention."[136] Impersonal conventions pertain not only to the
professional writing of literature but also to the beliefs, feelings, and performances of a willing British subject. In a famous moment of the *Reflections*,
Burke praises the "untaught feelings" of Britons; but the context makes it apparent that Burke has in mind the well-trained, conventional feelings that
easily surface in familiar public settings.[137] Indeed, Scott and Carlyle are fond
of invoking the figures of mechanical performance and mechanical writing, as
though Britain's literary-political public sphere could even dispense with the
need for humans to perform the routines of convention.

The questions, problems, and genres constructed by these particular writers also provide a way to observe some of the significant changes in Britain's
political constitution, economic structure, and imperial scope during this period. In 1790, Burke writes that "our thoughts of everything at home are sus-
pended, by our astonishment at the wonderful Spectacle which is exhibited
in a Neighbouring and rival Country—what Spectators, and what actors!
England gazing with astonishment at a French struggle for Liberty and not
knowing whether to blame or to applaud!"[138] In a spectacle most seductive to
some British audiences, revolutionary France dramatized the discovery of its
own agency. It discovered a capacity to prescribe its own structure and to direct its collective destiny. One radical writer, for example, typically compared
the "English Nation," which is merely "a passive mass acted upon . . . and
managed at the will and for the interest of particular orders," with the "French
Nation": "an organized body acting for itself," a "Prometheus, a moral agent
at liberty, and conferring heavenly blessings on the world."[139] In response,
Burke's *Reflections* suggests that Britain's political liberty arises mainly
through a tradition of ironic *and* enthusiastic complicity with political illusions. Burke also calls tirelessly in his other counterrevolutionary writings for
war against the "armed doctrine" of revolutionary France. And as a result
of the wars fought over the following decades, Britain not only expanded its
overseas empire to include southern Africa, Indonesia, Ceylon, and important Caribbean and Mediterranean islands but also built up a complex international network of trade that allowed it to exchange, for example, commodities such as Indian calico, guns, and spirits for African slaves, gold, and
ivory; slaves, gold, and ivory for Caribbean sugar, cotton, and tobacco, and
silks, spices, and teas from Asia; and these latter commodities for European
timber, pitch, iron, and grain, which were imported back into Britain.[140]
Ports such as Glasgow thus acquired a new prosperity and importance. With
its victory over Napoleon, Britain's world dominance seemed assured by
1815. Walter Scott's first set of historical novels performs the critical task of

examining the British nation's identity at this juncture. How is that identity related to militarism, on the one hand, and to the boundary-dissolving flows of commerce, on the other? What is the meaning of territorial boundary or of political allegiance in a commercial empire? How can British nationalism reconcile its devotion to inherited and timeless particulars with its tendency to draw all things into the ephemeral circuits of commodity-exchange? The period between 1790 and 1843, when Carlyle published *Past and Present*, also witnessed Britain's further dramatic industrialization; technological as well as social innovations in fields ranging from agriculture to cotton and iron production resulted, in one historian's words, in "a widening of economic horizons in both space and time."[141] From across a broad social spectrum, investment in fixed industrial capital and new infrastructure resulted in an explosion of productivity as well as in destabilizing economic crises. Ireland, too, though not undergoing the same degree of industrialization, showed itself deeply affected by the fluctuating prosperity of British capital. This British productivity forms the chief target of Carlyle's affirmative irony in the works leading up to and including *Past and Present*. He helps to redefine Britain's identity as an essentially productive one. Indebted more to the rhetorical analysis of social class than to that of the cultural nation, but still stubbornly evincing an outsider's view of "England," Carlyle addresses the British as self-conscious producers of commodities, forms of life, and political illusions. "How to deal with the Actual Labouring Millions . . . ? This is the imperatively pressing Problem of the Present, pressing with a truly fearful intensity and imminence in these very years and days," he writes.[142] Carlyle will turn to the absorbed, self-forgetful act of reading literature as a model for the disavowal through which Britain is to overcome class struggle. This act of disavowal he figures through the imperial trope of fetishism or deliberate self-subordination to the work of one's own hands.[143]

The intersections of irony and nationalism explored by these writers can be usefully viewed in light of the important changes in the public conduct and private interpretation of politics at this time. Rather than focusing on the theme of political and social reform, however, I want to look at a few indications of the changed forms and meanings of public deference: deference to the symbols, tropes, and ideas of the nation. Throughout the period, the French Revolution, reported by Burke and chronicled in Scott's *Life of Napoleon Buonaparte* (1827) and Carlyle's *History of the French Revolution* (1837), served as a mirror in which Britain could revise its self-understanding. As Britain's tradition of public, conventional deference came under review, a space was opened up for irony to be practiced and recognized, not without discomfort. By the time that Carlyle writes, "has not a French Revolution been? Since the year 1789, there is now half a century complete; and a French Revolution not yet complete! . . . These Chartisms, Radicalisms . . . are *our* French Revolution," he puts pressure on ironic deference to define itself differently, to distinguish itself from cynicism, and to ground itself in a subjectively held attitude rather than merely in convention.[144]

Traveling in France in 1789, the quintessential Englishman Arthur Young continually emphasizes the broad diffusion and the quality of the political intelligence that circulates in Britain — not only within London but also "from one end of the kingdom to another."[145] Unlike the French, British subjects of all ranks and social classes, he asserts, debate not only domestic politics but also the internal affairs of foreign nations with accuracy, practiced skill, and an astute sense of what is comprised in political calculation and judgment:

> Scarcely any politics [in French conversation], at a moment when every bosom ought to beat with none but political sensations. The ignorance or the stupidity of these people must be absolutely incredible; not a week passes without their country abounding with events that are analyzed and debated by the carpenters and blacksmiths of England. The abolition of tithes, the destruction of the gabelle . . . feudal rights destroyed, are French topics, that are translated into English within six days after they happen, and their consequences, combinations, results, and modifications, become the disquisition and entertainment of the grocers, chandlers, drapers, and shoemakers, of all the towns of England.[146]

With patriotic pride tempered by a hint of uneasiness, Young sees political debate in Britain as the recreation of the idle as well as the potential means of social change. What he points to is a mastery of the rhetoric of political analysis ("consequences, combinations, results, and modifications"), performed with more of an eye to "entertainment" than conviction. But as the revolution unfolds in France, Britain's actual politics can be seen retrospectively as a cynically calculated exercise in manipulating conventional deference, particularly toward that most important of national symbols, the king.[147] When the French royal family was forcibly removed from Versailles to Paris in October 1789, this event recalled to some British observers the Regency Crisis of 1788–89, when George III, suddenly mentally incapacitated, was, in Burke's notorious description, "plunged . . . into a condition which drew upon him the pity of the meanest peasant in his kingdom."[148] The ensuing struggle largely concerned which party would, through its royal figureheads, take over the monarch's patronage and power. What is most striking about the Parliamentary debates on the crisis is their confident presumption that awe and veneration for the king were not private feelings but conventional civic emotions that could be openly treated as such. Both parties fearlessly exposed the inconsequence of the king's presence, except as a constitutional fiction with high political stakes. Both sides, and Burke himself most sensationally, seemed to take an almost cynical pleasure in publicly describing their king as a mere "tool," to be stripped or decorated or displayed at will. The sovereign's duties to the nation could just as ably be performed, it seemed, by the Great Seal, "a certain composition of wax and copper [used] to represent the Monarch," as Burke complained.[149] In the debates that lasted from the winter of 1788 to the spring of 1789, when George III recovered, each side accused the other of trying "to make a King" either by dressing up the Prince Regent in "a mock crown, a tinsel robe, and a sceptre from the theatre, lackered over, and unreal" (again, Burke's words), or by producing the king "as a pageant, dressed up with useless splendor and degrading dignity, to serve the purposes of ambitious men."[150] Although such cynical manipulations were usually attributed to the other side and ostensibly deplored, the constant reiteration of this charge by both sides left little doubt that, whichever party was orchestrating the pageant at the time, it was still largely a show. Even Burke's sympathetic defense of the king rested on portraying him as permanently dispossessed of rational agency, destined to remain the ward or fetish that the monarch had perhaps been for a long time. Burke even suggested that George's "symptoms of sanity" could not be trusted when they reappeared, noting that "some of these unfortunate individuals after a supposed recovery, had committed parricides, others had butchered their sons, others had done violence to themselves by hanging, shooting, drowning, throwing themselves out of window, and by a variety of other ways."[151] Under the pretext of concern for the nation, Burke virtually consigns Britain's king to Bedlam, an institution that he commends for "the discipline throughout, and the wonderful order; in consequence of which so many persons were governed by a few."[152] The irony of holding up Bedlam as the model for state authority could have been savored both by the many who felt themselves subject to that authority and by the few who exercised some part of it.

Mary Wollstonecraft was one of the first to compare the Regency Crisis with the October Days; her goal was to expose the cynical heartlessness of Burke's professed tenderness toward monarchs:

> I have, Sir, been reading . . . your insensible and profane speeches
> during the King's illness . . . what but the odious maxims of Machiavelian policy could have led you to have searched in the very dregs of
> misery for forcible arguments to support your party? Had not vanity
> or interest steeled your heart, you would have been shocked at the
> cold insensibility which could carry a man to those dreadful mansions . . . to *calculate* the chances against the King's recovery.[153]

Wollstonecraft demands that Britons "tremble for humanity" at the sight of a suffering king, that they feel real sympathetic suffering for the symbols of the nation. Her dismay attests to the sufficiency of conventional deference in the public sphere; Wollstonecraft will call for a new and more heartfelt manner of conducting the business of politics. But demands for real public feel-ing, combined with a heightened concern for authority, open up a greater, though perhaps less public, space for irony. In his *Letter to William Elliott* (1795), Burke describes the changed ways in which authority was viewed af-ter 1789: "[a]ttacked on all sides . . . authority could not stand on authority alone. It wanted some other support than the poise of its own gravity. Situa-tions formerly supported persons. It now became necessary that personal qualities should support situations. Formerly, where authority was found, wisdom and virtue were presumed. But now the veil was torn."[154] What Burke means by authority here is not so much the formal power of the state and its laws. Rather, it is the practical power of social institutions and sym-bols to keep beliefs and performance from undergoing revolutionary change. Burke argues that in the past such authority relied on the merely conven-tional attribution of certain "personal qualities" to those in power. But with new ideals of believing in persons rather than simply deferring to their po-sitions, new solutions have to be found. Developing the same theme some years later in his essay on "The Spirit of the Age" (1831), John Stuart Mill emphasizes that both political and epistemological authority continue to be at stake: "Mankind will not be led by their old maxims, nor by their old guides; and they will not choose either their opinions or their guides as they have done heretofore."[155] None can agree on whom to follow, what to believe, what to take for granted as the common practice of others——the usual fall-back of conservative skepticism—or what would count as a legitimating ar-gument for authority.[156] Another politician suggests in the pages of *Fraser's Magazine* in 1835 that the authority to enjoin belief or performance encoun-ters a new skepticism when it claims to ground itself in a particular place or local tradition:

> The people in their several districts never will again bow down at the
> shrine of a mute idol,—no matter of what ancient reverence it may
> be. . . . The genius loci, the spirit of the place where in olden time the
> idol was reared, is now all powerless, except within the realms of
> poesy; in the stern realities which furnish forth the world of politics
> there is no longer . . . fane, shrine, or image, held in blind, unsearch-
> ing reverence.[157]

Here a romance of authority is constructed with a sentimental nostalgia not to be found in Burke's curt acknowledgments. Burke's own irony, taken up by Scott and Carlyle, responds both to the skeptical scrutiny of conventional deference and to this belated romance of authority. Their irony hints at a pos-sible power to move between heterogeneous feelings, conventions, argu-ments, and justifications, where the nation's authoritative symbols are con-cerned. It allows a monarch, for example, to be seen as a passive puppet, as a mere man, and as a signifier capable of eliciting powerful emotions: even as a fetish, a humanly constructed object purposively misrecognized. Carlyle remarks in his *History of the French Revolution*, "Finally, the King is shown on an upper balcony, by torchlight, with a huge tricolor in his hat . . . surely the New Era was born."[158] But with Carlyle, the public openness and private freedom of patriotic irony come to an end.

When Carlyle writes amid the turmoil of Chartism, conventions governing deference have clearly changed. Where Burke and Scott had seen more of an ironic complicity with conventions regarding authoritative symbols of nationhood, Carlyle stresses how subjects actively produce the very authority that keeps them in their places. This is not the impersonal production carried out by tradition, but rather the work carried out by Britain's embodied subjects: their material production of commodities, including the peculiar commodity known as literature.[159] The laws, the landscapes, and the collective property of Britain, Carlyle argues, are "all work and forgotten work," and certain genres of literature can both reveal and disguise this knowledge.[160] The fact of their having virtually created the state does not, as in liberal or radical thinking, give the nation's subjects a continuing right to control it. Instead, Carlyle argues that literature invites this consciousness of active productivity to lose itself in a special kind of self-forgetfulness, as the reader's creative labor comes to appear as an attribute possessed by the image that it has made. Bringing the rhetoric of fetishism from the margins of the empire to its very center, Carlyle suggests how literature can lead the nation to accept its dominant classes and culture in a manner that is disenchanted but heartfelt, voluntarily self-blinded but not entirely so. The political volatility and originality of this position become more apparent if we briefly consider the counterexample of Coleridge, an English conservative with strong intellectual ties both to Burke and Carlyle. Coleridge, too, invokes the notion of fetishism in an early essay written for *The Friend* (1809); by it he refers to the error of "connect[ing] with the objects of our senses the obscure notions and consequent vivid feelings which are due only to immaterial and permanent things"—"the Ideas of Being . . . Freedom, Immortality, God!"[161] For Coleridge, the first necessity of correct feeling (and correct politics) is ecstatic faith in the existence of the Absolute, "the true cause and invisible Nexus of the things that are seen," and in the "universal laws by which each thing belongs to the Whole, as interpenetrated by the powers of the Whole."[162] To do otherwise is to become a "Fetish-worshipper."[163] So, for Coleridge, the fetish arises when a concrete object, or the experience of it, is improperly invested with the feeling that belongs to genuinely ideal objects, notably the idea of the whole. Coleridge's scorn for the particular material object stems from a long tradition of argument, made in aesthetic, political, and philosophical discourses, in favor of aristocratic or elite rule.[164] Carlyle, too, believes that the few should rule over the many. But, for Carlyle, the fetish is neither simply an object available for sense-perception nor a part mistaken for the whole. Rather, as a thing or an idea that ironically disavows its own provenance, the fetish is a seductive but incomplete illusion of wholeness. It derives its apparently autonomous power through a half-forgotten history of its own production. In Carlyle's mode of fetishism, a sense of superiority can be both enjoyed and strategically disavowed in the act of submitting to self-created political illusions concerning the nation.

Is this fetishistic nationalism something that already operates in Romantic Britain? Or is it regarded as something that may or ought to come about in the future? At whom is their irony aimed? For whom is it meant? The unanswerability of these questions points to some distinctive features of the irony found in these writers. There is, first, their canny refusal to differentiate between constative and performative speech, between representations that describe something already existing and representations that aim to bring about a state of affairs not yet realized. Burke's *Reflections* and Carlyle's *Past and Present*, to take only two examples, present themselves as aiming to bring about change in the nation. But they try to do so, in part, by describing and quoting documents and actions from the past. The past is used to describe the present; the present is supposedly described so as to bring about a future. The statement of what was the case shades off into a programmatic vision of what should be the case. There is no uniform scheme of temporality in their writings that can be isolated from their pragmatic agendas, even when that agenda is carefully concealed, as in Scott's case. Corresponding to this is a distinctively self-conscious ambiguity about whom their works address. Written to a French correspondent, Burke's *Reflections*, for example, can be decoded only by British readers. French or English? Passive or active? Of what social class? Of what political persuasion? Sometimes this volatility of address is explicitly highlighted. It is thematized, for example, in *Past and Present*, which seems to test in an almost phatic sense the social limits of print as a way to pull a nation together. Carlyle's loud apostrophes invoke readers that range from "his Grace of Castle Rackrent" to "Advanced Liberal" to "ye workers."[165] Is there a single ratio of irony to nationalism that can fit these diverse audiences?

The paradoxically cohesive force of irony becomes clear when Carlyle invites his readers to occupy in imagination social positions radically different from those they presently inhabit. He invites them to emulate his own ironic agility. In this way, the distinctions between insider and outsider, have and have-not, Thady Quirk and master, are somewhat blurred. It is a poor substitute for the amelioration of material inequalities, but irony serves no one side. If it is true that ironic nationalism cynically recommends to the nation "to put up with the preestablished relations that it finds dubious, to accommodate itself to them, and finally even to carry out their business," it also rests on the imagination of a nation with a far more fluid, indeterminate social structure.[166] At its outermost limit, it imagines a nation that reposes its faith in no single class or political doctrine but rather in a constant habit of agile, deterritorialized movement between competing feelings and knowledges.

2

Edmund Burke's Pretexts for Politic Bodies

That Edmund Burke achieved his political ends through subtle, surreptitious, largely rhetorical means was a belief well established even in his own lifetime. An anonymous political cartoon from the Regency Crisis of 1788–89 shows Burke, along with Charles James Fox and Richard Brinsley Sheridan, trying to break into the house of the "Treasury," defended by Pitt from an upstairs window. Fox uses a pick-axe inscribed "Presumptive Right" (the presumptive right of the Prince of Wales to the regency); Sheridan uses the crowbar labeled "Begum Sophistry" (the Begums of Oudh, mistreated by the East India Company); Burke, hunched over, applies one from a set of keys to the padlock on the door. This ring of keys is labeled "Tropes."[1] This ephemeral satire raises lasting questions about how Burke uses tropes, and how such tropes are related to his political projects and intentions. Sophistry and even constitutional shibboleths are the equivalents of blunt instruments. Are Burke's rhetorical keys, then, legitimate means of entry into power? To whom do they belong and who has the right to use them? And what role do they play in the nation's self-understanding?[2]

The trope of prosopopoeia or personification provides a good point of entry into what is Burke's best-known and perhaps most influential work, his *Reflections on the Revolution in France* (1790).[3] It is this work, more than any other, that justifies Coleridge's remark in 1817 that "not only the debates in parliament . . . but the essays and leading paragraphs of our journals are so many remembrances of Edmund Burke."[4] And it is in this work, even more than in his Irish writings, that Burke develops his distinctive loyalist irony. To begin with, personified abstractions have an odd way of cropping up at crucial points in the *Reflections*. They take on lives of their own, sometimes clashing with other historical agents and sometimes expanding grotesquely into dense, compacted, miniature allegories, as in this notorious passage, where Burke is discussing the new political role of men of letters in the French Revolution:

> Learning [in the ancien régime] paid back what it received to nobility
> and to priesthood; and paid it with usury, by enlarging their ideas and

by furnishing their minds. . . . Happy if learning, not debauched by
ambition, had been satisfied to continue the instructor, and not as-
pired to be the master! . . . learning will be cast into the mire, and
trodden down under the hoofs of a swinish multitude.[5]

Both faithful debtor and practitioner of usury, Rousseauian tutor, Luciferian
rebel, and prodigal son, this personification of "learning" stretches and
mixes metaphors in defiance of the rules set for the correct use of figurative
language. In simply using abstractions such as "learning," Burke is far from
unique, of course; these figures form an important part of most political discourses.[6] But Burke's personified abstractions aim at and accomplish something quite different from what is seen in more conventional writers. They
remove the possibility of regarding the public sphere as a place regulated exclusively by either nature or artifice. In eighteenth-century rhetorical theory,
figures such as personification were usually understood to signify a subjective psychological state: "a state of violent emotion" in the speaker, according to Hugh Blair's influential treatise.[7] There are in fact two ways in which
such figurative language can appear unexceptionable: it can appear to emanate from violent emotion, or it can appear purely conventional. Usually,
in either case, "we make the proper abatement, and understand them according to their just value," often doing so unconsciously and instantaneously.[8]
But at other times, when there is something "striking and unusual" in a figure of speech, or something incongruous about its use, we see and notice it.[9]
And personification, we might notice, is "plainly the boldest of all rhetorical
figures."[10] Countless readers of Burke's *Reflections*, seeking to correlate such
figures to vehemence of emotion, were bewildered by the apparent lack of
cause, the radical improbability of Burke's violent tropes. Was it, in fact, genuine emotion, a simulacrum of feeling, or something else entirely?

Burke seems to have at once too much and too little control over his
tropes: too much for them to be spontaneous expressions of passion, too little for them to be conventional exercises in ornamentation. Burke's personifications seem to doubt their own credibility even as they insist on their
point. They led Mary Wollstonecraft, one of his most astute contemporary
readers, to wonder what Burke actually believed, if anything. His tropes irresistibly make her picture him as a "violent revolutionist," arguing for the
other side and exhibiting a purely theatrical emotion.[11] Burke's tropes have a
deterritorializing effect. Not only do they fail to testify to an unequivocally
held set of beliefs about meaning, but they also open up passages and connections between positions that are, in theory, diametrically opposed.

It is even more strange to realize that Burke's tropes in the *Reflections* pur-
port to designate the objects of patriotic or loyalist feeling: those institutions
that must be defended against revolutionary change. But when Burke defends the aristocracy, for example, through extended and elaborate figures,

the relations between object, subject, emotion, and trope become unfamiliar. In a naturalizing view, the object might be supposed to give rise to a strong feeling in the speaker, from which the trope proceeds. In Burke's case, however, the trope seems to give rise to a feeling, from which the value of the object is tentatively conceded. Burke is not merely showing how public emotion can be manipulated by rhetorically skilled politicians like himself. He suggests that openly manipulable artifice is the essence of civic emotion. In this chapter, I argue that Burke defines the public sphere, that zone where subjects come into contact with the state and its dominant ideologies, as a place of unmystified illusion. Though Burke does mention family and domestic life as examples or tropes for social ordering, he appears to be primarily concerned with the nation's public culture.[12] In particular, Burke challenges radicals' view of the public sphere as a space where individuals may exercise their unencumbered reason in defense of their own interests. In Burke's vision of the nation, the public sphere may be said to consist, rather, in the pretexts, the strategic namings and misnamings that are commonly acknowledged. Instead of asking which persons have the right to participate in the public sphere, Burke examines how tropes and figures provide pretexts for public feelings, affect the exercise of power, and hold a nation together.

Burke's own tropes thus stake out and defend the place of irony in patriotic culture. Turning away from the sublime that Burke had himself played an important part in theorizing, his tropes practically invite doubtfulness and deliberation. Instead of only using them at moments when powerful feeling might be expected, Burke often introduces hypertrophied conceits when he calmly assesses the value of institutions that are crucial to Britain's public sphere: the aristocracy, the church, the press, and other instruments of political oppression and opposition. Theorists such as Blair constantly warned orators to make sure that their audiences already shared their passions before attempting feats such as personification; otherwise, "We remain not only cold, but frozen," Blair writes, "and are at full leisure to criticise on the ridiculous figure which the personified object makes, when we ought to have been transported with a glow of enthusiasm."[13] Blair assumes that the rhetorician's goal is the production of the sublime. Burke had provided an influential definition of the sublime in his early *Philosophical Enquiry into the Origin of Our Ideas of the Sublime and the Beautiful* (1757): "the mind is so entirely filled with its object, that it cannot entertain any other, nor . . . reason on that object which employs it . . . the sublime . . . hurries us on by an irresistible force."[14] But when Burke comes to stipulate what is distinctive and, in his view, worth preserving about the British public sphere, he turns away equally from the sublime and the beautiful. The potential leisure to criticize, shunned by Blair as the frigid antithesis of aesthetic transport, is crucial to Burke. Burke finds his model of patriotic feeling in this leisure to criticize rather than in the collective transports of the sublime or the complacent social relaxation offered by the beautiful. Elaborate, static, self-involved, and sometimes grotesque, Burke's tropes demonstrate a highly resistible force— a tempered and qualified power that Burke would like to align with an ideal British way of governing. Burke's tropes incorporate this leisure to criticize, but they are not actually self-critical or parodic. Rather, they seem to culti-vate a particular kind of indifference: an indifference to the absence of pre-viously shared feeling or experience among the members of a public. The types of personifications that Burke likes to use do not claim in any simple way to articulate the common basis of individual experience. "Chivalry," for instance, fails to correspond to most people's experience of the British aris-tocracy, as Burke himself is quite happy to point out in works such as his *Letter to a Noble Lord.* Nor do they seek to impose a normative image of what ought to be general experience. According to one study of eighteenth-century poetry, personifications "[demand] that we attribute no value to whatever we do experience as individuals which does not correspond with common experience."[15] But Burke's strange personifications do not make such a demand. Rather, his obtrusive tropes gesture beyond what they locally represent to a larger tissue of social conventions: conventions of deference that are held in public and by a public, quite apart from individual experi-ence. When he writes, for example, that "[n]obility is a graceful ornament to the civil order. It is the Corinthian capital of polished society" (RRF 187– 88), Burke is exhibiting a social fiction that represents "what all its members share not individually but collectively, not privately but publicly" in the words of a recent critic.[16] Such a trope is itself an important example of "a public institution shared by its members . . . it is common to them not in a way that having two eyes is common to all human beings, but in a way that a dining table is common to those seated around it."[17] However, Burke's per-sonifications and other tropes do more than represent institutions that are held publicly and in common. They also represent the continual testing of that brittle consensus: on-going negotiations over which artificial ideals are appropriate to apply as pretexts or as self-descriptions in the public sphere.

Burke's well-wrought or over-wrought tropes are also important as highly visible examples of artifice. They are examples of making or of fabrication, offered at a moment when such concepts acquired charged political mean-ings. While indebted to the ideas of earlier conservative theorists like David Hume, Burke uses the concept of artifice in significantly different ways. For Hume, who fearlessly exposes justice to be an "artificial" rather than a nat-ural virtue, artifice refers to the ground of conventional behaviors, such as promise-keeping or respect for others' property, observed and praised by so-ciety as a whole. Such social behavior is regarded as artificial in that it fails to conform to Hume's vision of human nature as narrowly self-interested and swayed by that which is immediately present. Rules, for instance, are artifices contrived by conscious ingenuity rather than springing directly from the structure of the mind as Hume sees it.[18] They are followed for the sake of convenience, but for the most part unreflectively. [19] Habit and custom take over the regulation of action and soften the distinction between nature and artifice in practice and in theory. Artifice is after all simply a "more artful and more refin'd" version of nature.[20] Even if they were recognized to originate in human contrivance, Hume has little doubt that such rules would continue to be observed for their beneficial effects. But in the political climate in the 1790s, Burke could not take for granted the "commitments to institutional continuity, authority, [and] social hierarchy," that David Miller has shown could simply be assumed by Hume and Adam Smith. The terms as well as the stakes of political debate had changed.[21] What is at stake is the concept of self-determination. Radicals envisioned the public sphere as a metatopical space in which individual agency could be exercised to a particular end. In the public sphere, "private people," through the press or other organs of public opinion, would confront the state's authority, judging it by the standard of critical reason and shaping it to reflect their own interests.[22] The Revolution Society, a classic organ of the public sphere in this model, provides an example of such an independent agency. This voluntary association publicly passed a resolution approving the events in France and transmitted this resolution to the National Assembly. Burke censures and ridicules this radical club. But Burke does not advocate, as some of his followers do, a simple univocal loyalty, nor does he envision the public sphere as comprised of patriotic demonstrations alone. Burke eschews both the radical ideal of transparent agency and an opaque, unreflective adherence to the given. His tropes demonstrate a kind of making that is also a way of acting. Burke focuses on the fictions that mediate action in the public sphere. He reconstitutes the public sphere as a realm of convention: a thin but surprisingly resilient consensus about which pretexts can be summoned for action or emotion, how far they should be acknowledged, and when disavowed; and which conventional gestures of conciliation, deference, or unity can be performed, under what conditions.

Burke's vision of the public sphere shares the goal of building safeguards against the abuse of power. But instead of imputing such a force to organs of public opinion, Burke's *Reflections* looks at how public naming and misnaming, through tropes such as "inheritance," influence the ways in which political agents make choices and represent themselves. Burke often makes it appear as though the power of monarchs and legislative assemblies was controlled through their quasi-voluntary subordination to certain moral ideals. What is most quintessentially Burkean, however, is the way in which his rhetoric exaggerates the presence of a conscious confrontation with artifice. Burke's language even suggests that rhetorical artifices exert a ghostly agency of their own. In his *Letter to William Elliot* (1795), he writes that true citizens "would not suffer Monarchs or Senates or popular Assemblies . . . to shake off those moral riders which reason has appointed to govern every sort of rude power. These, in appearance leading them by their weight, do by that pressure augment their essential force"—an image drawn from the mechanics of plowing. The "riders" here are things, heavy moral ideals like "prudence and virtue" that weigh down those in power. But Burke immediately goes on to say:

> It is true, not only in the draught, but in the race. These riders of the great, in effect, hold the reins which guide them in their course, and wear the spur that stimulates them to the goals of honour and of safety. The great must submit to the dominion of prudence and virtue; or none will long submit to the dominion of the great.[23]

The passive weights become jockeys, spurring and guiding the aimless and inert holders of authority. The pun manages to suggest that the powerful are under the dominion not only of moral ideals but also possibly of persons who use those ideals to manipulate them. Personified ideals such as prudence and virtue can be forcefully misapplied to rulers as a means of stimulating them to reform: this is irony in the service of public spirit.[24] Burke also uses his powers of tendentious naming to challenge subalterns.[25] Eliciting an overwhelming public reaction full of angry pride, Burke's phrase, "a swinish multitude," gives radicals a crucial pretext to engage in public debate. Daniel Isaac Eaton's periodical, *Politics for the People, or a Salmagundy for Swine* (1793–95), was only one of innumerable radical pamphlets, serials, and broadsides called into being by Burke's notoriously dehumanizing personification.[26] Eaton and many other writers tried to construct their own political identities by appropriating that trope with a ferociously ironic deference to Burke's authority to misname them. Radicals often collaborated with Burke in making irony a recognized dimension of Britain's public sphere in this historical moment. They extended irony to the point where it can be difficult to distinguish radicals' voices from those of their avowed enemies: "The Swinish Multitude," one radical broadside promises, "will with the utmost Ease, and facility (to prove the exquisite refinement of their Taste) metamorphose a PALACE INTO PIG-STYE, and then transform a TREASURY CHEST INTO A HOG TROUGH," thereby seeming to fulfill the direst of Burke's predictions.[27] Burke's rhetoric provides pretexts to all sides.

By picturing a public sphere constituted by abstractions and personifications, Burke leaves strategically open the crucial political questions of who dominates, who submits, and whether this submission to power is sincere or merely politic. In his well-known discussion of chivalry, for example, Burke portrays chivalry as an oppositional force that "mitigated ferocity" and "subdued the fierceness of pride and power" (RRF 127). But he leaves it unclear whether it mitigated its own ferocity or that of its rulers, or perhaps accomplished the goal of subduing sovereigns by itself adopting a manner of ostentatious humility. In such careful evasion lies Burke's own politic irony, seemingly indifferent to the distinction between sovereign and subject. But Burke extends a particular consolation to those under the sway of another's power. Burke turns often in his revolutionary writings to the subject of the theater to describe feelings evoked by the spectacle of political power. For Burke, the theater represents a type of response to political authority that is not dependent on delusion: emotion that coexists with a detached, leisured awareness of how artificial conventions have mediated one's response. Such a response closely resembles the response Burke invites to his own rhetorical displays. The theater institutionalizes active complicity as a regular public experience. Burke wants to suggest that Britain's politics, unlike those of revolutionary France, rests on voluntary complicity with public illusions. Despite its movements of sympathy, the audience retains control over its own tacit feelings. (And indeed observers of post-Napoleonic France, including Walter Scott, noted just such a voluntary, even cynical complicity.) But what Burke says about the theater is designed to collapse distinctions between audience and actor, between conscious imitation and genuine feeling. Actors, audiences, and real participants in the public sphere all seem to create apparently genuine emotions in themselves by invoking abstract images and personified emotions—such as the useful civic emotions of "love, veneration, admiration, or attachment" (RRF 129). Sometimes but not always by design, actors and citizens work on their own bodies through a language of outward, conventional gesture so as to produce real, not merely feigned, feelings. What may begin as the conscious imitation of servility may even end up as a genuine sensation not amenable to control. In the end, Burke offers a strange, ironic image of the politic body of Britain's subjects: a body instinctively sagacious, astute, able to work on its own feelings through the application of abstract ideals, but in control of its doubleness only up to a certain point.

Far from being a spontaneous emanation of strong feeling, then, Burke's figurative language is important precisely for its avoidance of passion. It is not designed to be overlooked; defying abatement, it becomes itself a second-order figure for the mediated nature of political sentiments in the nation Burke is defending. In his *Reflections*, Burke comments on the recent revolutionary events in France as a way to offer to a broad public a particular image of Britain's own political culture. The image is not of Britain as it is, but as it could be imagined, and thus as it could actually become. To prevent the possibility of radical reform, he represents the public sphere as already working to curb power. But his picture of the nation is far from idyllic, idealizing, or sentimental. It does not merely assert the existence of certain natural feelings, relationships, rights, or capacities which, in the absence of artificial impediments, are bound necessarily to assert themselves through the actions of individuals or groups. In the public sphere that he describes, political outcomes are tied to the strange influence of tropes, pretexts, and other artifices.

Daniel Eaton, self-appointed spokesperson for the "swine," unintentionally confirms this view as he tries to undo what he sees as the black, Circean magic of Burke's rhetoric: "Thy magic rod, audacious Burke / Could metamorphize Man to pork, / And quench the Spark divine; / But Eaton's Wonderworking Wand, / By scattering knowledge through the Land / Is making Men of Swine."[28] Perhaps still too much under Burke's influence, Eaton portrays the restoration of nature not as the result of rational agency but as an act of countermagic.[29] Not only radicals but also conservative ironists such as Walter Scott and Thomas Carlyle ambivalently cooperated with Burke in his project of creating a stable, coherent modern nation out of a volatile mixture of prejudice, self-conscious enlightenment, civic feelings, civic ideals, and irony.

Radical Agency

In a letter written in August 1789, Burke sets up the coordinates of the position from which his first major counterrevolutionary work was to be delivered. He describes to the Irish peer Lord Charlemont the spectacle provided by English spectators:

> As to us here our thoughts of everything at home are suspended, by our astonishment at the wonderful Spectacle which is exhibited in a Neighbouring and rival Country—what Spectators, and what actors! England gazing with astonishment at a French struggle for Liberty and not knowing whether to blame or to applaud![30]

For Burke, not just the foreground of the spectacle but the show itself is provided by England rather than France. Burke directs his gaze anxiously at the faces of the rapt audience. The British reaction continues to be his chief concern in the *Reflections*, published the following year. Both in his private letters and his published works, Burke provides ample evidence of the intentions behind this work: to change the generally favorable, if not enthusiastic, British response to the French Revolution into one of "dread and apprehension from the contagious nature of those abominable principles, and vile manners, which threaten the worst and most degrading barbarism."[31] More particularly, what drives Burke to answer a brief enquiry from a young French aristocrat with an extended comparative analysis of England, ancien régime France, and revolutionary France is the wish to discredit and "expose," as he puts it, "to the hatred, ridicule, and contempt of the whole world" radical Whig aristocrats and their coterie, including, most notably, the Dissenting minister Richard Price.[32] It is well known that the event that prompted the

Reflections was a sermon Price delivered in November 1789 to the radical London Revolution Society, in which English habits of servility and stasis were compared unfavorably with French liberty and self-transformation.[33] But to understand why Burke portrays Britain as he does, we need to see the *Reflections* in the broader context of Burke's engagement with the Dissenting movement for reform. This movement generated a conception of political agency that could be used, Burke fears, to incite widespread revolutionary unrest in Britain. It is in response to this as much as to France that Burke represents Britain's public sphere as a space of irony and unstable duplicity.

Burke's relationship to Dissent was something of a puzzle; while Dissenters had historically been allied with the Rockingham Whigs, by the 1780s, Burke's attitude toward them seemed to be negative, to the surprise of many. The 1787 movement to repeal the Test and Corporation Acts had begun, it seems, with the expectation that Burke would lend his support; but the Dissenting delegates sent to sound out Whig leaders reported that Burke, unlike Lansdowne and Fox, did not receive the idea encouragingly.[34] Burke argued that Dissenters should not be permitted to enter politics because of the need for one officially recognized religion — a position that appears particularly odd considering that he supported the movement for Catholic emancipation in Ireland.[35] But it is worth noting that in the meantime, largely through the writings of Richard Price and Joseph Priestley, Dissenters had adopted in national political debate a discourse with characteristic themes and preoccupations. Most notable among these was the idea of political agency, conceived of as an individually possessed right. Price's *Observations on the Nature of Civil Liberty* (1776), which sold 60,000 copies, became one of the most influential publications in the debate over the American Revolution; in this work Price uses his defense of the American colonies to criticize British political culture in ways that would become deeply antipathetic to Burke at the outset of the French Revolution.[36]

Price's *Observations on the Nature of Civil Liberty* carries out its argument on many fronts, though always with an eye toward making the case for the extension of political rights within Britain. Its arguments against prosecuting a war with the colonies base themselves on "Justice," the "Honour of the Kingdom," economic policy, particularly the effects of paper circulation, and "[t]he principles of the constitution."[37] Most of all, though, it devotes itself to constructing the notion of agency as a simple abstraction. Through its manifold arguments, agency emerges as a single, unified idea that provides the ground of all legitimate politics and policy. Price begins by analyzing the different varieties of liberty: physical, moral, religious, and civil. "Physical liberty" is "that principle of spontaneity, or self-determination, which constitutes us agents, or which gives us a command over our actions, rendering them properly ours, and not effects of the operation of any foreign cause" (21–22). Several patterns can be noted in this definition. Liberty is rendered nearly synonymous with agency; agency is associated with command and with property/propriety, and most importantly the strong distinction is established between what is "properly ours" and what is "foreign." These patterns continue to be developed: moral, religious, and civil liberty are all defined as the power to reject influences external or extraneous to the self. "In all of these cases," Price sums up, "there is a force which stands opposed to the agent's own will, and which . . . produces servitude . . . [T]his force is incompatible with the very idea of voluntary motion; and the subject of it is a mere passive instrument which never acts, but is always acted upon" (22–23). Price stands strongly by this coupling of liberty with the notion of agency; in his *Additional Observations on the Nature and Value of Civil Liberty*, published a year later in answer to his many respondents, he reaffirms that "the liberty of men as agents is *that power of self-determination which all agents, as such, possess*" (76, emphasis added). It is noteworthy that Price seems deliberately to ignore the common usage of the word "agent" to mean representative or delegate; he is interested in establishing a very strong sense of agency as originary power.[38] Agency is the power of exerting one's own will, whether directly or through a proxy—a mode Price reluctantly admits in the face of the practical difficulties of direct democracy.

The relation that Price's notion of agency bears to the Dissenting reform movement becomes clear when he states that "the fundamental principle of our constitution . . . is that every independent agent in a free state ought to have a share in the government of it" (80). Ostensibly, he refers to the Americans; but he seems to have in mind also the Test and Corporation Acts, which prevented Dissenters from holding crown, state, military or municipal offices, and subjected them to numerous other penalties, unless they publicly participated in the rituals of the Established Church. These legal and social pressures to conform to beliefs accepted by others are clearly resented in the public statements issued in the 1787–90 campaign for repeal. In an address "To the People of England" from the committee in charge of the movement for repeal, the Dissenters "assert our claim to think and act for ourselves."[39] Yet in this statement, published in May 1790 after the motion failed yet again, and in many others, the Dissenting discourse of autonomy converges with the discourse of the French Revolution. The Dissenters make their appeal in two seemingly incompatible political languages: "Great Britain," the above address concludes, "will not permit herself to be exceeded by other countries in the regards which are due to the rights of men and of citizens and to the claims of faithful and loyal subjects."[40] The Dissenters portray themselves as loyal subjects, who unquestioningly accept their subordination, and also as citizens of a universal community of natural rights. The juxtaposition is not stable; neither was it found plausible.

Inherent in Price's concept of agency is a radical egalitarianism. In a free state, Price had written in the earlier *Observations*, "all the springs of action have room to operate and the mind is stimulated to the noblest exertions. But to be obliged . . . to look up to a creature no better than ourselves as the master of our fortunes, and to receive his will as our law. . . . What elevated ideas can enter a mind in such a situation?" (Obs. 29) Price draws attention to the degradation of heteronomy, of having another determine our will. The influence of this emotionally charged language of agency can be seen in any number of pamphlets written in response to the *Reflections* or to the French Revolution. For instance, in *Lessons to a Young Prince by an Old Statesman* (1791), the writer, David Williams, expounds to the future George IV the familiar radical tale of the corruption of the British constitution. Originally, before the Norman Conquest, freemen controlled the workings of government. In 1790, he asserts, utter corruption has set in: the "English Nation" at present is "a passive mass acted upon . . . the English Government is a machine acting on the people, and managed at the will and for the interest of particular orders."[41] The French nation, however, will become through its new constitution "an organized body acting for itself"—what Williams describes metaphorically as "Prometheus, a moral agent at liberty, and conferring heavenly blessings on the world."[42] The French are free, in short, to act in the original etymological sense of the word. As Hannah Arendt paraphrases its meaning, "To act . . . means to take an initiative, to begin . . . to set something into motion. . . . It is in the nature of beginning that something new is started which cannot be expected from whatever may have happened before."[43] The origin of this notion of agency in the classical ideal of virtue becomes apparent.

It takes little, however, to see that the radical idea of agency runs into trouble over the opposition between internal and external, self and other—the opposition on which its conceptual coherence depends. In social practice, "foreign causes" of one's actions or motions are not so easily distinguished from native causes, short of actual cases of physical restraint or force; the anticipated opinions and perceptions of others, for example, fall into neither category neatly. Conversely, the self, which ought to be united, separates into internal and external layers. Once embedded in a concrete set of circumstances, self-conscious agency starts to take on the features of theatricality or of action in the theatrical sense of the word: external gesture. This dynamic emerges in Price's 1789 sermon, *A Discourse on the Love of our Country*. The stated goal of the sermon is to reflect on the meaning of patriotism "and to make it a just and rational principle of action." [44] Discussing the response to the recent crisis of George III's illness, Price is moved to assert the need for Britons to assume their proper agency. He instructs his listeners to go forth and raise the consciousnesses of British subjects: "Enlighten them and you will elevate them. Shew them they are *men* and they will act like *men*. . . . In our late addresses to the King on his recovery . . . we have appeared more like a herd crawling at the feet of a master than like enlightened and manly citizens rejoicing with a beloved sovereign."[45] But what does it mean to "act like men"? Price writes:

> Had I been to address the King on a late occasion, I should have been inclined to do it in a style very different from that of most of the addressers, and to use some such language as the following:
> I rejoice, Sir, in your recovery. I thank God for his goodness to you. . . . May you enjoy all possible happiness. May God shew you the folly of those effusions of adulation which you are now receiving, and guard you against their effects. May you be led to such a sense of the nature of your situation and endowed with such wisdom as shall . . . engage you to consider yourself as more properly the *servant* than the sovereign of your people.[46]

Burke cites this as an example of strikingly uncouth manners. But there is an even more strikingly theatrical quality in both the situation Price chooses to imagine and the political action he models. Rather than imagining himself engaged in legislative action, or in any act of directing his motions by his own will, Price envisions a scene in which his external manner, bearing, and "language" are to represent both a larger body of people and a particular ideal of "manliness." He casts himself in a given role as the ambassador of the people and imagines the manner in which he would deliver his speech in a very public setting. He draws attention himself to his "style" and "language" as matters of primary importance, inviting us to imagine the suitable tone and gestures (action) that might accompany the delivered speech. And the theatricality runs even deeper: agency here means not acting according to one's own laws but rather acting in a way calculated to produce a certain effect on the minds of the audience in accordance with given norms of verisimilitude.

A similar dialectic can be seen in William Godwin's *Enquiry Concerning Political Justice* (1793), an expansion of many of the same themes and ideas that had emerged in Price's writings. Here, too, an ideal of independent action or agency comes to resemble its opposite: a mode of external action ironically at odds with the contents of subjective consciousness and allied instead with accepted social forms. Godwin advises his readers on the proper mode of action vis-à-vis the necessary evil of government: " 'Comply, where the necessity of the case demands it, but criticise while you comply. Obey . . . but beware of reverence. [Do not confound] things, so totally unconnected with each other, as a purely political obedience, and respect.' "[47] In short, Godwin counsels, act as though you respected your governors and superiors while scrupulously withholding from them any internal deference or confidence. Maintain an obedient exterior and a seditious mind. " 'Obedience and external submission is [*sic*] all you [the government] are entitled to claim; you can

have no right to extort our deference, and command us not to see, and dis-
approve of, your errors.'"[48] In both of these passages, speaking in an assumed
character and scenario, Godwin seems to counsel the practice of irony.

But how deep or how shallow is external submission? In the repressive political climate of the 1790s, this becomes a matter of practical urgency to radicals and to counterrevolutionaries alike.[49] What Seyla Benhabib has called
"the interpretive indeterminacy of action" becomes a charged affair particularly in the sedition trials of this period.[50] What constitute the boundaries
of an act? Does it begin with the motions of the body, as opposed to the mind?
Who is it that acts? Is it the truth that acts in or through us when we dissent
silently or audibly from the commands of power? Defending Thomas Paine
in December 1792, Thomas Erskine tried to draw the boundaries of action
and the sphere of agency:

> every man . . . seeking to enlighten others with what his own reason
> and conscience, however erroneously, have dictated to him as truth,
> may address himself to the universal reason of a whole nation. . . . All
> this every subject of this country has a right to do, if he . . . but seeks
> to change the public mind. . . . If, indeed, he . . . holds out to individ-
> uals that they have a right to . . . oppose by contumacy or force what
> private reason only disapproves . . . he is then a criminal . . . because
> such a person . . . excites to overt acts of misconduct.[51]

Trying to exculpate Paine from the charge of sedition, Erskine entangles
himself in the ambiguous relationships between truth, belief, agency, and action. In the end, Erskine drives a wedge between "the public mind" and
"overt acts." He almost suggests that good Britishness consists in private, enlightened disaffection, belied perhaps by outward acclamations of loyalty. Erskine, Godwin, and others inadvertently strengthen the case made by Burke's
Reflections. In the *Reflections*, Burke represents the nation's "public mind" as
a web of conventional tropes used to obscure questions of agency. In tropes
such as that of inheritance, distinctions between self and other, agency and
instrumentality, are strategically blurred.

Contemplating Inheritance

An important object of Burke's *Reflections* is to eclipse the radical ideal of
agency in the public mind. Burke does so by offering a description of the
British nation as a complex, ironic whole within which simple, decontextualized acts of individual will cannot be made out. In Burke's picture, rather,
the nation dedicates itself to equivocal forms and fictions of agency. Para-

mount in this representation is the theme of voluntary self-restriction; thus, the interpretation of the Glorious Revolution becomes crucially important. In his *Discourse on the Love of our Country*, Price insists that the people of England acquired in 1688, "the right to chuse our own governors, to cashier them for misconduct, and to frame a government for ourselves."[52] Radical arguments for political reform stress the loss of this right; David Williams, for example, sees in the 1790s "[t]he Body of the People variously operated upon, and amused by Forms, but having no election, choice, or share in the Political Government."[53] To this point, Burke argues that, if there was a choice made at the time of the 1688 Revolution, it was, paradoxically, a choice *not* to choose: "if we had possessed [the right to elect our kings] before, the English nation did at that time most solemnly renounce and abdicate it . . . for ever" (RRF 70). Burke daringly describes the nation's act as an abdication, associating it with James II's dereliction. Burke's use of the word is, however, ironic in that the right thus abdicated was of highly doubtful existence; Burke insists that the monarchy had always been a hereditary rather than an elective one. According to Burke, what England chose in 1688, "observing . . . the traditionary language, along with the traditionary policy of the nation" (RRF 70), was an old principle or paradigm of inheritance as the basis of its modern nationhood. Inheritance might seem to be a form of traditionalism, in that it includes a habit of considering everything as "handed down, to us and from us." But in Burke's hands this basis of national identity, semi-personified in elaborate ways, becomes more than an institution and more than a hermeneutic code, though inheritance is also both of these things. By its means, the British nation becomes a peculiar, ironic whole, whose parts continually have to resign themselves, in every sense of that word.

Burke claims that "it has been the uniform policy of our constitution to claim and assert our liberties, as an *entailed inheritance* derived to us from our forefathers, and to be transmitted to our posterity" (RRF 83, original emphasis). A mode of action, a uniform style of claiming and asserting is in question; but the agent's identity is far less clear. Syntactically, the agent is not a person but "our constitution"—recorded acts such as the Magna Charta and the Declaration of Right (both of which Burke cites). But there is a broader sense of the word in play as well: constitution as make-up, composition, or structure. In his *Philosophical Enquiry*, Burke had used the phrases "mechanical structure" and "natural frame and constitution" synonymously.[54] In the *Reflections*, "constitution" is surrounded with overtones less mundane than mystical, but it remains nevertheless a structure, that is, a necessary relation obtaining between parts. In this sense, "policy" and constitution pull against each other, and the moment recalls others when Burke suggests that necessity is often a pliable human invention. This is the first of Burke's crucial equivocations: England both can and cannot do otherwise.

Inheritance may reflect either a necessary constitution or a contingent policy or a dialectic of both. This constitution, whether framed or given, acts in history on the external world: it claims new rights, and more important, it *derives* old or existing distributions of power. It tells a story about itself: about how "our constitution preserves an unity in so great a diversity of its parts," and how certain "privileges, franchises, and liberties" were acquired. This story has a protagonist, but one that is not identified with a tangible social group, aristocrats or the people, Whigs or Tories, not identified even with an institution or a concrete social practice but rather with an idea: the idea of inheritance. "[T]he people of England well know, that the idea of inheritance furnishes a sure principle of conservation, and a sure principle of transmission" (RRF 83). Inheritance provides a certain formal unity for the description of English social and political life. But it is most useful to Burke for the ways in which it undercuts the ideas of agency, property, and proper agency. At Burke's hands, inheritance introduces notions of change, loss, and contingency. At the same time, it is familiar, even familial. A crude summary of Burke's doctrine of inheritance might state the following: as a mode of coming by and owning property, the social practice of inheritance provides a stabler ground of possession than theoretical right because it cannot be extricated from countless local contingencies. But part of the meaning of Burke's doctrine lies in its resistance to paraphrase: while Price's principles are meant to be summed up and easily retained, the concept of abridgement is the antithesis of inheritance. Inheritance is not something to be extracted and applied but rather experienced as a continual process of loss, resignation, and self-resignation. Individual possession is continually undercut, and thus, according to Burke's deeply paradoxical logic, made more secure. Finally, inheritance allows Burke to stress the role of contemplation in Britain's political culture and the ways in which such contemplation ensues in a civilized theatricality of action.

Burke imagines a place within his paradigm of inheritance for individual exertion, yet promptly subordinates it to the good of a larger whole—an "imaginary whole" in protest against which Wollstonecraft and others asserted the rights of the individual.[55] But at a critical juncture, Burke introduces into this story of accretion and aggrandizement a startling element of defeasibility. Burke begins by noting that inheritance does not "at all exclud[e] a principle of improvement. It leaves acquisition free; but it secures what it acquires. Whatever advantages are obtained . . . are locked fast as in a sort of family settlement; grasped as in a kind of mortmain for ever" (RRF 84). Active getting occurs in the margins as a sort of footnote to the main plot: the transmission through time of property, life, and government. In this transmission, though, nothing can be said to be either "properly ours" or "foreign." Actions are performed not as an expression of will but seemingly as an effect of concordance.

We receive, we hold, we transmit our government and our privileges, in the same manner in which we enjoy and transmit our property and our lives. The institutions of policy, the goods of fortune, the gifts of Providence, are handed down, to us and from us, in the same course and order. (RRF 84)

Burke transmutes these ambiguous types of action (receiving, holding, transmitting) into the static *attributes* of a particular kind of body: "a permanent body composed of transitory parts; wherein . . . the whole, at one time, is never old, or middle-aged, or young, but in a condition of unchangeable constancy, moves on through the varied tenour of perpetual decay, fall, renovation, and progression" (RRF 84). This body, the body of the English people and of their polity, is never identical with itself, making it inconceivable as a unified "moral agent at liberty." Moreover, the concept of *agere* (to set into motion) undergoes a curious revision. This body "moves through [a] varied tenour"; it moves only internally in its shifting composition, and only metaphorically moves itself through time. Inheritance has to do not with the transmission of external things, as we might expect, but with a perpetual balancing act performed by a body on its own parts. The narrative of inheritance is turned into a way to describe synchronically the structure of the nation's constitution at any given moment. What is most surprising, though, is the way in which Burke introduces "perpetual decay [and] fall" into what was supposed to be an endless accretion of benefits "grasped . . . for ever." The whole that Burke describes is not only heterogeneous but also constantly losing its grasp on parts of itself, revising itself and its fictions out of necessity.

Burke's assertion that the English constitution reflects a "choice of inheritance" is compromised by what follows. In a minor way it is qualified by Burke's claim that the constitution was shaped not through an independent act but in a condition of tutelage: "we are guided," he writes, "by the spirit of philosophic analogy." But the idea of choice is vexed even further. Burke's syntax reveals that, within the texture of English political and social relations, agency can become a matter of seeking or of positing relations in an attempt to bind the collective self together: "In this choice of inheritance, we have given to our frame of polity the image of a relation in blood; binding up the constitution of our country with our dearest domestic ties; adopting our fundamental laws into the bosom of our family affections; keeping inseparable, and cherishing with the warmth of all their combined and mutually reflected charities, our state, our hearths, our sepulchres, and our altars" (RRF 84). Burke associates the principle of inheritance with "domestic ties," as many readers have noticed.[56] Inheritance represents at one level the warm mutual embrace of politics and sentiment, laws and family; on another level, it suggests a dissolution of the boundaries (including that between animate and inanimate) on which action would depend. In the first person plural possessive, the collective agent certainly remains a presence, but it becomes blurred and attenuated through the anaphoric reverberations of "binding, adopting, keeping." The important "charities" are not ours but "their[s]", emanating from and belonging to the half-personified institutions of the hearth, sepulchre, and altar. The imagined totality of the nation continually binds itself up and together in a way that quietly implies its constant dissolution.[57]

Burke would argue that for the British, choice is something more to be contemplated than to be attempted. But his description of the "choice of inheritance" as an object to be "considered" leads him to yet another daring contradiction. Inheritance is supposed to be a name for the familiarity of the past and of the public; but Burke goes on to depict it as the very principle of strangeness, intimidation, and distance. He notes that the English "have derived several other . . . benefits, from considering our liberties in the light of an inheritance. Always acting as if in the presence of canonized forefathers, the spirit of freedom, leading in itself to misrule and excess, is tempered with an awful gravity" (RRF 84–85). These are the important consequences of an interpretive rather than an assertive act: "considering" or construing political rights in a certain way. The interpretation hinges on making a particular equivalence—seeing one thing or situation "as if" it were another thing. Within his own interpretation, Burke performs an important metaphorical substitution of great importance: for "the people of England" he discreetly substitutes "the spirit of freedom." Again, an intangible style or spirit is the agent. It is this "spirit of freedom" that seems to contemplate fearfully the "awful gravity" of "canonized forefathers." It disguises its natural character, suppressing its ebullience with a performance of dignity. Burke's "acting as if" gestures toward the theatricality that Price and others had refused to acknowledge. Price's radical logic could not admit the possibility that liberty could have this theatrical dimension. Burke goes on to personify the abstraction of liberty in such a way as to dissociate it almost completely from practical action. Made purely for contemplation, Burke's British liberty becomes a stage set—one that prescribes and prohibits actions through its powerful decorum. "Our liberty becomes a noble freedom. It carries an imposing and majestic aspect. It has a pedigree and illustrating ancestors. It has its bearings and its ensigns armorial. It has its gallery of portraits; its monumental inscriptions; its records, evidences, and titles" (RRF 85). English liberty, thus described, achieves nothing and is instantiated in no act. It is static, self-referential display. Through this moment of allegoresis, Burke manages to make liberty independent of actions and agents. The idea is not even given the attributes of a human agent. It becomes a place or a temple in Angus Fletcher's terms.[58]

By emphasizing how it is consciously contemplated, Burke suggests an essential estrangement, almost approaching irony, within the structure of inheritance. It is not an idea that unconsciously regulates acts or thoughts;

rather, Burke describes a self-conscious knowing that correlates to the quasi-theatrical "acting as if" that he praises. Burke's entire discussion of inheritance is framed within this critical assertion about the actual citizens of the nation: "The people of England well know, that the idea of inheritance furnishes a sure principle." The nation is not merely accustomed to this idea through habitual usage. Rather, Burke suggests, Britain recognizes how certain ideas can shape or conceal social reality. With the phrase, "choice of inheritance," he comes close to suggesting that England is in the ironic condition of having chosen its own limiting ideology, in the weaker sense of the word "ideology" as a constellation of ideas and beliefs or a political culture.[59] If we take Burke's formulation literally, the idea of liberty and the acts of piety that Burke enumerates are bound together by occurring within a medium to which Burke gives the name of inheritance. Inheritance is not so much an instrument by means of which ends are accomplished as a name for a larger, framing code within which national culture can be described and political decisions vindicated. The figure of inheritance is an artificial medium analogous to that "dense medium" of "common life" that refracts and redirects the abstract, universal rights of men, according to Burke.[60] To say that the actions of English rulers and subjects occur "[i]n this choice of inheritance" is both to recognize and to deny human agency on several levels.

Abstraction, Personification, and the Curtailment of Power

By emphasizing inheritance as a national trope, Burke may appear to be advocating a wholly passive attitude toward the constitution. But this is not the case. Rather than simply defending existing forms of power, Burke consistently turns his attention to the cultural conditions that enable political opposition. To one of these conditions he gives the name "chivalry." Burke offers high praise for chivalry as an effectual model for controlling and limiting sovereignty. But chivalry challenges power indirectly, even quixotically, through the defense of abstract ideals that are not embodied: ideals that exist only in the nation's imaginary. If the trope of inheritance bound the nation together as an ironic whole, Burke's scheme of chivalry assumes the nation to be divided between those with power and those without. With particular attention to those in subaltern positions, Burke here examines the role played by rhetorical illusion in the homeostasis of political struggle. From its first publication, the section of Burke's text devoted to the defense of chivalry has drawn the keenest criticism; with remarkable unanimity, critics, ranging from Thomas Paine and William Godwin to present-day readers such as Ronald Paulson and Claudia Johnson, have condemned this part of the *Reflections* for the way it seems to use heightened emotion or its textual counterpart to make a case for political passivity or outright servility.[61] Godwin, for example, establishes the link between Burke's revolutionary spectacles and absolutism:

> There are two modes, according to which the minds of human beings may be influenced, by him who is desirous to conduct them. The first of these, is a strong and commanding picture, taking hold of the imagination . . . the second, a distinct and unanswerable statement of reasons.[62]

But, even as it presents what many have experienced as an energetic picture, this section of Burke's *Reflections* relies most heavily on strangely abstract personifications. Burke even turns Marie Antoinette from a historical person into a fictive personification: the personification of abstract ideals that the real queen, unfortunately, failed to embody. The institution of chivalry also emerges as a notoriously ahistorical abstraction, though Burke praises it for its historical record of opposing centralized power. Yet this is one of the points that Burke wants to make: that using abstractions rather than proper names, and using words that have only conjectural rather than failsafe referents have been effective ways of changing the dynamic of power in the public sphere.

Burke sees chivalry as a form of political opposition that places illusion or nonexistence at its center. There is at least a partial precedent for this view. One of Burke's most important sources for his discussion of chivalry in the *Reflections* is the influential *Origin of the Distinction of Ranks* (1771) by the Scottish Enlightenment historian John Millar. Millar's account emphasizes two features of medieval chivalry: self-discipline, particularly in "rules and maxims" of warfare, produced by "notions of honour"; and "the passion between the sexes," which it raised to a historically new level of importance.[63] The latter receives more attention from Millar:

> Thus, while his thoughts were constantly fixed upon the same object [his lady], and while his imagination, inflamed by absence and repeated disappointments, was employed in heightening all those charms . . . his passion was at length wrought up to the highest pitch, and uniting with the love of fame, became the ruling principle, which gave a particular turn and direction to all his sentiments and opinions.[64]

Millar, like Burke, sees the cultural influence of chivalry on modern European culture as both deep and extensive and links it to the growing social empowerment of women in European modernity.[65] Burke also places an absent woman in a crucial role, but he tends to figure gender less directly, ascribing it to rhetorical figures rather than to concrete persons. Wollstonecraft found this relative deemphasizing of gender suspicious, even insidious.[66] But Burke subsumes gender difference within broader differences of power. Chivalry's imagined achievement, for him, lies in the tactics it inspired in social and political subalterns. The important point is that material effects follow from something that is not really there.

> Without force, or opposition, it subdued the fierceness of pride and power; it obliged sovereigns to submit to the soft collar of social esteem, compelled stern authority to submit to elegance, and gave a domination vanquisher of laws, to be subdued by manners. (RRF 127)

In this scenario, opposition is almost imperceptible. It does not operate through overt resistance or attempts to circumscribe power. Esteem and elegance are inessential, merely decorative supplements, but end up vanquishing power by being merely negligible. An inherent weakness in power seems to emerge under these cultural conditions.[67] In praising chivalry for bringing about these conditions, Burke is assuming that his readers have a strong interest in curbing power—that they imagine themselves in the position of political opposition. This is an attitude with which Burke consistently identified himself; at the end of the *Reflections*, for example, he depicts himself as "one who has been no tool of power" and describes "the tenour of his life" as a struggle against "tyranny" and a campaign "to discredit opulent oppression" (RRF 293).[68] Burke's oppositional stance rests on important assumptions about the nature of political power: for instance, that power, dominion, or the monopoly of force will always "survive the shock in which manners and opinions perish" (RRF 129). Power's sole aim is to preserve itself by perpetuating all forms of inequality. If not inwardly subverted by the spirit of chivalry, it will rely on "preventive murder and preventive confiscation, and that long roll of grim and bloody maxims, which form the political code of all power" (RRF 129).

It would have been easier for radicals to refute Burke if he could be seen as simply advocating servility or recommending that we "receive [another's] will as our law," in Price's words. But Burke praises chivalry because he sees ostentatious outward servility as a means of disarming the vigilance of power. That chivalry involves only a pose or pretext of humility Burke is careful to make clear, describing the institution as "that subordination of the heart, which kept alive, even in servitude itself, the spirit of an exalted freedom" (RRF 127). Throughout Burke's model, political action involves not the open interaction of equals, but a tactical and largely unspoken negotiation between commander and subaltern. And what he values in chivalry is the apparatus of consciousness that permits subalterns to maintain, surreptitiously and ironically, their own agency:

All the pleasing illusions, which made power gentle and obedience
liberal, which . . . incorporated into politics the sentiments which
beautify and soften private society, are to be dissolved. . . . All the super-added ideas furnished from the wardrobe of a moral imagination,
which the heart owns, and the understanding ratifies, as necessary to
cover the defects of our naked shivering nature, and to raise it to dignity in our own estimation, are to be exploded as a ridiculous, absurd,
and antiquated fashion. (RRF 128)

The subaltern's sense of dignity is ironic in its foreknowledge of its illusory
nature. Burke does go on to suggest that superiors are as much in need of this
imaginative "drapery" as inferiors; and one is tempted to object to the contention that kings and queens, who are already possessed of institutional
power, also need to be decked out with our thoughts. But in the context of
chivalry, Burke seems primarily to be concerned with the difficulties of imagining oneself as a public agent with an interest in "mitigating" power. Elsewhere he writes of the need to overcome the "natural . . . timidity with regard to power," the need to imagine oneself as qualified to act in a "liberal"
sense in a sphere outside private life.[69] The psychology of empowerment, the
relation between "our own estimation" of ourselves and political effective-
ness, and the conditions that ease the transition to public life and action, are
all subjects that consistently interest Burke. In an early publication, *Observations on a Late State of the Nation* (1769), Burke discussed the process by
which those new to public office or power become "formed to affairs." Neo-
phytes proceed from initial diffidence to confidence and, ultimately, to corruption or the abuse of power for their own ends.[70] Burke's writings on political party also form an important part of this strand of discourse; in his
Thoughts on the Causes of the Present Discontents (1770), for example, he defends the motives and the effects of political party in terms closely related to
his praise of chivalry in the *Reflections*. Like chivalry, which "incorporated
into politics the sentiments which beautify and soften private society" (RRF
128), political parties allow the individual to draw strength from the connections of "private honor" and "friendship" and thus establish a continuity between the realms of private and public feeling and action. They show "public and private virtues, not dissonant and jarring, and mutually destructive,
but harmoniously combined." They can be seen as "[bringing] the dispositions that are lovely in private life into the service and conduct of the commonwealth."[71] This is one of the "superadded ideas" that emboldened Burke's
party, and Burke himself, to oppose the monarch's influence and the power
and pride of the court faction.[72]

At the same time, Burke strategically blurs the distinction between opposition and obedience. The very same ideas, the same set of consciousness, can
inspire both, or an amalgam which makes the two indistinguishable and

which clearly works toward a conservative end. Private feeling not only emboldens "private men to be fellows with kings" but also apparently inspires them to be willing servants, at least outwardly. When Burke declares his emotions to have been particularly stirred by "the sex, the beauty, and the amiable qualities of the descendant of so many kings and emperors, with the tender age of royal infants" who suffered in the events of October 6, 1789, he seems to feel as a private, gendered being. The widespread disapproval elicited by his feelings for Marie Antoinette attests to this sense that Burke has crossed a line by bringing those most private of feelings, sexual feelings, into a public and political realm.[73] But if private sentiments are involved at all, they are surely curiously artificial ones. What rules out any personal element of feeling from this passage is the way in which Burke excises all that makes the queen into a particular being: all the scandalous material that constituted the historical Marie Antoinette.[74] He is not in the least concerned with her character, her desires, or even the concrete political force she was able to exercise. His feelings, he claims, are motivated solely by abstract notions of "sex," "beauty," "rank," "age," and the equally vague amiability that is conventionally deduced from these qualities. On the basis of these abstract or "superadded ideas," Burke feels sympathy not for a particular being but for the curiously bodiless suffering of an abstraction.

Devotion to the female sex as such is, of course, the characteristic of "foppery," and Burke's friend, Philip Francis, accuses him of precisely this affectation in the passage in question.[75] But Francis seizes on the abstract quality of Burke's feeling without discerning further. It is not simply a question of gender per se, but of the ancien régime's ordering of sex and rank into a baroque hierarchy. The queen represents, ex officio, the latter. In Burke's celebrated memory of having seen her as the dauphiness, she is literally a "vision" of an entire abstract order, presented allegorically.

> It is now sixteen or seventeen years since I saw the queen of France
> . . . at Versailles; and surely never lighted on this orb, which she
> hardly seemed to touch, a more delightful vision. I saw her just above
> the horizon, decorating and cheering the elevated sphere she just began to move in,—glittering like the morning star, full of life, and
> splendor, and joy. (RRF 126)

Like an allegorical image, as Angus Fletcher describes it, the queen of Burke's fond memory is "perfectly isolated, circumscribed," removed from narrative sequence or causality, and emblematic of a hierarchical order.[76] She symbolizes hierarchy for the same reason that, Fletcher argues, the astral image is favored by allegory: "astral imagery . . . displays the highest degree of symbolic isolation [distinctive of allegory as a mode], for not only are all stars all separated from each other . . . but they are even more distantly separated from man, who must adore and admire from a vast . . . distance."[77] This distance enhances the sense of almost overdetermined significance borne by the allegorical image and by Burke's image of the queen. Burke goes on to envision her in ways that make her status even more impersonal:

> Little did I dream . . . that she should ever be obliged to carry the
> sharp antidote against disgrace concealed in that bosom; little did I
> dream that I should have lived to see such disasters fallen upon her in
> a nation of gallant men, in a nation of men of honour and of cavaliers.
> I thought ten thousand swords must have leaped from their scabbards
> . . . But the age of chivalry is gone.

Marie Antoinette embodies honor (or at least carries the conventional emblem of it on her person, Burke imagines), which is the principle of monarchy, according to Montesquieu; she also theoretically inspires it in others— at least, in the ancien régime.[78] Like personifications in Spenserian allegory, equipped with their emblems and inflicting their own qualities on themselves, Marie Antoinette is both "agent and patient," in Coleridge's description.[79] Moreover, the queen bears in this passage two of the most salient characteristics of personifications, according to Steven Knapp: a "radical self-absorption" or absorption in the idea she embodies, and "overt fictionality."[80] This vision of Marie Antoinette, Burke insists, in his reply to Francis's letter, has its own truth quite independent of the empirical personage—"now I suppose pretty much faded."[81] It is not the actual woman he has in mind as an object of devotion.

Despite Francis's recommendation, Burke refuses to deplore Marie Antoinette's treatment by the crowd on the basis of the Queen's virtuous character or actions. He is concerned with the abstract notions of honor and virtue that could in the past be ascribed to her. What Burke laments is a failure of consensus around these conscious artifices. The flamboyant image of the "ten thousand swords" moving as one refers to the publicly, collectively held character of the system of illusions represented by chivalry. Burke admires the conscious artifice of chivalric feeling, its theatrical loyalty to illusion; he also admires how little regard it pays to individual possession. When Burke praises chivalry as "generous loyalty to rank and sex," he suggests that this loyalty or self-subordination is generous in overlooking the question of individual desert—the very question that Francis and others could not refrain from asking. Even more important, he implies the existence of a public, collective, even theatrical ethos. In the culture Burke defends, what commands collective loyalty, obedience, or affection is less the concrete person than the abstraction: the personification of kingliness, or womanliness, or, self-reflexively, even that of honorable subjection. In this passage on chivalry, Burke relies extravagantly on abstractions, impersonal nouns, and personifications, often impossible to visualize. Chivalry itself is described through a long string of strange half-personifications: "the nurse of manly sentiment and heroic enterprize . . . that chastity of honour, which felt a stain like a wound, which inspired courage whilst it mitigated ferocity" (RRF 127). Burke dares the reader to recognize these metaphors. There is a more than a casual continuity between his own efforts to embody abstract ideals rhetorically and the work done by the type of political constitution he praises:

> On the principles of this mechanic philosophy, our institutions can never be embodied, if I may use the expression, in persons; so as to create in us love, veneration, admiration, or attachment. . . . These public affections . . . are required . . . as aids to law. The precept given by a wise man . . . for the construction of poems, is equally true as to states. *Non satis est pulchra esse poemata, dulcia sunto.* There ought to be a system of manners in every nation which a well-formed mind would be disposed to relish. (RRF 129)

Burke's coy disclaimer—"if I may use the expression"—needs to be taken seriously. Embodiment is a metaphor for metaphor. Burke is not asking the question that some might justifiably see as all-important of whether actual institutions or persons empowered by the law deserve loyal obedience, veneration, or attachment. It is not admiration for the person of George III that is in question. It is admiration, even love, for a "system of manners" or a system of conventions. Under such a system, people conventionally agree to apply certain rhetorical descriptions, historical associations, and even private feelings to abstract ideals that may or may not exist. In his fourth *Letter on a Regicide Peace* (1795), commenting on a changed political world, Burke again remarks, this time cynically, on the power of rhetorical embodiment. In this later text, Burke complains about the practice, on the part of those advocating peace with France, of using the name "France" to refer to the revolutionary regime, "just as if we were in a common political war with an old recognized member of the commonwealth of Christian Europe." With ironic appreciation he goes on to note the benefits derived from using such personifications in a political argument:

> We thought that we had been at war with *rebels* against the lawful government. . . . But by slight [*sic*] of hand the Jacobins are clean vanished, and it is France we have got under our cup. Blessings on his soul that first invented sleep, said Don Sancho Pancha [*sic*] the wise! All those blessings, and ten thousand times more, on him who found out abstraction, personification, and impersonals. In certain cases they are the first of all soporificks. Terribly alarmed we should be if things were proposed to us in the *concrete*; and if fraternity was held

out to us with the individuals, who compose this France, by their
proper names and descriptions. . . . But plain truth would here be
shocking and absurd; therefore comes in *abstraction* and personification.[82] (original emphasis)

What Burke is criticizing here is the bad use that is being made of a legitimate
rhetorical resource rather than a device that is irrevocably tainted in its
essence.[83] In the case of the proposed "regicide peace," the function of abstract personification is abused. But it is neither difficult nor inconsistent
with Burke's usual practice to imagine cases in which this function is used
properly for an end he considers worthy—such as the creation of public affections. Indeed, Burke praises chivalry for how it mitigated the shocking
and absurd "plain truth" of power. If British politics remains true to its
chivalric heritage, it will continue to estimate properly the value of "shifting"
or "slipp[ing] the persons . . . out of sight" beneath the abstract ideals they
officially embody.

Theatrical Affections

Burke may appear to be recommending that subjects interpose pleasingly
vague, unlocalized abstractions to distort to themselves the nature of their
own actions or of their political rulers. But is it the case that Burke is merely
offering a cynical defense of mystification on the grounds of political necessity?[84] Burke's frequent references to the theater, concentrated in this section
of the *Reflections*, undergird the most inventive area of his thought. They
have often been misunderstood. When he remarks that "[s]ome tears might
be drawn from me, if such a spectacle were exhibited on the stage" (RRF
132), or praises the theater as "a better school of moral sentiments than
churches, where the feelings of humanity are thus outraged" (RRF 132), critics familiar with antitheatrical sensibilities might wish to equate theatricality
with pure factitiousness or illusion. But Burke sees the theater and its broad
range of associated critical discourses in a different way: as an institution that
explores and to a degree normalizes the phenomenon of complicity. In the
theater of Garrick and Siddons, the idea of illusion is strongly separated from
that of mystification.[85] Mystification results, in Thomas Paine's version of a
commonplace, from "the absence of knowledge."[86] It is seen as an unrepeat-
able condition: "when once any object has been seen, it is impossible to put
the mind back to the same condition it was in before it saw it."[87] But in the
theatrical criticism that Burke knew and himself produced, illusion is achieved
as the result of a particular competence—not only the actor's but also the audience's competence.[88] This competence involves manipulating a surplus of

knowledge and vision. That which is known must be discounted for theatrical illusion or actorly concentration to prevail. Burke aligns Britain's public sphere with the theater: both, he suggests, are paradoxical sites of well-rehearsed spontaneity. The public is both audience and actor. Civic emotions or public affections arise through careful practice and through the discounting of compromising knowledge. They can coexist with detachment. Civil illusions can be seen, Burke's writing suggests, not as imposed but as produced through active, even ironic, complicity. But conscious complicity may in turn produce emotions that feel genuine.

The links between theater and politics in Georgian Britain were many-sided and publicly acknowledged.[89] Garrick's biographer notes that the actor after his retirement often attended debates in the House of Commons "especially on such important questions as he knew would bring up all the best speakers of both parties." On one occasion in 1777, when a member objected to Garrick's sitting in the gallery and wanted to clear the House,

> Mr Burke rose, and appealed to the honourable assembly, whether it could possibly be consistent with the rules of decency and liberality to exclude from the hearing of their debates a man to whom they were all obliged; one . . . in whose school they had all imbibed the art of speaking, and been taught the elements of rhetorick. For his part, he owned that he had been greatly indebted to his instructions . . . [Burke] was warmly seconded by Mr Fox and Mr Townshend, who very copiously displayed the merit of their old preceptor, as they termed him.[90]

But going beyond the common parallels between political oratory and dramatic performance, Burke often focuses on the unstable duplicities of actor and audience. Burke began his career writing the kind of journalism that developed the technical critique of actorly performance, of "enunciations, tones, and attitudes," in Goldsmith's words.[91] Later in his career, Burke himself comes to embody the practical mastery of those techniques that also provided the chief subject of the elocutionary school of rhetoric.[92] What is innovative about Burke's application of this theatrical discourse to the public sphere is how he extends it not only to rulers but to subjects as well. Burke's knowing allusions to the theater suggest that the public emotions of actors and audiences, rulers and subjects, can be felt as natural and recognized as manufactured at the same time. They dwell in the zone between transport and frigid criticism. They may be generated by the artificial interposition of an abstract idea without losing their authenticity. Virtuous indignation, urgency, veneration, or admiration may arise not only through mystification but also as a result of lucid practice.

Both dramatic criticism and rhetorical theory in Burke's time investigated the problematic relationship between possessing feelings and evoking them in others.[93] In the case of Burke's close friend, David Garrick, public attention was overwhelmingly directed toward the ways in which, with "the Aid and Assistance of Articulation, Corporeal Motion, and Ocular Expression," he imitated "various mental and bodily Emotions," as Garrick himself put it.[94] Because Garrick's acting struck his audience as wholly naturalistic, reflecting genuine feelings rather than conventional "ranting, bombast, and grimace," theatrical criticism became preoccupied with the question of the actor's conscious lucidity or lack thereof.[95] In the debate over whether the actor must actually feel the emotions he represents or whether he maintains an undisturbed inward detachment, the French critic Diderot adopts one extreme position. He argues, against those who insist on the authenticity of the actor's emotions, that Garrick's "touching and sorrowful accents . . . are all planned":

> At the very moment when he touches your heart he is listening to his own voice; his talent depends not, as you think, upon feeling, but upon rendering so exactly the outward signs of feeling, that you fall into the trap. . . . The broken voice, the half-uttered words, the stifled or prolonged notes of agony . . . —all this is pure mimicry . . . [T]he grimacing of sorrow, the magnificent aping . . . leaves him . . . a full freedom of mind.[96]

The perfection of the actor's technique allows him to mimic emotions almost without thought or concentration; he enjoys a complete mental freedom to pursue calmly his private thoughts while directing the feelings of his audience. Diderot himself draws the analogy between this view of acting and the practice of politics: "is it to be believed that an actor on the stage can be deeper, cleverer in feigning joy, sadness, sensibility, admiration, hate, tenderness, than an old courtier?"[97] In rhetorical theory, too, often drawn from the same French sources, it was maintained by some that the orator, however he might display the signs of emotional transport or enthusiasm and seek to produce such effects in his audience, must retain a "fund of coolness" within, an ironic detachment from his own emotion.[98] These discourses adumbrate a certain concept of liberty that proves useful to Burke.

Other critics, including Burke himself in an early work, move toward a theory of acting in which the distinctions between feigning and feeling, artifice and emotion, are blurred. The paradox at the heart of this method, most fully described in Aaron Hill's *Essay on the Art of Acting* (1753), can be summed up as practiced feeling. Unlike spontaneous reflex or habit, such feeling arises from the interposition of an artificial method but is nonetheless held to be genuinely possessed. Hill, Garrick's "exorbitant panegyrist" and founder of a "Tragick Academy . . . for instructing and educating actors in the practice of dramatick passion," insists that the actor must in fact be possessed of the emotion he enacts: "the actor . . . must not, upon any account, attempt the utterance of one single word, till he has first compelled his fancy to conceive an idea of [the emotion]."[99] Ten different passions each give rise to distinct physical symptoms: in grief, for example, "muscles must fall loose, and be unbraced into a habit of languor," while joy expresses itself in a greater tension and uprightness of body. But the way for the actor to conceive the idea in his fancy is not by putting himself imaginatively in the situation of the dramatic character he plays and waiting for his body to reflect the impression made in his mind: rather, by carefully simulating the passion's outward symptoms in front of a mirror, he will come to imagine and then to possess the actual feeling.

> When [the actor] believes himself possessed of such an idea of joy . . .
> let him not imagine the impression rightly hit, till he has examined
> both his face and air, in a long, upright, looking glass; for *there*, only,
> will he meet with a sincere and undeceivable test of his having
> strongly enough, or too slackly, adapted his fancy to the purpose
> before him. If, for example, his brow, in the glass, appears bent, or
> cloudy, his neck bowing, and relaxed . . . his back-bone reposed, or
> unstraitened . . . any of these spiritless signs, in the glass, may con-
> vince him, that he has too faintly conceived the impression.[100]

The actor cannot know whether he really feels a passion until he sees the objective evidence of it in the mirror; he must put himself in the position of the detached spectator before he can be sure of his own feeling. But detached lucidity and absorbed involvement engage in a curious dialectic: "his voice also will associate its sound to the plaintive recognition of his gesture [of grief], and the result, both in air and accent, will be the most moving resemblance of a heart-felt and passionate sorrow."[101] By observing his own imitation of conventional gestures, the actor will be drawn in more and more until at last he comes to embody the feeling in question.

In the fourth part of the *Philosophical Enquiry*, Burke seems to rely on this theatrical method to dismantle even further the distinction between artificial and natural or practiced and spontaneous feeling. Burke wants to argue for the physiological basis of the sublime in a "tension, contraction, or violent emotion of the nerves," here using "emotion" as synonymous with motion.[102] But what mediates between body and mind, and between sensation and idea, is calculated action in the theatrical sense of the word as physical gesture:

> I have often observed, that on mimicking the looks and gestures, of
> angry, or placid, or frighted, or daring men, I have involuntarily
> found my mind turned to that passion whose appearance I endeav-
> oured to imitate; nay, I am convinced it is hard to avoid it; though one
> strove to separate the passion from its correspondent gestures.[103]

Burke seems to have discovered the cause of the sublime through the sort of acting exercise that Hill recommends to his aspiring actors; "gestures," a term repeatedly emphasized in this section, together with looks, are the staple of theatrical study. Advising not rulers and subjects but actors and actresses, Charles Gildon had written, "When you speak to Inferiours . . . and your own Quality is great, Authority and Gravity ought to be in your Face; as Submission, Humility, and Respect or Veneration, when you address those above you."[104] And how is this to be done? Through the "motions of the Feet, Hands," "Place and Posture of the Body," through the movement of the head and, above all, through the "Management of the Eyes."[105] Burke wants to emphasize the necessary reciprocal influence of mind and body on each other. The "disposition" of the body, he insists, is a necessary and possibly even sufficient condition of having feelings. Conscious reasoning has no place in the production of these sentiments.[106] But the body can be consciously arranged or disposed, it appears from his example, without damaging the authenticity of the feelings. It is the same dialectic of correspondent gestures, giving rise to inward passion giving rise to correspondent gestures, that we find in Hill; and, as in Hill, the interposition of artifice, or conscious mimicry at one level, does not affect the quality of the emotion. Unlike Diderot's ancient courtier, the subjects for whom Burke writes do not feign their sentiments; but neither are these affections entirely divorced from volition. Burke's participation in this discourse puts a new twist on the idea of "pleasing illusions" and on the relation between "public affections" and public embodiments.[107] As examples of civic emotions, Burke writes, "We fear God; we look up with awe to kings; with affection to parliaments; with duty to magistrates; with reverence to priests; and with respect to nobility" (RRF 137). Burke could be describing spontaneous emotions, outward motions of hands and eyes, or the passions that arise from a well-regulated mimicry.

The actor's use of artificial method to manipulate his own sensibility is mirrored by the theatrical audience in its relationship to illusion. The audience embodies, on the one hand, detached awareness, like Hill's looking glass. On the other hand, it suffers and enjoys the full extent of the feelings that the actor represents. What makes the institution of the theatrical audience so valuable to Burke's rendering of political society is the way in which lucid self-consciousness and spontaneous impulse are tightly bound in a relation of mutual dependence. As critics insist repeatedly, the recognition of theatrical artifice is not an obstacle but a necessary condition for the experience of emotional transport. Burke's friend Joshua Reynolds, for example, emphasizes that, in order to enjoy the rich range of affective possibilities offered by the theater, the spectator must have a highly developed competence with regard to theatrical conventions. If the spectator is not well versed in artifice, he will be unable to move beyond it in his experience.

> In theatric representation, great allowances must be made for the
> place in which the exhibition is represented; for the surrounding
> company, the lighted candles, the scenes visibly shifted in our sight,
> and the language of blank verse. . . . These allowances are made; but
> their being made puts an end to all manner of deception.[108]

Theatrical experience, Reynolds suggests, has to be mediated by the awareness of what the mind itself contributes to it—not because, as in the sublime,
the object is so initially overpowering, but because it is so obviously deficient.
This case of "making allowances" stands as a more exact antithesis than even
beauty of the Burkean sublime, in which "the mind is so entirely filled with
its object, that it cannot . . . reason on that object which employs it."[109] But
the purpose of making allowances is to experience the objects of theatrical
representation as sublime. If sublimity is the mode of despotic power, as
Burke suggests in the *Enquiry*, the peculiar transport theatrical audiences induce in themselves corresponds to the liberal politics Burke sets out to describe in his *Reflections*. In such a political culture, a sense of power is con-
ferred and controlled through the interlocking artifices of rulers and subjects.

The theater of Garrick and Siddons was not a deliberately nonillusionis-
tic theater; it aimed at producing, in the language of the trade, a convincing
"delusion," as Thomas Davies states in his *Memoirs of the Life of David Garrick* (1780):

> To render the pleasure of theatrical representation complete, the
> delusion must be uniformly supported in every thing which apper-
> tains to a play . . . every thing must contribute to the general decep-
> tion; dress . . . scenery. . . . Without this universal consent of parts,
> the pleasure will be imperfect, and the spectator deprived of one es-
> sential requisite in entertainment.[110]

But the pleasure seems to arise less from the actual experience of being deceived than from the judgment that the representation is convincing enough
so that someone else, hypothetically, might be taken in. When actual deception becomes a possibility, the reaction is far less genial. Davies complains,
for example, of the violations of theatrical "delusion" resulting from the
practice, largely reformed in England but still common in the French theater,
of seating the upper classes on the stage in full sight of the audience: "young
nobility [sitting on the stage] did not only accustom themselves to talk louder
than the players, but they were so intermingled with them during the time of
action, that you could scarce discover the real from the represented mar-
quis."[111] When there is a possibility of mistaking the real and the represented,
a chance of being involuntarily deceived, theatrical pleasure is jeopardized.
The transports offered by the theater, and even its potentially subversive so-

cial and political insights, rest on a confidence derived from the conscious negation of artifice. The experience of genuine feeling, however, is by no means eliminated as a result.

The audience of the theater thus becomes an important model for Burke's sketch, in the *Reflections*, of a liberal polity built on an ironic dialectic of delusion and lucidity. Burke's description of the theater as a place "where men follow their natural impulses" (RRF 132) is, on the face of it, an insult aimed at Price and other radical preachers: their churches and their doctrines are even more artificial, even more radically denatured and denaturing than the theater, Burke wants to say. But Burke goes on to describe the keen political insight that the theatrical audience possesses—a quality that many observers of Georgian theater audiences, in fact, noted.[112]

> No theatric audience . . . would bear . . . to see the crimes of new democracy posted as in a ledger against the crimes of old despotism, and the bookkeepers of politics finding democracy still in debt, but by no means unable or unwilling to pay the balance. In the theatre, the first intuitive glance, without any elaborate process of reasoning, would shew, that this method of political computation, would justify every extent of crime. They would see . . . that criminal means once tolerated are soon preferred. . . . Justifying perfidy and murder for public benefit, public benefit would soon become the pretext, and perfidy and murder the end. (RRF 132–33)

The conditions for the instantaneous flash of insight that Burke envisions are provided by the cumbersome apparatus of artifice that Reynolds and Davies describe. The political education that the theater provides, and the freedom of apprehension and reaction it offers, rest on that act of "making allowances," prior to that first glance. A very particular kind of complicity leads to an insight useful to political subjects with an interest in defending, once again, against the abuses of power. But Burke's use of theatrical metaphor is far from simple. He can use it to represent both the necessity of univocal, resolute action and the possibility of ironic detachment. In a letter to his friend and ally, William Windham, Burke writes, "We cannot be neuter. We are on the Stage: and cannot occasionally jump into the Pitt or Boxes to make observations on our brother actors."[113] In this instance, the metaphor of the theater conveys several key ideas: action that is constrained by circumstances or elicited by structure, necessity that excuses internal reservations, and the acknowledgment of a position from which lucid critique might, in theory, be practiced.

Pretexts, Agency, Allegory

The continual application of ideals to those in power as a means of tempering their ferocity; the pragmatic imitation of civic emotions like veneration until they begin to be felt: it is a delicate irony that Burke recommends to his British readers. It is dangerous as well, for revolutionary France, as many commentators including Burke himself pointed out, cultivated the practice of such a theatrical politics. There indeed theater became a political instrument by finessing the difference between artifice and reality, power and public opinion.[114] Predictably, Burke deplores in the French context the theatricality that he sees as a model of liberal politics in Britain, speaking of the French Revolution's "painted theatric sentiments, fit to be seen by the glare of candlelight," and describing the new government of 1795 as "revolutionary scene-shifters, second and third mob, prompters, clerks, executioners . . . murderers in Tragedies, who make ugly faces under black wigs; in short, the very scum and refuse of the Theatre."[115] But through this apparent inconsistency, Burke shows what ought to distinguish Britain from the theatrical political culture of revolutionary France: the determination to view what he calls "pretexts"—tropes, idealized persons and personified abstractions—with ironic tolerance, a balancing of disbelief and voluntary credulity. The idea of the pretext becomes central to Burke's vision of British history.

Burke's most direct defense of open pretexts in politics arises from his passionate protest against the French National Assembly's nationalization of church property. "Can one hear of the proscription of such persons, and the confiscation of their effects, without indignation and horror? He is not a man who does not feel such emotions on such occasions" (RRF 165). This is the root, as Burke sees it, of all other revolutionary evils: assignats, abolition of the aristocracy, and a general disregard for individual rights, legal precedent, religion, and "European" culture.[116] In the engineered anticlerical sentiment that gave popular support to the dispossession of the church, Burke sees a distorted version of the British mode of acknowledging fiction as a necessary part of politics. The revolutionaries

> rake into the histories of former ages . . . for every instance of oppression and persecution which has been made by that body [the clergy] or in its favour, in order to justify, upon very iniquitous, because very illogical principles of retaliation, their own persecutions . . . to take the fiction of ancestry in a corporate succession, as a ground for punishing men who have no relation to guilty acts, except in names and general descriptions, is a sort of refinement in injustice belonging to the philosophy of this enlightened age. (RRF 189)

This "fiction of ancestry in a corporate succession" strangely resembles the "policy" of inheritance, the soul of the English constitution as Burke interprets it. "Names and general descriptions" that can be comfortably extended over many particular individuals are crucial, as we have seen, to that tempered, self-regulated liberty that disdains revolution. The practical counterpart of this French "fiction of ancestry in a corporate succession" also mimics Britain's theatricalized polity. The historical tragedy, *Charles IX* by Marie-Joseph Blaise de Chénier, performed many times to public acclaim in 1789, produces a concrete representation of this corporate identity that asks to be taken for the real thing:[117]

> In this tragic farce they produced the cardinal of Lorraine in his robes of function, ordering general slaughter [of Protestants at the massacre of St. Bartholomew]. Was this spectacle intended to make the Parisians abhor persecution . . . ? No, it was to teach them to persecute their own pastors . . . the archbishop of Paris . . . is forced to abandon his house . . . because, truly, in the sixteenth century, the cardinal of Lorraine was a rebel and a murderer. (RRF 191)

Instead of writing that an actor played the part of the cardinal of Lorraine, Burke simply states that "they produced the cardinal" on the stage, thus suggesting that for the Parisian audience's purposes, the actor is the same as the cardinal, the cardinal of the sixteenth century the same as that of the present, and the archbishop of Paris the same as any of these. All are seen as mere embodiments. The hatred thus aroused is the inverted reflection of the critical distance that exists alongside theatrical veneration in the British public sphere that Burke imagines.

Burke wants to defend the French clergy, to evoke "indignation and horror" at what they have suffered in their natural persons. But he does so in a surprising way. He defends them not only as individual victims suffering pain and indignity but also, even more passionately, as mere *pretexts* that should have been left alone.

> History consists, for the greater part, of the miseries brought upon the world by pride, ambition, avarice, revenge, lust, sedition, hypocrisy, ungoverned zeal, and all the train of disorderly appetites, which shake the public with the same
> — troublous storms that toss
> The private state, and render life unsweet.
> These vices are the *causes* of those storms. Religion, morals, laws, prerogatives, privileges, liberties, rights of men are the *pretexts*. The pretexts are always found in some specious appearance of a real good.

. . . As these are the pretexts, so the ordinary actors and instruments in great public evils are kings, priests, magistrates, senates, parliaments, national assemblies, judges, and captains. You would not cure the evil by resolving, that there should be no more monarchs, nor ministers of state, nor of the gospel; no interpreters of law; no general officers; no public councils. . . . Seldom have two ages the same fashion in their pretexts. . . . The very same vice assumes a new body. The spirit transmigrates; and, far from losing its principle of life by the change of its appearance, it is renovated in its new organs with the fresh vigour of a juvenile activity. It walks abroad; it continues its ravages; whilst you are gibbeting the carcass, or demolishing the tomb. . . . It is thus with all those, who, attending only to the shell and husk of history, think they are waging war with intolerance, pride, and cruelty, whilst . . . they are authorizing and feeding the same odious vices. (RRF 189–90, original emphasis)

We might expect Burke to condemn the clergy's sufferings, like the monarch's humiliation, and to raise ethical questions about their treatment. He does this elsewhere. But here, he defends them as *mere* "actors or instruments," carefully conflating the two. What he means to say is that they are simply the passive medium through which national history moves. These institutions and persons should be respected because they are of no consequence. The true drama is performed by "pretexts": "morals, laws, prerogatives, privileges, liberties," all of the most deeply contested and politically significant parts of the nation's constitution. These pretexts are "bodies" through which human vices act. They are also merely "the shell and husk." Burke comes close to suggesting that the nation's laws, manners, and its entire constitution are themselves simply ephemeral figures of speech.

It is no less striking to realize that when Burke describes the true agents of history, he gestures toward a conspicuously artificial, archaic mode of allegory. In oblique defiance of the neoclassical opinion that allegorical abstractions should not act in historical genres, Burke makes history itself into a parade of abstractions.[118] Burke's direct quotation, from Book II, canto 7 of Spenser's *Faerie Queene*, flaunts the original source: similar tableau and parades are found in this canto, where "Cruell Revenge, and rancorous Despight, / Disloyall Treason" are among Mammon's gatekeepers.[119] There is also the parade of sins in the first book of Spenser's poem—Pride, Lechery, Avarice, and "fierce reuenging Wrath" prominent among them, each with its characteristic emblems and quaint insignia. This antiquated moral allegory, rather than the psychological discourse of the passions one finds in Burke's contemporary, Joanna Baillie, for instance, is the mode he chooses to adopt at this juncture.[120] Indeed, when he describes how "the very same vice assumes a new body," he practically offers an allegory about allegory itself.

In a sense allegory is the logical outcome of Burke's rhetorical maneuvers as well as his ironic politics. Defined as a "continued metaphor," allegory requires "great nicety," in Hugh Blair's words, "so as neither to lay the meaning too bare and open, nor to cover and wrap it up too much."[121] It is the essence of the "well-wrought veil," whose operation in politics Burke praises. It involves a tranquil oscillation between abstract ideal and perceptible embodiment. But allegory also threatens to separate permanently into two levels or parallel series: an independent literal or surface speech, and a hermetically concealed, inaccessible "other speech."[122] Burke seems, in fact, to embrace without fear the very doubleness of allegory and the larger duplicities it invokes. In Book Two of *The Faerie Queene*, Britain's history is figured in terms of an irreducible duplicity. Just before the passage quoted above, Burke offers the following image of history: "In history a great volume is unrolled for our instruction, drawing the materials of future wisdom from the past errors and infirmities of mankind" (RRF 189). He seems to allude here to the end of Book Two in the House of Temperance, where there are exhibited not one but two such great volumes of history.[123] Prince Arthur and the knight of Temperance, Guyon, are given to read, respectively, "A chronicle of Briton kings, / from Brute to Vthers rayne. / And rolles of Elfin Emperours, / till time of Gloriane."[124] History is divided or doubled into two parallel modes. The chronicle Arthur reads, "Briton moniments," redacts historical material from Geoffrey of Monmouth and Holinshed; but Guyon's "great / And ample volume" "That hight Antiquitie of Faerie lond," belongs to a different realm.[125] Between the origin of "Prometheus" and the telos of "Gloriane," the exploits of Elfe, Elfin, Elfinan, and their entirely mythical progeny display the self-consciously idealizing artifice of invention.[126] There is Britain's history, with the sufferings of "natural persons," and alongside it the world of national myth. Parallel to the monarchy run its various mythical embodiments. Despite a general feeling of congruence, the two levels cannot be mapped onto one another with any degree of exactness. Burke's vision normalizes an openly disjunctive relation between these levels of historical Britain and mythical Britain, between actual politics and idealized tropes.[127] Pretexts and fictions and temporary artifices are defended as such, not on aesthetic but on pragmatic grounds. But in an irony that he could not have foreseen, Burke's own legacy was to be a divided one: some would take his defense of a culture's pretexts as a defense of tradition's truth. But there would also be others, such as Walter Scott, who would elaborate a more capacious, flexible, and practically indefeasible counterrevolutionary irony.

3

Sir Walter Scott on the Field of Waterloo

In the summer of 1815, as Walter Scott's new career as a novelist was beginning to take shape, an event occurred which put a decisive end to twenty-two
years of war for the British nation: the battle of Waterloo, where "the terrific
spectre of Bonaparte's power . . . [broke] into thin air at the talismanick touch
of English steel," as one contemporary observer described it.[1] Together with
many other curious Britons, Scott came to the field of Waterloo that summer
hoping to collect some fragments of that talismanic steel. Many British
tourists who visited the battlefield expecting sublimity experienced awk-
wardness instead, and even a sense of interdiction; the strangely flat, unin-
spiring landscape left them tongue-tied.[2] But in *Paul's Letters to his Kinsfolk*
(1815), the account of his European tour, Scott embraces the unexpected banality of the Waterloo battlefield, its absence of pathos:

> Bones of horses, quantities of old hats, rags of clothes, scraps of
> leather, and fragments of books and papers, strewed the ground in
> great profusion. . . . The tall crops . . . were trampled into a thick
> black paste . . . the ground was torn in many places. . . . Yet, abstract-
> ing from our actual knowledge of the dreadful cause of such appear-
> ances, they reminded me not a little of those which are seen upon a
> common a few days after a great fair has been held there.[3]

Practicing a curious technique of double vision that his fictional creations like
Waverley also exercise, Scott applies to the field two incommensurable perspectives.[4] In the patriot's eyes, informed by the "actual knowledge of the
dreadful cause," the scene inspires awe. But from another unnamed perspective that has quietly bracketed this knowledge, the "celebrated scene of
the greatest event of modern times" (146) seems inevitably to recall the site
of the most mundane event of modern times: "a common, a few days after a
great fair has been held there." In the way he proceeds to conduct himself
while touring the area, Scott suggests the truth of both these views, for he is
there as an antiquarian.

Scott's third novel, *The Antiquary* (1816), worked out during the same summer, is set during the British wars against revolutionary and Napoleonic France. The advertisement notes, "The present Work completes a series of fictitious narratives, intended to illustrate the manners of Scotland at three different periods . . . the *Antiquary* refers to the last ten years of the eighteenth century," ending with a false invasion scare that occurred in Scotland in 1804.[5] The indebtedness of Scott's historical novels to antiquarian research and discourse has long been acknowledged. Scott himself remarks in the preface to *Ivanhoe* (1819) that as a novelist he had merely "availed himself . . . of the antiquarian stores which lay scattered around him," ready to be animated by a self-effacing creativity.[6] Among recent scholars, Ina Ferris, for example, has stressed Scott's reliance on the characteristic media of antiquarian history: "unofficial historical memory and record . . . marginal kinds of writing and print, like the letter, tracts, pamphlets and private memoirs"; his self-conscious deference to "official . . . standard narrative history" is also typical of antiquarianism, she notes.[7] But Scott's novels do not always express a uniform relation to antiquarianism. Using Sharon Turner's history of Anglo-Saxon culture as a source for *Ivanhoe*'s details of costume and setting, or deriving incidents and characters from collections such as George Ellis's *Specimens of English Romance*, is not the same thing as constructing a novel such as *The Antiquary*, in which the "office of an antiquary" is assumed by practically every character, from wandering beggar to nobleman. Antiquarian activity here does not remain discreetly in the conceptual background or in the editorial apparatus of the novel; antiquarian tracking, deciphering, arguing, collecting, and remembering are the primary activities performed within its pages. It is far from easy to see why Scott would write a novel that not only foregrounds antiquarianism but also makes it a collective obsession, and the puzzle is compounded by the fact that Scott chooses to situate it during a period of feverish counterrevolutionary enthusiasm.[8] Set on the coast of Scotland, taking for its villain a "foreigner" and "alien," the swindling German *Illuminé*, Dousterswivel, *The Antiquary* would appear to emphasize Britain's identity as a unified, clearly bounded, self-consciously Protestant nation. How, then, is the figure of the antiquary related to the enterprise of British patriotism that was undertaken with such apparent fervor during these decades of war? We need to ask, in other words, how antiquarianism is related to the patriotic ideologies that, with the help of repressive force and legislation, "brought about," in Coleridge's words, "a national unanimity unexampled in our history since the reign of Elizabeth."[9]

Scott's antiquarianism does more than provide an innocuous source of historical embellishment or a legitimating framework of erudition for his novels. It plays an unusual but critical role in pacifying Britain as the pressures of war receded. The peculiar finality of Waterloo, as that event was characterized by contemporary observers, brought about the need to consolidate and to maintain at a higher level the patriotic unity that war had been able to produce. The active repression and even persecution of political dissent and the enforcement of order had found an excuse in the exigencies of the French wars; but with the apparently decisive defeat of this enemy it became less clear how this superficial "unanimity" could be maintained. Tropes, exhortations, proclamations that acquired plausibility from an acute sense of urgency could no longer count on the same response when no external threat existed. Once the royal dynasties of Europe have been unequivocally reinstated, revolution at home, not merely imitative of the French example but deeply rooted in internal social causes and class antagonisms, becomes a more distinct possibility. In light of this imminent rupture of national solidarity and the weakening of the urgency that had lent plausibility to highly conservative ideologies of order, the figure of the antiquary as constructed and embodied by Walter Scott becomes useful.

The usefulness of antiquarians for the British nation at this moment is linked with the curious blindness they were thought to embody. The political implications and the cultural standing of antiquarian knowledge were both ambiguous. Well known for their defenses of national or regional culture but just as often deeply engaged in debunking the myths of nationalist histories, antiquaries did not always put their knowledge to politically predictable uses.[10] They were equally difficult to categorize or judge on epistemological grounds. Antiquaries were traditionally derided for their infatuation with the past and their inability to distinguish forgeries from authentic relics. Their exceptional susceptibility to deceit constitutes a well-worn literary topos: "He is a man . . . enamored of old age and wrinkles, and loves all things . . . the better for being moldy and worm-eaten. . . . Beggars cozen him with musty things which they have raked from dunghills, and he preserves their rags for precious relics."[11] Yet the antiquary often adopts the stance of the demystifier, the enlightened detective of fraud and ideological imposture.[12] On the politically charged issue of Scotland's past, eighteenth-century antiquaries like Thomas Innes had been instrumental in debunking the putative origins of the Scottish monarchy and the idea of a Scottish ancient constitution.[13] Learned and naïve, suspicious and credulous, cultural authority and dupe by turns, the antiquary can thus figure, at a moment when questions of truthfulness and knowledge become highly political, the strange mutual imbrication of enlightenment and susceptibility to delusion. Distinguished equally by an attitude of confidence and a constant underlying anxiety about its own truthfulness, antiquarian knowledge comes to reflect a nation afflicted with a similar ironic undecidability—in Carlyle's description of Scott's audience, "fallen languid, destitute of faith and terrified at skepticism? Or . . . all in peaceable triumphant motion?"[14]

Even more specifically, antiquarianism provides a way of dialectically cancelling another discourse that had dominated national sensibilities during the years of war: patriotic pseudo-Burkean traditionalism. Not so much in the complex satires of the *Anti-Jacobin* as in the broadsides and ballads that inundated the country at each threat of French invasion or military supremacy, some of the ideas of Burke's *Reflections* were extracted and naturalized into a number of highly conservative traditionalist themes. According to this latter discourse, the nation's essence, not only its political institutions but also its habits and dispositions, its character, had been transmitted as a miraculously unbroken whole from the past to the present. Faced with crisis from within and without, all classes of British society during these years of war were called to draw on an undivided cultural inheritance in order to reenact the military triumphs of ages remote in time. The emphasis fell not on the transformations, the uneasy unions and rebellions that had shaped the nation over the course of actual history, but rather on the abstract temporal distance over which Britain's putative identity had been transmitted marvelously intact and there for the invoking.

Tacitly questioning this theory of the nation's undivided inheritance, and ambiguously related to the trope of voice that typically sustained the popular rhetoric of nationalist historicism, antiquarianism was directed, particularly in the context of eighteenth-century Scotland, toward the gathering of scattered material and discursive fragments.[15] Even when, as in the case of Scott's own *Minstrelsy of the Scottish Border* (1802–3), these acquisitive efforts were aimed at popular or folk ballads, the orality of such traditions was arguably secondary in importance to their vanishing status and gave way in any case to the textual bias of antiquarianism.[16] But it was neither this textual bias nor the empiricism of antiquarians that stood in such awkward relation to the discourses of patriotism. As David Simpson has argued, English empiricism, in its capacity to be opposed to French theoretical abstraction, played a crucial role in the construction of national character.[17] Rather, the dimension of antiquarianism that could be seen as objectionable or embarrassing lay in the untheorized assumptions about national history behind its characteristic activities of gathering, collecting, and compiling. While those activities may often have proceeded from a conscious sentimental desire to preserve or to restore a national patrimony (however the boundaries of that nation were defined), the very egregiousness of this antiquarian foraging drew attention to the troubling processes of loss and extinction that made the retrieval necessary.[18] If patriotic traditionalism portrayed the nation as undivided and self-inheriting, continuously bequeathing institutions and character to itself, antiquarian practice could appear to belie those assumptions: like the curiosity that greets it, the existence of the antiquarian object is contingent on processes of obsolescence and fragmentation. The possibility of antiquarian knowledge, of the type that Scott produced, rests to a large extent on the prior division, erasure, and epistemological or material forfeiture of what may be construed as a nation's culture.

It is not the case that antiquarian knowledge explicitly opposes traditionalist discourse on ideological grounds: it is generally a reverence for tradition that motivates the pursuit of that knowledge. But as an activity based ultimately on the individual's elective affinities, antiquarianism contrasts strongly with the passive, collective reception of the immaterial treasures of the past enjoined by patriotic traditionalist propaganda. If that propaganda removed Burke's idea of inheritance from that complex tissue of self-conscious artifice in which he had involved it, Scott's antiquarianism, in particular, reminds his readers that inheritance and transmission take their places among other chosen fictions and chosen acts in the context of a commercial society.[19] *The Antiquary* repeatedly emphasizes the elective rather than prescriptive nature of Oldbuck's antiquarian activities; as one character puts it, "Mr Oldbuck . . . you . . . may . . . indulge yourself in the researches to which your taste addicts you—you may form your own society" (Ant 124). Oldbuck's antiquarian activities signify his freedom from the strictures of tradition: "I am master of my acres . . . they cannot oblige me to transmit my goods, chattels, and heritages, any way but as I please. No string of substitute heirs of entail . . . to cumber my flights of inclination, and my humours of predilection" (Ant 125). As a mode of activity, antiquarianism's incompatibility with traditionalism appears also in its family resemblance to commerce, both in its busy acquisitiveness and its intuitive understanding of the contingency of value. As Scott's own practice on the field of Waterloo shows, antiquarianism, like the marketplace—a phenomenon tactfully deemphasized during the national crises of the period—saw the value of its objects as depending not only on cycles of supply and demand but also on broader movements like the decline and collapse of cultures, nations, and empires.[20] The principle of scarcity supplies much of the meaning as well as the drama of antiquarian activity. Fragments, traces, and inscriptions become collectible, valuable, seductively indecipherable, and endlessly debateable in one and the same process of obliteration. The pricelessness of antiquarian relics was not inherent but obviously contingent on the interplay between scarcity and demand, as well as the vagaries of personal choice and whim.

Scott's novel also makes much of the fact that antiquarianism relies on many of the same habits necessary for success in the domain of commerce. Oldbuck, the scrupulous keeper of time and of money, is derided by his aristocratic rival for his "habit of minute and troublesome accuracy," his "mercantile manner of doing business" (Ant 41). Throughout, traditionalist credulity is associated with the farcical, the fanatical, and the delusive. It is opposed to the critical and investigative stance of Oldbuck, busily detecting as well as acquiring hidden objects and causes, and applying his habits of accuracy to the resolution of mysteries. *The Antiquary* even seems to regard as heroic the demystification of fraudulent forms of veneration. But Oldbuck's disavowal of the mythologies of patriotic traditionalism hardly ensures his freedom from other forms of delusion and distortion. A posture of knowingness or an obsessive drive to discover the truth does not of itself guarantee true knowledge. In Scott's novel, the antiquarian's drive to unearth hidden causes, to authenticate the relics of the past and to establish their value—and to some degree nearly everyone in this novel is an antiquarian—is seen as ultimately no more perspicacious than the blind embrace of the mythology of inheritance. Scott's novel suggests that antiquarianism constructs its own cherished fictions even in the very act of detecting fraud. If antiquarianism negates the traditionalist interpretation of national history, Scott, in turn, ironically negates that negation, mocking it for its pedantry, omnivorous eclecticism, and confident belief in its own privileged access to truth.[21]

Burkean Themes and the Disavowal of Antiquarianism

Antiquarian knowledge emerges in a curiously negative light in one of the most canonical texts of British counterrevolutionary nationalism. Far from being revered as guardians or trustees of the nation's historical knowledge, antiquarians were singled out for disapproval in a text of major importance for patriotic traditionalism, Burke's *Reflections on the Revolution in France* (1790). Burke's tropes and his distinctive tone of mingled defensiveness and pride were imitated by many who sought to mobilize a sense of nationhood in the ensuing decades of war against France. But important changes took place in the underlying argument. As we have seen, Burke's *Reflections* works against any simple or literal understanding of the nation or of its history. While Burke dramatically exhibits on other occasions a profound regard for the archives and repositories of British history, he emphasizes in the *Reflections,* the fictions, evasions, and figures of speech that constitute an indispensable layer of the nation's political culture. Rather than essentializing national character, Burke suggests that Britain chooses to see itself through the glass of conventional tropes and conventional emotional responses.[22] A decision to embrace the trope of inheritance, for instance, leads the British to regard not only property but also the existing disposition of political power and social privilege as though these were legacies rather than negotiable impositions: "We have an inheritable crown; an inheritable peerage; and an house of commons and a people inheriting privileges, franchises, and liberties, from a long line of ancestors."[23] Burke praises the determination to view the constitution in this light, insofar as it requires a skilful, subtle blindness to actual British history. While inheritance is a legal institution, as a description of the constitution it is rather closer to fiction, as Burke makes painfully clear in his writings and speeches about colonized Ireland and India. It is at this moment in the *Reflections,* though, that Burke goes out of his way to deplore antiquarianism: "By adhering in this manner and on those principles to our forefathers, we are guided not by the superstition of antiquarians, but by the spirit of philosophic analogy" (84). Not only the methods but also the attitudes of antiquarianism are unequivocally repudiated, linked through the term "superstition" with the forms of heteronomy rejected by the British.[24]

In the broader context of this passage from Burke's *Reflections*, antiquarianism is associated with the idea of a short-sighted literalism, lacking imagination and for that reason prone to "superstition." The contrast between the letter and the spirit of the law, the despotic old and the liberal new dispensation, is important to Burke's argument, though not in the ways imagined by those who see Burke as simply an authoritarian traditionalist. Assuring his readers that a pedantic scrutiny of the past insults Britain's self-conscious theatricality, Burke shrewdly aligns antiquarianism with the idolatry that blindly worships the letter of the law—as opposed to the "spirit of philosophic analogy." What Burke wishes to invoke by means of the latter phrase is an attitude at once rational and generous, practical and humane: a civilized Whig traditionalism that knows the importance of liberal paraphrase, adaptation, and the "well-wrought veil" of artifice. The security and prestige of this position seemed to Burke to depend on excluding antiquarians from this struggle to define the proper orientation toward the past. The antiquarian's concern for establishing the objective authenticity of the past needs to appear supererogatory and even ungrateful. Antiquarianism constructs the object of its searches and researches in a particular fashion: it targets the discrete historical object or artifact.[25] Valued to the extent that it crumbles or disappears, the antiquarian object is to be bought, sold, collected, deciphered, and authenticated. Burke's idea of the national entity, in contrast, emphasizes the elusive immaterial continuities that could be self-consciously constructed with the institutions handed down from the past.[26]

The disavowal of antiquarianism in Burke's *Reflections* rests, then, on Burke's desire to win recognition for the pretexts that Britain's subjects and rulers need to maintain. The analogy that can be drawn between inheritance and the protocols of English constitutional reform earns his praise not as a fact but as a lucid, elegant contrivance. But this dimension of Burke's thought falls away when the idea of inheritance emerges as the dominant theme of patriotic propaganda during the years of war with revolutionary and Napoleonic France. In this patriotic rhetoric, the conscious analogies to which Burke draws attention give way to assertions of identity with a simple personification of the past and a reified national character. Relying on a simple, exaggerated traditionalism to mobilize the British nation and to fill the ranks and coffers of regular and volunteer forces, this discourse cuts away that ironic, reflexive dimension characteristic of Burke's argument. Instead, it stresses the urgency of publicly declaring and believing in certain traditionalist articles of faith. As Linda Colley, David Simpson, and others have recently shown, an artificial solidarity was manufactured in this period by means of a "mythology of national character": miscellaneous ideals such as common sense, untaught feeling, and domesticity were combined into a factitious national identity, neatly posed over against caricatures of the French.[27] During the French invasion threats of the 1790s and early 1800s, this ideological effort took on a new concentration and visibility through the inauguration of a national patriotic broadside campaign of unprecedented scope.[28] The *Gentleman's Magazine* noted in September 1803, "30,000 copies of one of these publications, called 'John Bull,' have been sold within a few weeks; the very beggars come to the shops for them."[29] Intended to provide the nation with a common political language in a moment of crisis, these broadsides and ballads turn Burke's intricate presentation of inheritance as a praiseworthy contrivance into a straightforward historicization of national character. Burke saw inheritance as a paradoxical choice not to choose, as something that both familiarizes and estranges the possessions of the present. But inheritance here becomes the basis of a simple antirevolutionary Francophobic ideology. Despite the conspicuous industrial expansion and administrative rationalization that accompanied these wars, Britain relied for its ideological mobilization on a narrative that overwhelmingly emphasized the wealth and strength of the past and the continuous transmission of an unchanged national character over time.

A brief glance at this patriotic traditionalism explains its hostility toward antiquarian activity that treated the past as defunct, illegible, and marginalized. The propaganda generated by the periodic threats of French invasion suggests that the mythology of national character, so useful in visual form as the figure of "John Bull," was inseparable from an ideology that established this character firmly in the past. The motive and emotive power of the idea of native character depended on the belief, reiterated in countless broadsides and pamphlets, that this character was not of recent vintage. Rather, it was presented as rooted in the past, nurtured in past struggles against the French, and unconsciously passed on from generation to generation. In a way that was required to be felt as miraculous, the continuity given the name of national character spanned the gap of time between progenitors and descendants. Here the past had no need to be recovered, deciphered, mediated, or imaginatively constructed: it was still alive, though unconscious, and had only to be awoken and called into public action. As one patriotic broadside affirmed, "The Descendants of the heroes of Cressy, Agincourt, &c . . . are animated with the same Soul, possess the same Courage and unshaken Zeal for their country, which glowed in the Breasts of their Forefathers."[30] The magnitude of the chronological passage of time was acknowledged only so that it could be invested with the glamor of a lengthy descent: "Shew them that age to age bequeaths / The British Character complete."[31] No patriotic subject is excluded, none is exempt from this inheritance. Moreover, as these examples suggest, this trope of inheritance played a crucial role in the construction of a masculinity appropriate to the occasion: "Oh! call to mind the gallant deeds / Your noble Sires have done, / And may the Spirit of the Sires / Descend upon the Son!"[32] The simple act of historical recollection becomes a sacramental event for the male Briton—provided that history be remembered only as a narrative of heroic exploits, transmitted in spirit from father to son without editorial, curatorial, or restorative intervention. Despite the patriotic motives they often shared, the antiquarians, who traced actual genealogies and authenticated concrete artifacts, did not fit well into this ideological fantasy.[33]

The literalism of antiquarians with regard to the vestiges of the past and their concern with the authenticity of scattered artifacts rather than the cultural authority of intangible dispositions gave sufficient grounds for their exclusion from this phase of the counterrevolutionary ideological project, even as they had earlier distanced themselves from what J.G.A. Pocock has called "the cult of the 'ancient constitution.'"[34] If patriotic propaganda hinged on the assumption that tradition was self-evident and self-interpreting, and that being part of a tradition meant knowing instinctively how to act, antiquarian research emphasized the need for collection, retrieval, and decipherment. The aphorism, practice, or "unwritten story fondly traced from father to son" was removed from the context of local, everyday use and resituated in an environment of private intellection.[35] Since inheritance or unbroken transmission provided patriotic traditionalism with its master narrative, the anxiety with which antiquarianism was regarded is understandable: the antiquary did not claim to inherit nor did he aspire to transmit. The bulk of his activity, pursued in a spirit of conspicuously bourgeois leisure, consisted in amassing objects, deciphering scattered fragments of the past, and producing rather obviously contingent forms of knowledge. For all its sentimental attachment to the value of the past, antiquarianism assumed the already accomplished or imminent demise of tradition as a matter of continuous, practical usage. Antiquarians sought out, as François Furet has noted, "coins, stones, inscriptions, and portions of monuments—the random remains of a fatal shipwreck": the trope of catastrophe rather than the narrative of inheritance seemed to structure the practice, if not the discourse, of antiquarian history.[36]

The patriotic propaganda of these years reveals yet another reason for the repression of antiquarianism by the popular discourses of patriotism: the class-exclusive associations of antiquarian activity. Though the subjects of antiquarian foraging ranged from titles and genealogies to folk ballads, the enquiry itself was neither equally open nor equally intelligible to all classes. In the rhetoric of patriotic traditionalism, however, the divisive notion of class difference was displaced by the theme of national sympathies and antipathies inherited from the past. As this example shows, national antagonism superseded and rendered irrelevant any difference of class: "Our ancestors declared, that One Englishman was ever a match for Three Frenchmen. . . . We have but to feel these sentiments to confirm them; you will find that their declaration was founded on experience."[37] Class distinction was eclipsed by the revelation of a common inheritance. A key figure was Henry V, remembered not in his historical but in his dramatic incarnation. "Shakespeare's Ghost," the incarnation here not of theatricality but of native genius and collective expression, proclaims, after a lengthy pastiche of Shakespeare, "We too are Britons;—-Let, then, all who claim that Title, and whose Veins flow with British blood, emulate the Ardour, the Courage, and the Glory of their Ancestor [Henry V] . . . and strive to preserve that Renown for their posterity, which the Heroes of Agincourt and Cressy have transmitted to us."[38] In one stroke, all Britons are ennobled in name if not in fortune, provided that rigorous scrutiny be withheld from this dramatic genealogy.

These broadsides carefully obscured the material basis of social distinction. Material artifacts and property were deemphasized wherever possible. "Publicola's Postscript to the People of England," published in July 1803, brings up the question of cash only to transform it ostentatiously into a trope for national spirit: "By general circulation, [gold] might diffuse comfort and happiness around; by being hoarded, it baffles the use and purpose for which it was ordained. Even so, my COUNTRYMEN, is this high pride, this feeling, this spirit of the British character."[39] The lukewarm patriot, materially impoverished, is cleverly invited to view himself as a miser, thus obtaining the privilege of the rich man's guilt without his actual property. Hannah More's "Ploughman's Ditty" suggests that what matters is less the quantity or the quality of possessions than simply the abstract concept of property itself, applicable to anything that could be named or imagined, whether animate or inanimate, collective or individual: "My cot is my throne, / What I have is my own, / And what is my own I will keep, Sir. . . . Now do but reflect / What I have to protect . . . King, Church, Babes, and Wife, / Laws, Liberty, Life; / Now tell me I've nothing to lose, Sir."[40] In this song for the have-nots, a hearty compensation for poverty is found in the contemplation of public and private institutions. "What I have is my own": private property is an English institution that must be protected—not sought. In these broadsides, acquisition is an event always assumed to have occurred in the past, and distribution is motivated by generosity and public spirit rather than a desire for profit. Having, defending, keeping rather than getting comprise the nation's vocation; commerce, the principle of mobility and profit-motivated exchange, threatens to undo the model of national solidarity, generated by the threat of French invasion.

Even traces of engagement in commerce were implicitly disavowed by the very classes most directly involved: the "Merchants, Bankers, Traders and other Inhabitants of London" insist that "we fight . . . to maintain the spotless Glory which we have inherited from our Ancestors."[41] Through this rhetoric of inheritance the notion of capital could be tactfully deemphasized. As the merchants, bankers, and traders of London conclude, "we will rather perish together, than live to see . . . that *noble* Inheritance of Greatness, Glory, and Liberty destroyed, which has descended to us from our Forefathers" (original emphasis). The suppression of commercial principles by patriotic ideology brings us to the last fact betrayed by the disavowal of antiquarianism: antiquarians supplied, however innocently, the inadmissible links between national legacy and class interest, between history and profit. In Walter Scott's case, his practice revealed clear points of resemblance between antiquarian value and market price: both were contingent on the relation between scarcity and generalized demand. Far from constituting an undivided and priceless ideal legacy, relics of the national past were bought and sold— exchanged for money or for less tangible profits.

Scraps, Relics, and Commodities

From the start, Scott's career was characterized by a conflation of antiquarian and military, literary, commercial, and patriotic activities. The publication of his *Minstrelsy of the Scottish Border* in 1802 and 1803 coincided with the second period of growing alarm over French invasion. A letter from this time, written to his antiquarian correspondent George Ellis, shows the aplomb with which Scott negotiates between patriotic and antiquarian discourses; after remarking how, as a member of the Volunteer Cavalry, he has been "occupied with Armies of Reserve, and Militia, and Pikemen, and Sharpshooters, who are to descend from Ettrick Forest to the confusion of all invaders," Scott takes up their ongoing antiquarian conversation, only pausing to remark, "I am interrupted by an extraordinary accident, nothing less than a volley of small shot fired through the window . . . To return to Sir Tristrem."[42] Since Scott's antiquarian researches of this period have been seen as expressing his naive infatuation with military heroism, it is worth noting how he discriminates to almost ludicrous effect between these two areas of activity. But more than in his letters or poetry of this period, it is in an account written at the conclusion of the war that Scott most effectively explores the irony required to bridge the implicit tensions between his roles as antiquary and as patriot. The biographical detail of Scott's having collected scraps from the battlefield is well known; it is too often assumed that Scott was engaging unreflectively in an act of sentimental patriotism. But in *Paul's Letters to His Kinsfolk* (1815), Scott presents himself on the field of Waterloo as a self-consciously awkward-distinguished public figure on the stage of history. Unlike other tourist narratives, which concentrated on the mental re-creation of the events of the battle, Scott's account focuses on the detritus of the battlefield and, more particularly, on the way in which these antiquarian relics generate a marketplace. Scott seems to enjoy the salutary discomfiture of patriotic traditionalism as it is forced, through his own antiquarian zeal, to confront its own ideological disjunction from material and commercial real-ities. Bargaining heroically for the relics on sale, Scott ironically conjoins the habits of commercial society with the dispositions of a patriotism that thought itself above commerce.

Since Waterloo was the event that brought to a close the years of war fu-eled by the traditionalist propaganda discussed above, it was only appropri-ate that Robert Southey among others should celebrate it in a rhetoric by now familiar: "The glory of all former fields seemed . . . to fade before that of Waterloo. At Cressy, Poictiers, at Agincourt, the ease with which victory had been obtained appeared to detract from the merit of the conquerors. . . . Blenheim had been . . . less momentous in the consequences."[43] But Southey's remarks already show how disenchantment with the nostalgic ori-entation of patriotic rhetoric might begin to be felt. Agincourt and the ex-ploits of revered ancestors suddenly diminish in monumentality. Amid the triumphalism of the present, the gesture of mere historical recollection be-gins to seem irrelevant or hollow. The editorial conspectus for the *Gentle-man's Magazine* in 1815, for example, refrains from retracing the familiar narrative of transmission:

> it is impossible to overlook this prominent fact, that the history of
> mankind does not exhibit as resulting from one conflict, however glo-
> rious it may have been, consequences so important, so extensive, so
> beneficial to mankind, as those which progressively ensued, and are
> still succeeding to the Victory of Waterloo.[44]

From the metaphorical prominence of the present moment, the future looks different. The rhetoric of inheritance from a remote past gives way to a be-lated acknowledgment of the nation's modernity. Even where historical ret-rospect is taken, a commercially inflected discourse appears alongside a Burkean vocabulary of legacy, inheritance, and nobility.[45] One typical British account of the Waterloo tour begins:

> the voice of history is likely to sustain to the full our present estimate
> . . . the battle in question will always be described . . . as a fit compan-
> ion to the finest achievements either of ancient or modern times, that
> have been picked out to stand prominent illustrations to the honour
> of human enterprizes, and to give the effect of sublimity to the annals
> of human affairs.[46]

As "gallant deeds [of] noble sires" give way to "human enterprizes" and "human affairs" as privileged tropes for history, patriotism begins to acquire a subtly commercial flavor. The metaphors seem to recall, even if the writer chooses not to, a nation less concerned with winning honor and chivalry than with calculating and enjoying profit.

Scott fearlessly invokes, as we have seen, the similarity between sacred relics of national history and the detritus of a marketplace.[47] His own performance on the field of Waterloo shows how antiquarianism can weld together public spirit and private gratification, patriotic nostalgia and commercial ambition, into an ironic whole. *Paul's Letters* mediates self-consciously between two spheres. There is the world of sacralized events and emotions, national glory and collective destinies; then there is the life of ordinary labor, perceived through the simple logic of individual profit and loss. Scott embodies the former perspective in the figure of the English tourist and the latter in the Flemish peasant:

> The honest Flemings were at first altogether at a loss to comprehend the eagerness and enthusiasm by which their English visitors were influenced in their pilgrimages. . . . With them a battle fought and won is a battle forgotten, and the peasant resumes his ordinary labours after the armies have left his district, with as little interest in recollecting the conflict, as if it had been a thunder-storm which had passed away. (PL 147)

Scott evenhandedly extends his irony to both the patriotic pilgrim, such as the Englishman who buys the door of the farmhouse on the battlefield ("I own I was myself somewhat curious respecting the use which could be made of the door of La Belle Alliance" [PL 159]), and the peasant, tied to his life of toil. He ultimately does not trace the difference in vision to nation or to class but rather suggests that these radically contrasting modes of valuation may constitute two halves of a whole: an ironic whole that the patriotic antiquary is well suited to reveal through his awkward enthusiasm.

The banality of commerce confronts the "sublimity" of nationalism in one particular feature of the Waterloo tour. The battlefield of Waterloo had, in fact, been transformed into a marketplace of souvenirs, and Scott is unusual among British tourists in noting this transformation without disapproval: "A more innocent source of profit has opened to many of the poor people about Waterloo, by the sale of such trinkets and arms as they collect daily from the field of battle. . . . Almost every hamlet opens a mart of them as soon as English visitors appear" (PL 157). Other British tourists still entrammeled in the rhetoric of national glory found it difficult to countenance what they saw as tasteless commercial opportunism. But in Scott's account, the canny exploitation of this world-historical event by Flemish peasants was

clearly one of its most interesting and characteristic features. More than anything else, the peasants' ability to extract a tangible profit from military heroism, national rivalries, and anachronistic patriotic sentiment drew attention
to what might lie beneath these ideologically charged representations. In at
least one instance, Scott willingly collaborates in this project with a peasant,
formerly Napoleon's guide on the day of battle, who was now acting as tour
guide:

> He complained that the curiosity of the visitors who came to hear his
> tale, interfered a good deal with his ordinary and necessary occupa-
> tion: I advised him to make each party, who insisted on seeing and
> questioning him, a regular charge of five francs, and assured him that
> if he did so, he would find that Bonaparte had kept his promise of
> making his fortune, though in a way he neither wished nor intended.
> Pere de Coster said he was obliged to me for the hint, and I dare say
> has not failed to profit by it. (PL 149)

As Scott seems to be the first to perceive, De Coster's experience as Napoleon's guide enables him to produce a sought-after commodity: by "seeing
and questioning him," tourists acquire (secondhand) experience of the battle. By making, on Scott's advice, "a regular charge of five francs" for the secondhand experience he retails, De Coster merely completes the circuit of exchange. In comparison to the self-induced ideological frenzy of British
tourists, the Flemish peasants appear to good advantage in Scott's narrative
as examples of shrewd, if not exactly amiable, economic rationality. "The
good old Flemish housewife, who keeps the principal cabaret at Waterloo . . .
had learnt the value of her situation, and charged three prices for our coffee,
because she could gratify us by showing the very bed in which the Grand
Lord slept the night preceding the action" (PL 146–47). Here the exchange-
value of history is clearly and unsentimentally recognized; and it is in this
world that Scott, as modern antiquarian, seems to find himself comfortably
at home.

Whatever his motives for coming to Waterloo, Scott lingers on out of a
sharp antiquarian acquisitiveness; the "great object of my ambition," he
notes, "was to possess the armour of a cuirassier" (PL 157), as well as other
relics of national historical interest. Yet he has no illusions about the mode in
which these relics were to be acquired or the source of their value. The objects sold in the markets, according to his narrative, were "things of no in-
trinsic value, but upon which curiosity sets a daily increasing estimate." The
curiosity in question can refer to the subjective desire of patriotic tourists to
possess some authentic souvenir of the great victory. It primarily refers, however, to the objective phenomenon that generated the market value of these
things—their scarcity in relation to demand.[48] "These memorials . . . rise in

value as they decrease in number" (PL 157). As an antiquarian, Scott is well aware that these objects possess a dual nature as relic and as commodity, as food for future patriotic fantasies and as investments of monetary value. With an ironic flatness of tone, Scott remarks, "Crosses of the Legion of Honor were in great request, and already stood high in the market. I bought one of the ordinary sort for forty francs" (PL 157). While honor is always "in great request," it has not always been the case that it can be purchased so easily for forty francs. In its subtly ironic appreciation of the clash between laws of political economy and codes of aristocratic ideology, Scott's Waterloo narrative suggests that his novels, and *The Antiquary*, in particular, should not always be read as elegies for bygone feudal glories. Rather, they critique the ways in which outdated ideologies cycle and recycle through capitalist societies: even when symbols of honor can be purchased for forty francs, they can still always be imagined to belong to some other order of value.

The significance of Scott's antiquarian exertions becomes clearer in a broader context. Even as he bargains for nationalist relics, he reconciles two social or ideological formations, whose incompatibility had long been assumed: civic virtue, on the one hand, and commercial society, on the other. Both themes had been extensively explored by Adam Ferguson, John Millar, William Robertson, and other Scottish Enlightenment figures, who had instructed and influenced Scott.[49] Ferguson, in particular, along with Dugald Stewart, Scott's teacher at Edinburgh, who disseminated many of Ferguson's ideas and methods, was preoccupied with the political consequences of economic development. Ferguson's *Essay on the History of Civil Society* (1768) traced disapprovingly the inevitable collapse of the political public sphere in highly developed commercial societies: "To the ancient Greek, or the Roman, the individual was nothing, and the public every thing. To the modern . . . the individual is every thing, and the public nothing."[50] Ferguson clearly held to the classical ideal of the public sphere: "To act in the view of his fellow-creatures, to produce his mind in public . . . seems to be the principal calling and occupation of [man's] nature."[51] Ferguson found a bitter irony in the fact that, while it ought to be man's greatest happiness to "glow with an ardent zeal" for the "general good," the members of commercial society are consistently seduced by the false pleasures of "practising apart, and each for himself, the several arts of personal advancement, or profit."[52] Social relations become reified—"he deals with [his fellow-creatures] as he does with his cattle and his soil, for the sake of the profits they bring"—, and civic consciousness and civic virtue become impossibilities.[53] The choice is clear in Ferguson's eyes: either profit or patriotism.

The immediate context of Ferguson's concern was the loss of Scotland's political autonomy after 1707, its turn away from nationalist zeal, from "ardent attachment to . . . country" and "zeal for maintaining political rights" to pursue commercial profit and individual pleasure. Ferguson himself founded the Poker Club in 1762 to "stir up" interest in a Scottish militia, which would have expressed civic virtue, even more clearly than the voluntary societies, debating clubs like the Select Society, and other cultural institutions that flourished in post-Union Scotland.[54] But his larger concern was with the social effects of economic development, the increasingly intricate division of labor on which it depends, and the resulting elimination of political activity that comes to resemble in some ways the torpor of a despotic regime: "[men] have no common affairs to transact, but those of trade: Connections, indeed, or transactions, in which probity and friendship may still take place; but in which the national spirit . . . cannot be exerted."[55] Ferguson reserved his greatest contempt for those who only want to acquire things, who "value their houses, their villas, their statues, their pictures, at a higher rate than they do the republic."[56] Objects—particularly objects that can be bought and sold—stand as the antithesis of the public action that is the highest expression of patriotic zeal in the eyes of Ferguson and other theorists unsympathetic to the commercial society that many parts of Britain had become.

But Scott constructs the antiquarian object as a peculiarly ironic synthesis of opposing tendencies. In 1815, the antiquarian object of desire is simultaneously patriotic fetish and commodity. Objectively, the battlefield relic comes into being through the strange cooperation of militaristic nationalism and commercial enterprise. The antiquarian's drive to acquire such objects both stems from national spirit and satisfies a private desire. Scott's indefatigable exertions as antiquarian collector are also performed in full public view:

> The eagerness with which we entered into these negotiations . . .
> rather scandalized one of the heroes of the day, who did me the
> favour to guide me over the field of battle, and who considered the
> interest I took in things which he was accustomed to see scattered
> as mere trumpery upon a field of victory, with a feeling that I believe
> made him . . . heartily ashamed of his company. (PL 158)

The scandal arises from the seamless convergence in Scott's behavior of a narrow personal acquisitiveness with a virtuously archaic collective identification. Marketplace haggling and disinterested patriotic veneration find themselves equally well accommodated in Scott's antiquarian zeal. As the complex meanings of the word "interest" make clear, it is not a case of simple sentimentality. Scott notes that relics of the world-historical battle, proofs or tokens of British greatness, "were sold when I was there à prix juste, at least to those who knew how to drive a bargain" (PL 157). Much later in the history of nationalist rhetoric, Ernst Renan would write, "A heroic past, great men, glory . . . this is the social capital upon which one bases a national idea."[57] The heroic past, great men, and glory are shown by Scott's anti-quarianism to be a national legacy that is all too commensurable. Not despite but rather because of the piety of Scott's motives, his antiquarian activity in the summer of 1815 proves Britain to be a commercial society, modern rather than archaic. Even the attempt to preserve the past and every scrap of it draws attention to the occasion of this act—the evanescence not only of his-torical events but also of nationalist fervor. It also draws attention to the char-acteristic means of commercial society: private acquisition. The antiquarian's pious ambitions to acquire, "à prix juste," the relics of national glory reveal, somewhat scandalously, how intimately ideological fantasy and capital are linked. Benjamin Constant's tract, *On the Spirit of Conquest and Usurpation* (1814), had argued that commerce, "the spirit of the age," disregards national borders, discredits nationalist ideologies, and "opposes its irony to every real or feigned enthusiasm."[58] Scott's bargaining for battlefield scraps suggests how antiquarianism visibly mediates between the world of British commerce and the cherished patriotic notion of a priceless history that holds together and is held in common.

Antiquarian Knowledge, Antiquarian Fictions

Set in Scotland at the height of panic about French invasion, *The Antiquary* puts to good use the same equivocal zeal that Scott's eminent military friend found so scandalous on the field of Waterloo. Scott's peculiarly demonstra-tive enthusiasm, shown in his avid bargaining for arguably sacred national relics, paradoxically generates an attitude of skepticism about the value of such relics. The novel, whose title had been settled before the European tour and which was written immediately following the completion of *Paul's Let-ters*, further develops and unfolds this skepticism beneath the same anti-quarian pose of innocence.[59] Rather than celebrating the national unity that prepared the way for the triumph of Waterloo, this novel's version of history unapologetically inverts margin and center: ideological frenzy and military mobilization are merely the subject of intermittent rumors and occasional complaints, while the social and economic interactions of eccentric anti-quarians occupy center-stage in this extremely theatrical novel.[60] Since it could be said, however, that the logic of this national crisis consisted precisely in the sudden cathexis of the social margins and geographical borders of the nation on the one hand, and of domestic space on the other, it is important to note that *The Antiquary* does more than simply shift attention away from the "central" developments and events of the time. It represents the period and culture of war as driven by the production of knowledge. It is knowledge not in a scientific but in a social sense that the novel's society devotes its energies to acquiring: knowledge of others' identities, movements, aims, anxieties, and, above all, of the bearing of the past on the exigencies of the present. This knowledge does not issue from institutionalized or authoritative sources: enquiry and interpretation are informal, endemic, usually carried out in marginal spaces or self-consciously marginal activities like antiquarianism. Both the adherents of patriotic traditionalism and those skeptical of that attitude, most notably Jonathan Oldbuck, generate this type of knowledge, seeking to uncover the true nature of the existing social world and the relevance of the past. Both parties are liable to be grievously mistaken in their conjectures. But antiquarianism as pursued by Oldbuck, much along the lines of Scott's own practice, emerges in a better light because of its own self-conscious ideological impurity. It embraces sentiment and cynicism, avows its imbrication in the inauthenticity of the marketplace, and acknowledges its dialectical relationship to mystification. In Oldbuck's hands, antiquarianism defines itself in opposition to the false stories, conspiracies, and rumors that proliferate throughout this novel; it is, officially, the bearer of demystification, the exploder of myths and superstitious dreams. But his antiquarianism is also distinguished for its persistence in clinging to stories known not to be true. Elevating inconsistency, heterogeneity, and whim to constitutive principles, Oldbuck's antiquarianism allows the novel ultimately to celebrate the nation's unity in this period as an improbable but profitable and oddly comfortable fiction.

Patriotic traditionalism is represented in this novel by Oldbuck's chief rival in antiquarian studies, Sir Arthur Wardour, "a baronet of ancient descent, and of a large but embarrassed fortune" (Ant 37). It is not a flattering portrait. Mentally feeble and socially snobbish, Wardour studies antiquities — primarily his own family history and the history of the Scottish monarchy — in order to reinforce his own claims to social superiority. His "chivalrous" defense of Queen Mary of Scotland, for example, is intended to distinguish himself and his class favorably from the "boorishness [that] still flows in the blood" of the Oldbucks (Ant 40). Wardour is obsessed with the idea of impurity; his antiquarian studies have done little more than bolster his "horror and antipathy to defiled blood and illegitimacy, which has been handed down to me from my respected ancestry" (Ant 99). Wardour's pedigree serves, then, to guarantee the integrity of the identity that has been likewise "handed down"; but his embrace of the rhetoric of inheritance has another, more material purpose. Wardour is deeply in debt (though the history of that debt is never fully explained) and threatened with immediate bankruptcy. His obsessive recurrence to the idea of inheritance serves as a way to conceal this condition and also as a means, he hopes, of remedying it. In one of the novel's subplots, Wardour is led by a German swindler to invest ruinous sums of money in a scheme for mining copper ore on a part of his property; his firm belief in the immense quantity and the purity of this buried inheritance leads him to transfer his hopes to finding "the precious metals,—gold and silver" (Ant 182) beneath the ground of a ruined abbey on his estate. Discovering this vein of treasure would, Wardour hopes, both justify his faith in the power of origins and save him from the debtor's prison. Wardour's belief in the existence of this inheritance, then, stems directly from his actual and desperate impoverishment; it is a humiliating and literally costly way to defer the acknowledgment of this truth. It is Wardour, though, together with his daughter Isabella, who represents the British nation in peril. The threat is not only one of internal collapse, of the inability to support the dreams and the rhetoric of inheritance with anything more material. It comes from outside as well. In one episode, in which Wardour and his daughter are trapped on a beach by a storm while walking home, the scene conspicuously invokes the standard rhetorical topoi of Napoleonic despotism:

> towering clouds . . . assembled on all sides [of the sun], like misfortunes and disasters around a sinking empire and a falling monarch . . . forming out of their unsubstantial gloom the show of pyramids and towers. . . . The distant sea, stretched beneath the varied and gorgeous canopy, lay almost portentously still. (Ant 54)

Here Napoleon's empire is represented as already "sinking" under the weight of its own Egyptian pyramids and towers; in its emphasis on gorgeous show and lack of substance, the passage also echoes the themes of anti-Gallican rhetoric. But motifs of Oriental splendour and despotic imperial display give way to a more active sense of danger as the tide rapidly enters the bay along which the Wardours are walking: "Each minute did their enemy gain ground perceptibly upon them!" Trapped on a small ledge, the Wardours are rescued by the combined efforts of the community, under Oldbuck's efficient direction. But the means of their rescue is fraught with irony: the local fishermen use the same apparatus they used for smuggling "kegs o' gin and brandy lang syne" (Ant 62), hoisting them up with the help of a ship's mast and tackle. Even at this critical moment, as Wardour is being pulled up to safety, Oldbuck sarcastically suggests that there might be a difference between the objective value of the cargo thus secured and Wardour's importance in his own eyes: "canny wi'him—a pedigree of a hundred links is hanging on a twalpenny tow" (Ant 64). Wardour is also rescued, more than once, from financial collapse and imprisonment for bankruptcy. One notable recruitment comes in the apparent form of ancestral treasure buried in the ruined chapel. But it is characteristic of this novel that the discovered inheritance is factitious in a number of ways, known to all except Wardour himself. The silver was planted there secretly by a conspiracy of sympathetic strangers, in an antique chest randomly acquired. Its form is bullion, with "neither inscription nor stamp upon them" (Ant 193); in one version of the novel, it comes from Lovel's ancestral plate, melted down—an inheritance not only surreptitiously transferred but defaced as well.[61] Finally, it is found in the tomb of Malcolm Misticot, as supposedly belonging to the latter; but Misticot is the bastard of family legend, the twelfth-century usurper and family outcast, whose ancestry Wardour so firmly disavows. On the very sepulchre that contains the treasure Oldbuck traces "the baton-sinister, the mark of illegitimacy" (Ant 192). Thus, in both its actual and its putative provenance, this inheritance shows itself to be neither pure nor authentic. Nevertheless, Wardour's traditionalist beliefs are permitted to stand and even to be indulged by others.

Jonathan Oldbuck, generally referred to as "the Antiquary," appears to be Wardour's antithesis. Though Oldbuck is the proprietor of a landed estate inherited through several generations, he is self-consciously free from the prejudices of the class to which he objectively belongs. He boasts of his descent "from a man of more sense than pride. . . . No string of substitute heirs of entail, as empty and unsubstantial as the morsels of paper strung to the train of a boy's kite" (Ant 125). The ancestor in question is Aldobrand Oldenbuck, Reformation printer and descendant of "one of the original printers of Germany," who was exiled for his Protestant faith and eventually domiciled in Scotland (Ant 13). Oldbuck pointedly contrasts "the diffusion of Christian and political knowledge," the cause for which this ancestor "labour[ed] personally at the press," with the "effusion of blood," chivalry's only social accomplishment (Ant 85–86). Indeed, he sees Aldobrand, whose mechanical trade he takes no pains to hide, less as an ancestor than as an exemplum of "independence and self-reliance" (Ant 85). The ancestor whose spirit and whose practice Oldbuck invokes at every turn is, in fact, a whimsically chosen, elective one: "John o' the Girnell, remembered as the last bailiff of the abbey who had resided at Monkbarns," Oldbuck's estate (Ant 87). Emphasizing this dual line of descent, one real and the other fictive, Oldbuck takes delight not in the imperturbable transmission over time of an undivided inheritance but rather in the complex and unforeseeable historical contingencies through which he has come to possess his estate. Wardour's antiquarian studies terminate in the reaffirmation of royalist or traditionalist articles of faith: "Sir Arthur would have deemed himself guilty of the crime of leze-majesty had he doubted the existence of any single individual of that formidable bead-roll of one hundred and four kings of Scotland, received by Boethius, and rendered classical by Buchanan" (Ant 38). Oldbuck, though, "was apt to cavil at this sacred list" and other fetishes, particularly those, like Ossian, in which national pride is at stake. Instead, he devotes himself to detecting fraudulence or discovering unsuspected value. Originally "destined . . . to a share in a substantial mercantile concern" (Ant 14), Oldbuck retains, in Wardour's description, a "habit of minute and troublesome accuracy [that] leads to a mercantile manner of doing business" (Ant 41). He frequently vaunts his own powers of discernment.

His chief business lies in generating antiquarian knowledge; his drawers are stuffed with productions like the "Essay upon Castrametation, with some particular Remarks upon the Vestiges of Ancient Fortifications lately discovered by the Author at the Kaim of Kinprunes" (Ant 29). But Oldbuck produces other forms of knowledge as well; as a Justice of the Peace he investigates social mysteries and suspicious appearances. The Gothic subplot of the Glenallan family turns out to have been traced already in the past by Oldbuck himself; before his enquiries were eventually blocked by the family, he suspected the existence of "a counterfeit marriage, or that very strong measures had been adopted to stifle and destroy the evidence of a real union" between Eveline Neville and Lord Glenallan, resulting in their suicide and madness, respectively, and a lost child. The results of his researches are produced when Lord Glenallan comes to ask his help: "Mr Oldbuck opened a drawer of the cabinet of his ancestor, Aldobrand, and produced a bundle of papers . . . labelled, Examinations &c taken by Jonathan Oldbuck J.P. upon the 18th February 17–" (Ant 280). The reference to Aldobrand suggests that Oldbuck still sees himself as actively promoting the "diffusion of knowledge." Forensic, legal, and antiquarian knowledge are almost ludicrously intertwined in Oldbuck's practice, as we see when he proposes to clear up the Glenallan mystery by writing to "a literary friend at York, with whom I have long corresponded on the subject of the Saxon horn that is preserved in the Minster there; we interchanged letters for six years, and have only . . . been able to settle the first line of the inscription" (Ant 282–83). Oldbuck's correspondent is the soon-to-be-proverbial Dr Dryasdust.

As Whig calculator and Jacobite aristocrat, debunker and defender of mysteries, Oldbuck and Wardour would appear to be related antithetically to each other; and the narrative does suggest such a relation. They disagree on virtually every point, and their political and antiquarian disagreements even appear to reflect a clash at a different level: "Sir Arthur always wished to borrow; Mr Oldbuck was not always willing to lend" (Ant 40). Their ideological hostility seems merely to reflect this fundamental material conflict.[62] But the novel, in fact, explores their curious and complex symbiosis: each had become "essential," "necessary" to the other (39). Locally, the narrative explains this through the psychology of habit, together with a shrewd understanding of the sociology of boredom. In the absence of other suitable activities and admissible society, the two men have grown used to each other's company. But all the complicated transactions of the plot suggest that they are linked by a deeper and less easily deciphered necessity. Not only these antiquarians but also all the citizens of wartime Fairport are obsessed with the deciphering and interpretation of signs. In one extraordinary scene, for example, the town postmistress and her two cronies tamper with, try to decipher, and make reckless conjectures about the day's mail. Out of malignant curiosity, they examine each piece, scrutinizing its shape and seal, holding it up to the light. The scene is punctuated by their clamors: "Shew me! Shew me!" and "Lord's sake, let's see, lass! Lord's sake, let's see!" (Ant 110–12). The objects have fallen randomly into their hands, but offer ample material for ingenious conjecture, particularly in the symbols on the seals used to close the letters: "the seal [on one letter] has an anchor on't. . . . Here's a letter . . . frae [Wardour's] son . . . the seal has the same things wi' the Knockwinnock coach" (Ant 110–12). They draw broad and dramatic conclusions concerning the circumstances and destinies of their fellow townspeople from exceptionally poor evidence. The scene parodies not only philosophical investigation—"Nothing could be gathered from the outside [of one letter], except remarks on the various properties which philosophers ascribe to matter—length, breadth, depth, and weight" (Ant 112–13)—but antiquarian investigation as well. Oldbuck is typically engaged, for example, in trying to decipher the form and meaning of inscribed shapes, letters, and symbols. Unlike the results of the antiquary's researches, the knowledge which these "weird sisters" (Ant 110) produce is vital to the community: "like the sybils after consulting their leaves, [they] arranged and combined the information of the evening, which flew the next morning through an hundred channels . . . through the world of Fairport" (Ant 114).[63] This community thrives on the production and circulation of spurious knowledge. But this comic scene, like the tragic scenes of discovery in the Glenallan subplot, is distinguished by the absence of that necessary and productive tension between credulity and suspicion, belief and knowingness, Wardour and Oldbuck, that characterizes antiquarianism in this novel.

This tension appears not only in strictly antiquarian debates but also in other moments, in which a supposed message of social and individual importance—a message from the past—is at stake. A much-noted example is Lovel's dream.[64] Frustrated in his courtship of Wardour's daughter by his supposed illegitimate birth, Lovel dreams one night in the tapestried chamber of Oldbuck's house that Aldobrand Oldenbuck appears to him, bearing a cryptic message:

> Aldobrand held up his finger . . . and began deliberately to unclasp the venerable volume which occupied his left hand . . . raising his figure to its full dimensions, and holding the book aloft in his left hand, pointed to a passage in the page which he thus displayed . . . [Lovel's] eye and attention were both strongly caught by the line which the figure seemed thus to press upon his notice, the words of which appeared to blaze with a supernatural light, and remained rivetted upon his memory. (Ant 79)

The scene blends together disparate ideological discourses. As the figure of the father interpellates the "son," the obscure and classless Lovel glimpses the legitimacy of a long descent. But in *The Antiquary*, the conservative form of legacy and inheritance is retained while the content changes: what is actually transmitted in this scene is a motto of progressive, meritocratic ideology, disguised by the dream in German: "Kunst macht Gunst," or, in the delayed translation offered, "skill [as opposed to inherited status] wins favor." The ancestor in question, far from being noble, is Aldobrand Oldenbuck, artisan-printer. Notably, the transmission of this wisdom is not oral but textual; as an indecipherable inscription, it falls within the proper domain of the antiquary, removed from practical application. Lovel, however, is preoccupied with the idea that it pertains to his present activity. When he later learns its meaning, he confides to Oldbuck that he sees the phrase as "a motto which encouraged me to perseverance . . . a lesson which I could so plainly apply to my own circumstances" (Ant 104). But Oldbuck's reaction is deeply revealing: "The Antiquary burst into a fit of laughing" (Ant 104). The notion of ancestral sanction makes perfect sense as a wish-fulfilling dream, "one of those juggling tricks," in Oldbuck's words, "which the sagest of us play off now and then to gratify our inclination at the expense of our understanding" (Ant 104); the idea is thus both retained and cancelled.

Lovel's dream finds a number of important echoes in other scenes, where ancestral wisdom or knowledge is supposedly handed down to the present.[65] One of the most remarkable follows Wardour's discovery of the "inheritance" of the silver bullion. Having remained behind with Dousterswivel, Edie Ochiltree, the sage beggar, holds up for the swindler's scrutiny the cover of the chest in which the treasure had been found: "'Now look at this board. . . .' There was a word and a number on the plank, and the beggar made them more distinct by . . . rubbing off the clay by which the inscription was obscured. It was in the ordinary black letter. 'Can ye mak ought o't?' said Edie to the adept" (Ant 197). Edie helps him spell out the inscription as "Search Number 1," that is, an injunction to search further for another buried treasure. Thus, he lures the German back that night for a bout of comic retribution. The comedy of the scene arises from the violent tension in Dousterswivel's mind behind credulity and suspicion: as a professional impostor, he understands the arts of imposition all too well. He ultimately emerges as the credulous dupe to Ochiltree's superior knavery: "The features of the old man . . . seemed in this instance so keenly knowing, than even the assurance of Dousterswivel . . . sunk" (Ant 196). What Ochiltree knows, however, is that there is nothing to be known: only a spurious meaning to be constructed from an inscription that happens to be the name of the boat from which the chest was borrowed. The scene aims its parodic energy at both traditionalist ideology, the belief that the past can offer wisdom and guidance to the present, and at antiquarian investigation, based on the idea that the past bears a different type of value.

There are a number of intriguing links between Dousterswivel and Jonathan Oldbuck: like the antiquary, for example, Dousterswivel sees the past (or traditionalist prejudices concerning the past) as something that can be mined for objects of material value. Oldbuck, on overhearing an archaic word in an old ballad, exclaims (only half-facetiously) "the word's worth a dollar" (Ant 311); Dousterswivel's more sinister projects concern the "dirty Fairport bank-notes" (Ant 187) that he hopes to extract by exploiting Wardour's credulous belief in a buried inheritance. Other details provided by the narrative link the two characters. Dousterswivel is first described as a "High German landlouper" (Ant 101), and this descent establishes an important tie with Oldbuck, of whom Wardour observes, "the German boorishness still flows in the blood" (Ant 40). Dousterswivel's descent is emphasized not only by his fractured English but also by the fantastic tale of Martin Waldeck, translated by Wardour's daughter, which, set in the Harz forest, establishes Germany as the locus of superstition and magic. Oldbuck possesses and uses an antique candlestick, "wrought out of the silver found in the mines of the Harz mountains" (Ant 74); this candlestick had belonged, we are told, to Aldobrand Oldenbuck, and thus the possibility is opened up for regarding Aldobrand's "kunst" as related to the mystical "art" that Dousterswivel practices on his credulous client. The German swindler blends "the terms of science with a strange jargon of mysticism" (Ant 101); he discovers treasure, Wardour believes, "by the use of his art" (Ant 189). "Art" thus includes scientific knowledge and mystical jargon, artifice and merit. And, in fact, Oldbuck boasts that his ancestor, the champion of Reformation and enlightenment, "was a chymist, as well as a good mechanic . . . qualities . . . sufficient to constitute a white witch at least" (Ant 73).

The links between the two Germans in this novel do not impugn Oldbuck's credibility or character. Rather, they reinforce an essential quality of antiquarianism as represented by this novel: as a form of knowledge, antiquarianism is impure, chaotic, vulnerable to exposure, and politically valuable for these very qualities. The first important set-piece of the novel, the description of Oldbuck's study, takes up the traditional topoi of antiquarian satire in order to stress the idea of chaos:

> a chaos of maps, engravings, scraps of parchment, bundles of papers, pieces of old armor, swords, dirks, helmets . . . busts and Roman lamps . . . portraits in armor . . . a profusion of papers, parchments, books, and nondescript trinkets . . . which seemed to have little to recommend them, besides rust and the antiquity which it indicates. In the midst of this wreck of ancient books and utensils, sat a large black cat, which, to a superstitious eye, might have presented the genius loci, the tutelar demon of the apartment. The floor . . . was overflowed with the same mare magnum of miscellaneous trumpery, where it would have been as impossible to find any individual article wanted, as to put it to any use when discovered. (Ant 20–21)

The antiquary describes this space as his "sanctum sanctorum," a masculine space set apart from the rest of the household, jealously guarded from the intrusions of domestic order, and dedicated to the preservation of the past. Yet the joke is that many of the objects so vigilantly protected are of dubious provenance and questionable historical significance; they are more likely to be ordinary "trinkets" and "utensils" than ancient artifacts. The antiquary's study stands in an equivocal relation to patriotic traditionalism. Burke had thus summed up the usefulness of the discourse of inheritance: by venerating Britain's past as an inheritance, "our liberty becomes a noble freedom. . . . It has a pedigree and illustrating ancestors. It has its bearings and its ensigns armorial. It has its gallery of portraits; its monumental inscriptions; its records, evidences, and titles."[66] The sacralizing accoutrements of inheritance, and the paraphernalia of legal, political and military tradition are literally present in the antiquary's study, lovingly collected and preserved with a sentimental, even superstitious reverence for the past. But it belies the fundamental assumptions of traditionalism in some important ways. According to patriotic traditionalism, it is as incorrect to say that history randomly accrues as to believe that it leaves behind masses of wreckage for which no use can be found. National unity depends on seeing history as itself an ennobling order, a grand and impersonal rhythm, and the purpose of such a vision is eminently practical: to inspire certain forms of action and belief. But in the antiquary's study, the relics of history are radically decontextualized and chaotically jumbled together under the master-trope of "wreckage." No use can even be envisioned for these objects, or for the eclectic past, random, untotalizable, and uncontainable, conjured up through their juxtaposition. The parts fail to add up to any coherent meaning; much less is the owner ennobled in any way by the proximity of the past. The description concludes with a double impossibility: the impossibility of imposing any order on this chaos of history and the impossibility of devising any practical or moral use for it. In its rhythm, Scott's description echoes his representation of the detritus, the "mere trumpery," littering the battlefield of Waterloo.

Oldbuck's antiquarianism is self-consciously a private affair. The fervor with which he collects historical objects, records, and evidences reflects no desire to participate in a public or national history. What welds the miscellaneous collection into an artificial totality is the fact that each object has been personally acquired, discovered, or shrewdly purchased: "Mr. Oldbuck . . . taking a pleasure in the personal labor of forming his library, saved his purse at the expense of his time and toil" (Ant 23). The value of his acquisitions, however, does not rest on pure, private sentiment alone. For Oldbuck, each antiquarian discovery needs to have its value reflected, as it were, through the money-form.[67] When Wardour, heavily in debt to Oldbuck, presents the latter with a collection of antique coins as a "gift of friendship," Oldbuck accepts the curiosities only "on condition that you will permit me to mark the value according to Pinkerton's catalogue and appreciation, against your account in my red book" (Ant 185). Oldbuck's antiquarian pleasure is grounded in calculating the exchange value of ancient texts and objects, as his tale of Caxton's "Game of Chess" suggests. This rare book, Oldbuck rhapsodically recounts, was "originally secured, by skill and research, for the easy equivalent of twopence sterling" by an antiquarian and eventually "purchased by Royalty itself for one hundred and seventy pounds!" (Ant 24) It is in the secondhand marketplace, rather than on the imaginary stage of national history, that the antiquary comes into his own:

> How often have I stood haggling on a half-penny, lest, by a too ready acquiescence in the dealer's first price, he should be led to suspect the value I set upon the article! how have I trembled. . . . And then . . . . the sly satisfaction with which one pays the consideration, and pockets the article, affecting a cold indifference, while the hand is trembling with pleasure! (Ant 24–25)

Like Scott, Oldbuck knows "how to drive a bargain" (PL 157). The value of the article is an index not only of his own desire but also of the object's scarcity: "There was, it seemed, no peculiar distinction, however trifling or minute, which might not give value to a volume, providing the indispensable condition of scarcity . . . was attached to it" (Ant 25). Oldbuck's pleasure, too, is mediated through others: "Then to dazzle the eyes of our wealthier and emulous rivals by shewing them such treasures as this . . . to enjoy their surprise and envy." These are described as "the white moments of life!" (Ant 25). The novel suggests that antiquarian knowledge is not distinct from class consciousness and commercial calculation but rather flourishes as a displacement of these. In Oldbuck's antiquarian researches, we can see the incomplete sublimation of his tendencies toward "frugality and industry" (Ant 15).

Though Oldbuck congratulates himself on his "superior knowledge and dexterity" (Ant 25), his antiquarian theories are hardly above reproach. They are, as the episode of the Kaim of Kinprunes shows, exceptionally vulnerable to exposure by the first person who happens to come along—usually Edie Ochiltree. Having purchased a hilltop common in the belief that it was a Roman camp and site of an important ancient battle, Oldbuck describes to Lovel the scene: "Agricola . . . looked forth on the immense army of Caledonians, occupying the declivities of yon opposite hill, the infantry rising rank over rank as the form of ground displayed their array to its utmost advantage" (Ant 30)—only to be interrupted by Ochiltree, who reveals the true and humble origins of the mound, a recent, rustic, ad hoc construction. Oldbuck's discomfiture, however, is only momentary; he soon recuperates his exploded knowledge as fiction. Oldbuck proposes to Lovel that the latter write an epic poem on this same battle between the Caledonians and the Romans: "The Caledoniad, or Invasion Repelled—Let that be the title—It will suit the present taste, and you may throw in a touch of the times" (Ant 107). When Lovel points out that the Roman invasion "was *not* repelled," Oldbuck cheerfully argues that poets are "free of the corporation, and as little bound down to truth or probability as Virgil himself" (Ant 107). As Lovel and others realize, antiquarian discourse avails itself of a similar freedom. Oldbuck's antiquarianism is distinguished not only by its acute reckonings of value but also by its easy embrace of extravagant fictions as acceptable simulacra of knowledge.

The novel's conclusion vindicates Oldbuck's antiquarianism. Rumors of French, rather than Roman, invasion intensify, and suddenly the warning beacon is seen. The town gathers in the marketplace in the middle of the night:

> The windows were glancing with a hundred lights, which . . . indicated the confusion within doors. The women of lower rank assembled and clamored in the marketplace. The yeomanry, pouring from their different glens, galloped through the streets. . . . The drums and fifes of the volunteers beating to arms, were blended with the voice of the officers, the sound of the bugles, and the tolling of the bells from the steeple. . . . Such was the scene of general confusion. (Ant 350)

The scene strongly recalls, in Lockhart's words, "that old Border life of war, and tumult, and all earnest passions" that Scott's antiquarian studies had supposedly implanted in the British imagination.[68] Scott had described such a scene in the introduction to his *Minstrelsy of the Scottish Border*:

> These enterprising chiefs . . . had reached Stirling in a night march from Edinburgh . . . seized the principal street of the town. . . . The borderers had dispersed to plunder the stables of the nobility; the infantry thronged tumultuously together on the main street. . . . Their alarm was increased by the townsmen thronging to arms.[69]

But even more curiously the description of the nocturnal social coil recalls the picture of the antiquary's study: overflow, the mixing of disparate and "irregular materials" (Ant 350), chaos and "confusion." Most of all, the scene is characterized by a lack of truth and reality: the alarm of invasion is, embarrassingly, discovered to be false. The watchman had mistaken the bonfire made by burning Wardour's mining equipment for a beacon; the destruction of one duplicitous scheme gives rise directly to another fiction. Social or national harmony is revealed to be spurious in its occasion if not also somewhat factitious in substance. However, the triumphalism of the scene is not diminished but rather domesticated by being thus ironized.

In a final twist, Scott informs the reader in a footnote that the story of the false alarm is historically true, taken from "a real incident . . . on the evening of the 2d February, 1804. . . . The circumstances of this false alarm may be now held of too little importance even for a note upon a work of fiction; but at the period when it happened, it was hailed by the country as a propitious omen."[70] The remark is equivocal in a familiar way: the manufactured value of the national interpretation of the event as "propitious omen" stands without eclipsing the banality of this footnote to a history that never occurred. To borrow from Freud's description of the dynamics of the dream-work, we can say that according to Scott's interpretation of national history, the ideology of patriotic traditionalism, like the unconscious wish, furnishes the capital required by the entrepreneurs of the dream—or of the fantasies of nationhood.[71] Fittingly, the same moment provides the original capital for Scott's successful venture in the form of this historical novel.

Obsolescence

The disavowal of antiquarianism was repeated by nineteenth-century historians, whose quest for professional legitimacy was based on their claim to lay an indispensable groundwork for the ideology of the British nation.[72] Antiquaries continued to produce local or county histories, typically consisting, according to Philippa Levine, of "accounts of local superstitions and customs alongside discussions of medieval land holdings, of monasteries dissolved under Henry VIII and transcripts of epitaphs on old tombs."[73] However patriotic their intentions, such heterogeneous and disjointed productions were greeted with the contempt of professional historians such as Edward Freeman:

> There are men who busy themselves with buildings or primeval monuments or actual objects and relics of early times . . . whose interest ends in the objects themselves . . . [but] Unless it . . . goes on to their higher value as forms part of a greater whole, antiquarian study is a mere matter of curiosity.[74]

Again the problem of antiquarianism is cast in terms of a problematic of value: antiquarians see only the "curiosity" of objects instead of their "higher value." If the narrative of national history resembled, in Lionel Gossman's words, "a well-known tale whose general contours were fixed and unchanging,"[75] antiquarianism could problematize such master-narratives, not least by appearing to ignore them in favor of discrete facts and strange objects.

But Scott's novel suggests that antiquarian appreciation may not be ignorant of master-narratives so much as cognizant of their enabling conditions. At one moment, reflecting on Wardour's imminent bankruptcy, Oldbuck pauses to admire the elegance of the legal fiction, whereby "nobody can be arrested in Scotland for debt":

> the truth is, the king is so good as to interfere at the request of the creditor, and to send the debtor his royal command to do him justice within a certain time . . . the man resists and disobeys: what follows? Why, that he be lawfully and rightfully declared a rebel to our gracious sovereign. . . . And he is then legally imprisoned, not on account of any civil debt, but because of his ungrateful contempt of the royal mandate. (Ant 307)

Over the objections of his listeners, Oldbuck praises "the elegance of the legal fiction, and the manner in which it reconciles that duress which, for the protection of commerce, it has been found necessary to extend towards refractory debtors, with the most scrupulous attention to the liberty of the subject" (Ant 307–8). What the antiquary finds so elegantly illustrated in this example is the use of a legal fiction to create continuity between an archaic sovereignty and the modern economic reality of Scottish commercial practice. More important, by disguising debt as "ungrateful contempt of the royal mandate," this commercial society uses a fictive king to uphold a narrative about the liberty of the British subject. Other fictions, too, must be tolerated to preserve this grand narrative, as Oldbuck is blithely aware. The empire of his obsession is the Roman one, and his quest has been to possess that ground on which Scotland's natives made their last stand. When his successful acquisition turns out to be a humiliating mistake, he knowingly turns to the displacements of fiction. Counseling Lovel to write an epic poem that makes the Scots victorious in their resistance against empire, Oldbuck brazenly distorts history in order to preserve the myth of British—or, at least, Scottish—liberty. Finding equal grandeur in both empire and imagined resistance, Oldbuck reveals an oddly relaxed ambivalence toward imperial projects.

Freeman deprecates antiquarianism as a "mere matter of curiosity" for its failure to integrate its knowledge into a larger narrative about "a greater whole." But Scott's antiquarianism constitutes itself around the relation between part and whole, considered not abstractly but historically with regard to the imperial British nation. Scott's own antiquarianism bears an uncanny relation to the idea of the British nation, revealing the seams that ought to remain hidden within the larger whole, and pointing to the contingent movements of imperial history.[76] In an essay on "Border Antiquities" published in 1806, Scott notes that the antiquary's field of activity comes into existence only upon the demise of a living political, cultural, or ideological formation. Because continuous usage brings about continuous revision and rebuilding, "The frontier regions of great kingdoms, while they retain that character, are unavoidably deficient in subjects for the antiquary.[77] It is only when nations disappear that the spectral domain of the antiquary arises: "The case becomes different, however, when, losing by conquest or by union their character as frontier, scenes once the theatre of constant battle, inroad, defence and retaliation, have been for two hundred years converted into the abode of peace and tranquillity."[78] There is something chilling about the apparent naiveté with which he obscures the difference between conquest and union. Scott situates the modern antiquary as not a melancholy but a hearty, cheerful presence amid the "mouldering ruins" of defunct polities. As a classic paradigm of obsolescence, the former border between Scotland and England becomes a favorite haunt. But the "peace and tranquillity" achieved by the union come to be appreciated primarily as the condition that allows antiquarians to pursue their busy curiosity—curiosity aimed, moreover, at continually unearthing the material remains of conflict and resistance. Even when written to celebrate British unity in the face of French invasion, the antiquary's productions possess a scandalously dialectical character: they inevitably draw attention to the brevity, discontinuity, and factitiousness of the nation's history.

Scott's "Dedicatory Epistle" to *Ivanhoe* uses a discussion of antiquarian authorship, its difficulties and privileges, as a means of both self-consciously affirming and slyly crossing the border between Scottish and English history. In part, this border is constituted by the prejudice of "the English reader." Because of his general belief in the "wild and extravagant" character of that other part of Britain, the English reader, Scott argues, is disposed to accept the inherently bizarre work of antiquaries when this is placed in a Scottish context.[79] But antiquarian researches into English history are likely to be rejected by this same reader because of his stubborn refusal to acknowledge the alterity of his own country's past: "the same worthy person . . . is not half so much disposed to believe that his own ancestors led a very different life from himself . . . that the shattered tower, which now forms a vista from his window, once held a baron who would have hung him up at his own door without any form of trial."[80] Disrupted by antiquarian research, or even by antiquarian novel-writing, the homogeneity of England's past and present is revealed to be a complacent ideological illusion. The antiquarian's task, as Scott presents it here, is strangely double. On the one hand, he is charged to remember "that extensive neutral ground, the large proportion . . . of manners and sentiments . . . which, arising out of the principles of our common nature, must have existed alike in either state of society."[81] On the other hand, the antiquarian author, with his superior knowledge, is peculiarly obliged to be the guardian of "legitimate bounds": "The painter . . . must not plant cypress trees upon Inch-Merrin, or Scottish firs among the ruins of Persepolis; and the author lies under a corresponding restraint."[82] Obvious solecisms are easy enough to point out, of course; but the "neutral ground" Scott celebrates is largely conjectural, located in the past like the commons that were also disappearing. Extending this analogy with painting, Scott compares "the antiquarian details" of a novel with "the peculiar features of a landscape" that must be captured: the "feudal tower," rock, and waterfall. But he plays with this metaphor of "neutral ground," transforming neutrality into a matter of indifference: "herbs, flowers, and trees with which the spot is decorated . . . are . . . subject to the artist's disposal, as his taste or pleasure may dictate."[83] Decorative flora are indifferent, even whimsical matters until their relationship to the represented place comes into dispute. Scott suggests that what is really at stake is the politicization of the local. The antiquary stands at this conceptual border: the moment when the merely particular becomes consecrated as the local, claimed by a community, and defined in opposition to an imperializing universal. But the antiquary does not so much police that border as make its crossing a matter of everyday routine.

In the end, it is a taste for obsolescence that makes antiquarians uneasy sharers in the celebrations of a purportedly timeless patriotic ideology. Rather than continuity, transmission, identity, and wholeness (the touchstones of traditionalism), obsolescence, scarcity, strangeness, and fragmentation (the formal expressions of irony) are the conditions of antiquarian value. And this value is understood to be commensurable with other forms of currency, including the currency of fiction. In his polemical tract, *Letters of Malachi Malagrowther* (1826), Scott writes at one point of "an old boundary stone, half-sunk in earth, half-overgrown with moss"; with what appears to be typical antiquarian zeal for the obsolete object, he warns, "'Remove not the old land-mark.'"[84] But this old land-mark, the antiquarian's material fetish, is, in fact, a metaphor for Scotland's distinctive banking practices. The tract argues against the proposed English reform of Scotland's system of informal paper currency that circulated in lieu of coin. Even as a local rhetorical gesture, Scott's antiquarianism unabashedly reveals the imbrication of profit, tradition, knowledge, credulity, fictions, and the history of nations. It will be Thomas Carlyle's task to relate these ideas in new ways and to make of history a self-consciously occult principle of national cohesion.

4

A Nation's Fetish:
Carlyle and the Work of Literature

Thomas Carlyle's 1838 review of J. G. Lockhart's *Life of Sir Walter Scott* does more than insult that biography's famous subject. It maps out the relationships between literature, the marketplace, the British nation, and its history in a way that secures a place for Carlyle as one of Britain's foremost men of letters. Throughout this essay, Carlyle disparages Scott's historical novels as nothing more than commodities: "The great fact about them is, that they were faster written and better paid for than any other books in the world."[1] Unlike genuinely valuable creation, which emerges from inordinate struggle, accompanied by "severe pains" (WS 458), Scott's novels provide the writer with an easy surplus of profit. Indeed, they even assume all the agency that rightfully belongs to the author: "the Waverley Novels circulated and reigned triumphant" (WS 437). They provide a classic illustration of commodity-fetishism. The commodity's origins in social labor are forgotten, so that things seem to enter into relations with each other directly. Thus, Carlyle describes the intimate network created by Scott's novels, money, land, and other commodities: "fast as the new gold comes in for a new Waverley Novel . . . it changes itself into moory acres, into stone, and hewn or planted wood" (WS 442). While Scott's novels briskly form relationships with other commodities, hacked or hewn, they also function as signs in the scramble for distinction that occupies Britain's reading classes, at the risk of their masculine virtue. Any one of the nation's "indolent languid men . . . might fling himself back, exclaiming, 'Be mine to lie on this sofa, and read everlasting Novels of Walter Scott!'" (WS 452). The privileged, effeminate indolence cultivated by these novels forms the basis of a bogus community of "tourists, wonder-hunters, and all that fatal species of people" (WS 445). This community of Scott's readers is not at all anomalous; it represents an entire British nation "fallen languid, destitute of faith and terrified at scepticism" (WS 431). The novels retail a simulacrum of agency perfectly suited, Carlyle argues, to a nation in such a condition. Even Scott himself knows better than to set store by his own creations: he was "writing daily with the ardour of a steam-engine, that he might make 15,000 a year, and buy upholstery with it . . . cover the walls of a stone house in Selkirkshire with knick-knacks, ancient armor, and genealogical shields" (WS 51–52).

At this point, however, Carlyle performs an important equivocation. Do the novels really "change themselves" into commodities? Or is the author himself, however mechanical his habits of production, converting his novels into other forms of value? If the latter, is Scott's alienation of his own labor the sign of a pathological "delirium"? Carlyle is initially tempted to see it as a megalomaniacal derangement, Scottish-style: "That tract after tract of moorland . . . should be joined together . . . and named after one's name,— why, it is a shabby small-type edition of your vulgar Napoleons!" (WS 452). But Carlyle can also see in Scott's easy disavowal of his own labor a sign of the "health" that he elsewhere in this essay singles out for praise. Carlyle finds the most telling sign of Scott's instinctive virtue in the public anonymity the latter maintained as the author of Waverley, the canny ironic self-erasure that made him "like a king travelling incognito" (WS 437). This is not involuntary self-forgetfulness but a publicly performed, strategic act. Through this disavowal, taken to the point of theatricality (as Lockhart informs us), Scott even seems to magnify what his novels can accomplish for the nation. Carlyle derives a number of crucial insights from the example of Scott's literary production. Carlyle will come to define a literary ideal antithetical to the Waverley Novels. While the Waverley Novels promote relaxation, Carlyle's ideal literature foregrounds productive struggle. It should represent, embody, and promote struggle in the form of labor that is not merely solitary but social, not mechanical but human. If Scott's novels exist in order to circulate and to exchange themselves for other commodities, Carlyle believes that literature should turn its back on the scramble for material and cultural capital. But Carlyle does realize, however disdainfully, the role that the Waverley Novels played in unifying the nation.

> Hardly any literary reputation ever rose so high in our Island. . . .
> Walter Scott became . . . the favourite of Princes and of Peasants, and all intermediate men . . . Solitary Ettrick saw itself populous: all paths were beaten with the feet and hoofs of an endless miscellany of pilgrims . . . male and female; peers, Socinian preachers (WS 255, 263)

However banal they might be, as Carlyle's metaphor of the beaten path suggests, Scott's novels became a ground on which different classes, ranks, genders, religions (and possibly even species) could meet and go through the same paces together. While Scott turns his novels into private land "joined together," those novels also join the national island together, giving it a certain unity. Carlyle wants his writings to hold the nation together less speciously, giving it an identity beyond that of geographical contiguity or even shared taste. And here he discovers something exemplary in Scott's famous self-forgetfulness. While Scott continues to receive the profits of his writings, he refrains from asserting other claims over his work. Scott even publicly disavows his own labor, allowing his novels to take on a semiautonomous social existence. The Waverley Novels make clear literature's status as a commodity. As such, literary texts constantly raise questions about the conditions in which they are produced and, especially, consumed. Carlyle's strongest interest concerns the labor performed not by the author but by the reader of literature: the work of deciphering, understanding, interpreting, sympathizing. In an early published essay, a curious image describes the work he expects: "[w]ere there but on the reader's part . . . a kindred spirit of endeavour! Beshone strongly, on both sides . . . this poor opaque Intrigue . . . might become quite translucent between us; transfigured, lifted up . . . ; and might hang there like a smallest Diamond Constellation."[2] For a text to be transformed from an opaque thing into a sign, public, visible, and yet subjectively meaningful, the reader must provide a luminous, connective force through his own labor. But this labor, too, can be forgotten, and even disavowed. Carlyle represents and even demonstrates the act of reading as an abstract, strangely self-forgetful struggle—a struggle, like nearly all other forms of Carlylean labor, carried out by men alone.[3] But instead of creating a material thing that the reader might claim to possess, the labor of reading dissolves it and forgets itself. Carlyle's reader labors to erase the text or to make it, in one of his favorite metaphors, translucent. This is not the translucence of the universal emerging through the particular, but, in the case of history, the shining-through of a particular existence from the past, compelling enough to eclipse the reader's own. In this ironic intersection of work and deferential forgetfulness lies what literature can potentially do for the nation.

Though the concept of the fictive is essential to his thinking, Carlyle rejects the literary genres of fiction. Instead of the novel, history is presented as the most meritorious form of literary discourse.[4] In his histories, Carlyle's working methods do conform to the protocol of the "respectable" historians that he disparages; he claims to have written with "the strictest regard to chronology, geography . . . documentary evidence, and what else true historical research would yield"(DN 232). Carlyle's concept and practice of history, however, are deeply idiosyncratic, and his rhetorical techniques and stances obviously owe much to fiction, despite his disclaimers.[5] In his 1837 essay, "The Diamond Necklace," an account of a famous scandal in ancien régime France, Carlyle makes it clear that his history will not repeat the "empty invoice-lists of Pitched Battles and Changes of Ministry," from "Constitutional History" or the history of "wretched politico-metaphysical abstraction[s]" (DN 227–28). It will differ perhaps most radically from the Scottish Enlightenment version of conjectural or philosophical history that emphasizes a society's impersonal but guaranteed progress through stages of socioeconomic development. Carlyle's goal is not to lay bare the laws of historical development. Nor is it to legitimate a particular political right or claim; nor is it even to create a common political memory for the nation.[6] Rather, his purpose is to create a shared, endemic forgetfulness with important political consequences. If his histories have the effect of "deepen[ing] the possession of the past," as J. W. Burrow phrases it, Carlyle's most urgent aim is to persuade important segments of the nation to forget the claims to which the past might entitle them.[7] And this is to be accomplished through the reading of history. Ultimately, what distinguishes history for Carlyle is simply its claim to be read in a particular way: with absorption in the sense of recovering something real. This absorption is to be so deep that it cancels out the awareness of the reader's needs and manifold labor in the present moment. Such an enchantment comes about not passively but through the act of overcoming historical distance or opacity. The reader must perform strenuous hermeneutic labor to transform "dumb idols . . . inwardly empty, or full of rags and bran" into a "living Picture" full of meaning (DN 133). But Carlyle also suggests that the reader's work, without which meaning could not be produced, needs to be misrecognized in an important way. Literature derives its power from the way in which it can evoke, exercise, and cancel the reader's self-consciousness about his own powers of creation. Carlyle's major historical lectures and narratives often construct mobile frames for acts of self-conscious interpretation. He draws attention to the frame, to the sharp visual focus it makes possible, and to the sense of artifice it creates; the spectator is almost theatrically self-aware. At the same time, he constantly urges his readers to merge or dissolve themselves into the picture, forgetting their "kindred" participation in the animation of the scene.[8] In his lectures *On Heroes, Hero-Worship, and the Heroic in History* (1841), a scene of fetish-worship both exemplifies and self-reflexively illustrates this strategy. Fetishism, as this chapter will show, becomes a crucial figure not only for reading but also for participation in the discourse of the nation.

> The poorest mortal worshipping his Fetish, while his heart is full of
> it . . . surely cannot be an object of hatred. Let his heart *be* honestly
> full of it . . . let him entirely *believe* in his fetish,—it will then be, if
> not well with him, yet as well as it can readily be made to be, and you
> will leave him alone, unmolested there.[9]

Here the reader, explicitly figured and addressed, discovers his double in the fetish-worshipper, observed in a quasi-historical setting. Initially, he is the imperial observer, deeply prejudiced in favor of his own civilized beliefs. This spectator is critical, unable to sympathize, tempted to protest. But Carlyle strategically plays with the related phenomena of critical distance and sympathy. He assumes that the spectator bases his judgment on an act of sympathy, measuring the worth of what he sees by his ability to sympathize with the action. But if the spectator can envision the possibility of the worshipper's impossible belief, he can also reproduce its extent, which is willed rather than involuntary. The imperial reader comes to mirror the fetishist's silent absorption, deferring to a partially misrecognized image of his own making. Carlyle's reader, in turn, figures the British subject contemplating his own sublime image of the nation, forgetting his own role in the creation of that plenitude.

The new national role that Carlyle imagines for literature comes to rely on the topos of fetishism.[10] Later critics have seen fetishism as an unconscious feature of Carlyle's writing related to sexuality.[11] But Carlyle's works allude to this phenomenon in a broad range of contexts related to Britain's imperial political culture. Without receiving the kind of insistent emphasis that turned concepts like hero-worship into bywords for Carlyle's thought, the topic of fetishism becomes central to the ways in which Carlyle represents the act of reading, the practice of conservative nationalism, and the relationship between the two. Derived from imperial ethnography as well as Enlightenment histories of religion, the idea is summed up in Carlyle's assertion that in primitive social states "men . . . worshipped their poor fellowman as a God, and not him only, but stocks and stones, and all manner of animate and inanimate objects" as well as "the poor image his own hands had made."[12] Throughout this chapter I will consider as comprising one discourse of fetishism, Carlyle's references to the worship of objects, talismans, and figures known to be of contingent human provenance. Most often, in his scenarios, they are constructed through the interposition of clothes and texts. Carlyle occasionally seems to use the term, "fetish," to refer to what Mungo Park calls, in his *Travels in the Interior Districts of Africa* (1799), "charms or amulets called saphies . . . prayers or sentences" written down and then worn on the body (or in some instances consumed) to protect the possessor.[13] Park notes that "similar charms or amulets, under the name of . . . fetich, &c. . . . are common in all parts of Africa" (57). This type of fetish is particularly interesting in Carlyle's case because it assumes an occult power attendant on the consumption of the written word; however, Carlyle seems most often to use the term "fetish" without this specific a reference. The idea of fetishism as the earliest primitive theology was common; it can be found, for example, in the writings of Carlyle's contemporary Auguste Comte.[14] But Carlyle applies it in the contexts of France and Britain as a trope rather than a literal description.

As a figure that can be adapted to different circumstances, the fetish permits him to address issues of crucial political importance and to link them to one another. First is the material want that Carlyle and later theorists see as having driven the French Revolution—in Hannah Arendt's words, "the immediacy of suffering . . . the exigencies of liberation not from tyranny but from necessity."[15] Instead of taking issue with political forms and principles, the French Revolution arose, Carlyle insists, from material need as well as from the inherent inadequacy of material, "inanimate" objects, however plentiful, to supply human needs. The fetish's inherent inadequacy as object, its "untranscended materiality," as a recent theorist describes it, alludes to this problem and figures it in a coded and yet recognizable way.[16] Carlyle diverges from other discussions of fetishism in emphasizing the manufactured nature of the fetish even more than its animated character. This topos of worshipping what one's "own hands had made" addresses a problem that had become even more pressing for Britain as a result of its own industrial revolution: the consequences of material productivity when it becomes the basis of a self-conscious political identity. Political claims came to be grounded in the consciousness of being able to produce things of material value. Even before the 1832 Reform Bill, the National Union of the Working Classes and radical papers like *The Pioneer* divided society into "those who do labour" and "those who produce nothing."[17] Conservatives as well spoke of "the unproductive classes" and "the productive classes."[18] In *Sartor Resartus* (1838), Carlyle deliberately exaggerates the division of Britain into two hostile "sects" with no shared experience or even communication. Those who labor and suffer from material want are confronted with the material affluence of those who do nothing; thus, the consciousness of laboring "work[s] unweariedly in the secret depths of English national existence; striving to separate and isolate it into two contradictory, uncommunicating masses."[19] This open secret of self-conscious labor is a force fraught with political peril in the eyes of a conservative such as Carlyle, who wishes in the end, despite his indignation at injustice, to retain existing structures of power. It can lead to the almost total revolutionary subversion of existing orders, as in his description of the Terror: "[a] nation of men, full of wants and void of habits! . . . men . . . have, on the spur of the instant, to devise for the want the *way* of satisfying it. The Wonted tumbles down; by imitation, by invention, the Unwonted hastily builds itself up. What the French National head has in it comes out."[20] Rather than marking a return to civic first principles, such revolutions arise from the full unleashing of a quintessentially modern inventiveness and energy—the same energy that animates British industrial production.[21] This is the energy that produces the "two-hundred thousand shirts [and] trousers" that Carlyle's *Past and Present* shows heaped up in ominous "mountains."[22]

Finally, the topos of the fetish alludes to the problem of cultural and political authority under such conditions: the failure of hierarchies on the basis of which national parts are delineated and ranked. The fetish acknowledges what a contemporary of Carlyle's described in *Fraser's Magazine* in 1835 as "the stern realities which furnish forth the world of politics": "there is no longer . . . fane, shrine, or image, held in blind, unsearching reverence."[23] Traditional representations of the nation are feeble, known to be constructed and only contingently legitimate, however conservatives might insist on the sacredness of king, magistrate, and other institutions.[24] Under the type of radical scrutiny that Carlyle himself provided early in his career for the *Edinburgh Review*, already-instituted forms of authority can be seen as mere fabrications, "chains of our own forging, and which ourselves also can rend asunder."[25] But Carlyle is unable to imagine an order that is not a hierarchical one and unwilling to embrace a radical transformation of political representation. The topos of fetishism allows Carlyle to create an ironic alliance between radical self-consciousness and conservative ends, radicalism and conservatism being, as he lamented to Emerson, "the grand Categories under which all English spiritual activity . . . must range itself."[26]

The constellated political meanings of fetishism give us another way to understand the pronounced ironic self-reflexiveness of Carlyle's writings.[27] Works such as *Sartor Resartus* use the resources of Romantic irony to present themselves as works-in-progress, as collated fragments laboriously produced and contingently pieced together by an editor-figure who stands in for the reader. All of Carlyle's writings require an equally arduous and self-conscious effort from the reader. Yet their meaning depends on overlooking this productive "endeavour" and the contingent nature of its success. Grappling with the formal complexities of Carlyle's texts models a larger contemplation: reading the "hieroglyphic page" (DN 136) of national history. Carlyle's histories develop on a thematic level many of these same concerns. There is, first, the theme of radical contingency, often linked with the figures of the marketplace, and of the nation as marketplace writ large. In the essay "The Diamond Necklace," Carlyle carefully traces how the jewels in the Queen's necklace, as well as the actors in that affair, are "united, in strange fellowship, with comrades blown together from all ends of the Earth . . . made to take rank and file, in new order . . . and parade there for a season. . . . In such inexplicable wise are Jewels, and Men also . . . jumbled together and asunder, and shovelled and wafted to and fro" (DN 234–35). This line of emphasis recalls Scott, though Carlyle will not, to the same degree, savor the discrepancies between the nation's essential contingency and its ideological fantasies. In strong contrast to Scott's novels, Carlyle's histories place against this backdrop of contingency the theme of heroic physical labor, again given a specific gendered character as "man's force": "The very shilling that thou hast was dug, by man's force, in Carinthia and Paraguay; smelted sufficiently, and stamped" (DN 235). The less muscular version of this we have seen in Burke's stress on the nonnatural harmony of Britain's public life. Both of these subjects, reiterated and developed in Carlyle's longer histories, bear directly on how he wants the nation to be understood. They militate against the habit of conflating the nation with commerce, which Carlyle sees as an impersonal, routine, anonymous circulation with just enough connection to half-perceived meanings and desires to preempt reflection. Instead, Carlyle's histories reveal the nation as the product of absolute contingency on the one hand, an "inexplicable" jumbling; and, on the other hand, the product of labor that stands in a dialectical relation to that contingency. *Past and Present* describes Britain's constitution, landscape, language, cultural and social forms as "work and forgotten work," performed by "[t]he hands of forgotten brave men" (PP 130). Carlyle displays the labor that has produced the nation, labor that contains its own moral necessity. But at the same time he stresses the contingency inherent in the nation's formation and in the recording of its history. The concept of forgotten labor, of work that creates a "new order . . . for a season" before being returned to the jumble of contingency, becomes central to Carlyle's idiosyncratic blend of radicalism and conservatism. Thus, he turns to the practice of the fetish-worshipper, who disavows his own role in producing the authoritative wholeness to which he defers. The hope is that the productive classes will follow this example, foregoing the claims to which their own labor might entitle them. Carlyle's most important model of labor, however, is not industrial production but the amnesic struggle carried out in the act of reading. Reading also crosses heroic labor with contingency and self-forgetfulness. There is a discernible link between Carlyle's conservative public fetishism, designed to promote both reverence and irony, and the discourse of open political artifice in Burke. Scott's antiquarian, too, bequeaths his knowledge of compromising histories to Carlyle's fetish-worshipper. Carlyle's greatest debt to Burke and Scott resides in his conviction that Britain's imperial unity could rest on an uncanny alliance of knowledge and disavowal, carried out in the privacy of reading.

Yet there is an attempt to move beyond irony that distinguishes Carlyle's writings from theirs, a desire to see irony as an initial stage in forging a less volatile bond to the nation. Carlyle's essay on Scott, for example, opens with a description of literary celebrities ("lions") at a soirée, the "crowning phenomenon, and summary of modern civilisation." Again, Carlyle uses literature as civil society's exemplary institution:

> Glittering are the rooms, well-lighted, thronged . . . behold there also flow the lions, hovering distinguished, oracles of the age. . . . Oracles really pleasant to see . . . [but] Utterance there is not . . . For which reason it has been suggested . . . Might not each lion be, for example, ticketed, as wine decanters are? Let him carry, slung around him . . . his silver label with name engraved; you lift his label, and read it . . . and speech is not needed at all . . . it is most true that there is "an instinctive tendency in men to look at any man that has become distinguished." . . . It is indeed curious to consider how men do make the gods that themselves [*sic*] worship. (WS 400–01)

Carlyle reveals his distinctively keen insight in this odd fantasy. Through the pervasive force of commodification, literary texts and producers have become consumable objects. Corresponding to this in an ironic way, the act of consumption has become textualized to the extent that it consists primarily in reading labels. Utterance, hearing, and consumption lose their distinctiveness, blending into one act of reading. Reading may be another crude transaction with a material commodity: it stands here as the essence of commercial culture. But its participation in this debased culture, in Carlyle's eyes, is what allows reading to point the way toward a renovated system of social relations. In this scene, the quasi gods of the cultural world arise only as a result of the aimless, lazy curiosity of the reading public. But reading will take on the features of fetish-making in a less ironic way in Carlyle's later works.

Habits of Irony and Beyond

Carlyle's first major published work, *Sartor Resartus* (serialized in *Fraser's Magazine*, 1833–34), radically questions what constitutes a nation, what creates its subsidiary social distinctions, and what role metaphor can play in holding it together. Carlyle's answer takes the form of a rhetorical question:

> looking away from individual cases, and how a Man is by the Tailor
> new-created into a Nobleman, and clothed not only with Wool but
> with Dignity and a Mystic Dominion,—is not the fair fabric of Society
> itself, with all its royal mantles and pontifical stoles, whereby,
> from nakedness and dismemberment, we are organised into Polities,
> into Nations . . . the creation . . . of the Tailor alone? (SR 219)

Sartor Resartus is the dramatized exposition of a fictive German Romantic philosophy, summed up in the contention that "Society . . . is founded upon Cloth" (SR 48). The curious nature of this work arises from the incomplete metaphoricity of Carlyle's controlling metaphor: fabric or cloth. On the one hand, cloth is clearly a metaphor for the arbitrary and yet collectively recognized authority of convention. In a sense, it is a metaphor for metaphor itself. Yet Carlyle's cloth is also always a substance, woven, cut, and sewn: a substance whose sheer material presence (when worn, for instance, as a magistrate's robe) prompts unreflective acts of obedience. *Sartor Resartus* shows its indebtedness everywhere to the Revolution controversy and, in particular, to the debates of Edmund Burke and Thomas Paine. The radical Paine had asked in his *Rights of Man*, "what is this metaphor, called a crown, or rather what is monarchy? Is it a thing, or is it a name, or is it a fraud? . . . Doth the virtue consist in the metaphor, or in the man? Doth the goldsmith that makes the crown, make the virtue also?"[28] Paine's question about the goldsmith is not meant to be answerable. Yet Carlyle applies it seriously to that complex word at the heart of Burke's counterrevolutionary writings: habit.[29] Protesting against the revolutionary dichotomy of nature and artifice, and against the definition of life as bare life, Burke had accused French radicals of tearing off the "decent drapery of life . . . the super-added ideas, furnished from the wardrobe of a moral imagination."[30] In an equally famous passage, Burke refers to the "coat of prejudice" that clothes "the naked reason," only to undo this dichotomy himself by concluding that "[p]rejudice renders a man's virtue his habit. . . . Through just prejudice, his duty becomes a part of his nature" (RRF 101).[31] We have seen that Burke uses his metaphors theatrically; and that such theatricality, in turn, signifies how Britain's choices have been made in the context of a political culture receptive to irony. But in *Sartor Resartus*, metaphors do more than register a tolerant acceptance of artifice. Carlyle's "Clothes-Philosophy" also draws on the particular semantic complexity of the metaphor of habit. Using it as a synonym for both external covering and interior organization, Carlyle reanimates Paine's question: Does the tailor or the weaver that made the habit produce the virtue also? Carlyle's concern with the material provenance of the social signs whose existence Burke takes for granted reflects his different historical circumstances. But he also points to an inherent illogic in Burke's positions. Bring together Burke's ironic deference, Carlyle seems to say, with Burke's defense of habit, and in the end you will get to the source of Britain's unrest: the hungry body, or the worker who is called on to defer to the hierarchy that his own labor has produced. *Sartor Resartus* is structured by the tension between questions of truth and questions of justice, habit as epistemology and habit as textile. On the one hand, it wants to critique jaded ways of seeing and knowing; on the other hand, it wants to press the claims of those concerned less with truth than with survival. The work's irony becomes the formal figure of this tension and points the way toward Carlyle's interest in the fetish.

Carlyle emphasizes the ingrained but also adventitious, even bureaucratically managed nature of habit. A significant portion of *Sartor Resartus* is devoted to rehearsing the "Sans-culottic" critique of habit in ways that also reflect the arguments of Wordsworth and Coleridge. Inveighing against the way that "Custom . . . [,]the greatest of Weavers" (SR 196), breeds blindness and indifference, Carlyle enjoins his audience to look through habits "till they become transparent"(SR 52). This act would require a certain violence that Carlyle is willing to entertain, for subjectivity has been colonized by the nation's conventional decencies and habitual hypocrisies: "these considerations, of our Clothes-thatch, and how, reaching inwards even to our heart of hearts, it tailorises and demoralises us, fill me with a certain horror"(SR 45). As Carlyle plays on the trope of "habit," he shifts the external sense of habit-as-costume toward that of costume-as-sign. Clothes provide an inward sense of coherence, but more important they also function as a system of signs within which social distinctions, and the oppressive enforcement of such distinctions, become possible: "Clothes gave us individuality, distinctions, social polity" (SR 32) or, as he repeats, "Politeness, Polity . . . Police" (SR 50). Taking up the favorite eighteenth-century historical theme of the origin of social ranks, Carlyle ironically describes the political order as based on nothing more than the signs worn on body and head. The man "dressed . . . in coarse threadbare Blue . . . marches sorrowfully to the gallows. . . . How is this . . . ? Has not your Red, hanging individual, a horsehair wig, squirrel skins, and a plush gown; whereby all mortals know that he is a JUDGE?" (SR 47–48) The red gown, the conventional sign of authority, gives the judge authority; the blue smock, the conventional sign of poverty, makes the poor man guilty. Thus do signs function according to Carlyle's radical semiotics. With an apparent faith in the value of such critique, Carlyle tries to dismantle a condition in which social and natural worlds appear, in Georg Lukács's words, as "petrified factuality . . . in which the reality that just happens to exist persists in a totally senseless, unchanging way."[32] The laws to which men submit are merely fetishes of their own making, to whose frangibility they have simply become blind through the reifying forces of habit. "Strange enough," Carlyle remarks, "how creatures of the human kind shut their eyes to plainest facts; and, by the mere inertia of Oblivion and Stupidity, live at ease" (SR 45). The means Carlyle uses to defetishize national life, and the energy with which he pursues this project, echo Jacobin discourse of the 1790s. The radical Jacobin newspaper, *Le Père Duchesne*, for instance, had asked, "What next, after having put paid to all the petty squires of the ancien régime . . . after having forced all those bewigged and brainless heads of the parlements to hang up their red robes?"[33] Carlyle likewise reduces nations to a piece of cloth, "a piece of glazed cotton," or to a metallic crown, "an implement . . . in size and commercial value, little differing from a horse-shoe" (SR 168). Habit blinds nations to the "plainest facts" about the oppressive forces that keep them together while treating their parts unequally. But Carlyle's reference to "commercial value" signals his ironic dissent from the critique that he has articulated. Commerce is as false a measure of value as the habitual ideological inflation of these symbols. *Sartor Resartus*, in fact, engages more than simply the metaphor of habit; it takes up Burke's irony and gives it a further twist.

Carlyle expands the irony that Burke himself used to unsettle the connections between public conventions, civic veneration, and the nation's constitution. *Sartor Resartus* elaborately practices an ironic deference toward conventional ascriptions of meaning and value but ends up halfway repudiating it as a facile political solution. Looking through habits until they become transparent also means looking at habits as opaque and material. Social conventions depend on a material infrastructure that comes to exist through the labor of a particular class. Unlike Burke, Carlyle is keenly aware of a class that has acquired numbers and visibility, a class "sighing indeed in bonds, yet sighing towards deliverance" (SR 220): the British laborers that have produced the very habits that keep them in thrall. "[H]aggard hungry operatives" (SR 205) produce signs under specific conditions: "clothwebs and cobwebs . . . woven in Arkwright looms, or by the silent Arachnes that weave unrestingly in our Imagination" (SR 52). He emphasizes the literal and particular constructedness of the social order and compares the imagination's private acts to the industrial production of British mills. Even when Carlyle claims to be enunciating a doctrine of mediation, a theory about the "Forms whereby Spirit manifests itself to Sense"(SR 205), declaring that "the parchment Magna Charta . . . the Pomp and Authority of Law, the sacredness of Majesty, and all inferior Worships . . . are properly a Vesture and Raiment"(SR 205), he makes clear that the vestures in question are not the legacy of an impersonal tradition. Nor are they merely the products of a poet's imagination. That passage goes on irresistibly to posit the "weaving-shops and spinning-mills" wherein such "Vestures," both material and metaphorical, are spun. This class creates the signs that organize nations. In Friedrich Engels's words, "the workers who by their inventions and labour have laid the foundations of England's greatness . . . those who are now daily becoming more and more aware of their power . . . are pressing more and more strongly for their share of the social advantages of the new era."[34] Rather than neutralizing this self-awareness of the working classes, *Sartor Resartus* aggressively contributes to their potential knowledge of the illegitimacy of the social and political order. Carlyle practices the defetishizing criticism that makes these workers aware of what their labor accomplishes: in the end, their labor produces a "fictile" (SR 8) order and keeps them in thrall to it.[35] Carlyle's word "fictile," apparently bringing together "fictive," "tactile," and "textile," marks the point at which ideology knots itself into materiality.

Yet having produced this knowledge, Carlyle fails to find an adequate practical end for it. Among Paine's radical articles of faith was the notion that demystification was an irreversible process: "Ignorance is of a peculiar nature; once dispelled, it is impossible to re-establish it. . . . The mind, in discovering truth, acts in the same manner as it acts through the eye in discovering objects; when once any object has been seen, it is impossible to put the mind back to the same condition it was in before it saw it" (RM 357). As a conservative critic, Carlyle's self-created dilemma is to persuade himself and his readers of the contrary. As he puts it in another essay, the challenge is to "voluntarily become involuntary," or to willingly relinquish (or disavow) the agency that one has discovered how to use.[36] One strategy is to point to the inherent banality of this knowledge: "Small is this which thou tellest me that the Royal Sceptre is but a piece of gilt wood" (SR 170). This acknowledgment moves Carlyle toward an ironic embrace of arbitrariness. But the vehicle Carlyle finally chooses in *Sartor Resartus* is rather surprising: courtesy. Making impossible a naive subjection to exploded forms of authority, *Sartor Resartus* turns to the social institution of courtesy, exaggerates its inherent irony, and recommends its practice to the subaltern. The notion of courtesy finesses some difficult problems associated with the conservative defense of social hierarchy: it is described as an inherently "noble" form of self-abasement, both conscious and grounded in habit, both natural feeling and supremely artificial. "Teufelsdröckh, though a Sansculottist, is in practice probably the politest man extant: his whole heart and life are penetrated and informed with the spirit of Politeness; a noble natural Courtesy shines through him" (SR 181). In light of Teufelsdröckh's theoretical hostility to artificial social and class distinctions, the praise of his manner as both "noble" and "natural" is ironic, to say the least. But Carlyle goes on to exaggerate this self-abasement in a way that clarifies its irony. He stipulates that such deference is not to be extended to embodied authority, lest the gesture "go to the pocket of Vanity"(SR 182). Instead, the subaltern's courtesy is to be shown merely to the clothes that invest that body. Carlyle writes, "The gladder am I . . . to do reverence to those Shells and outer Husks of the Body, wherein no devilish passion any longer lodges . . . I mean, to Empty, or even to Cast Clothes": "[t]hat reverence which cannot act without obstruction and perversion when the Clothes are full, may have free course when they are empty . . . so do I too worship the hollow cloth Garment with equal fervour . . . nay, with more, for I now fear no deception, of myself or of others." (SR 182). In this ironic deference to the hollow carapace, Carlyle follows Burke's example in *A Letter to a Noble Lord* and elsewhere of using deference as a form of critique. More broadly, Carlyle takes up the Burkean idea of embracing Britain's artifices and Scott's way of putting this idea into practice. He envisions an exaggerated show of deference to the nation's extinct ideologies, inadequate measures of justice, outmoded and meaningless conventions. Only defunct authorities, he suggests, may be safely and honestly obeyed. Irony smoothly takes the place of "deception" and seems to promise the continuity of social order.

But *Sartor Resartus* uses the resources of Romantic irony yet again to disavow this ironic complicity. The above remarks on "Clothes-Philosophy" and deference toward "Old Clothes" are presented as supposed fragments from the writings of the German philosopher Diogenes Teufelsdröckh.[37] At this moment of Teufelsdröckh's "worship," Carlyle, posing as editor, explicitly disavows the act: "His irony has overshot itself; we see through it, and perhaps through him" (SR 217). The curious metaphor reveals irony to be too thin a response and too risky a basis of community.[38] The ironic deference of old-clothes worship, by exaggerating its own fetishism, ends up invoking what it sought to remove: the British bodies that wear and produce the clothes. The problem is clearly stated in Carlyle's description of the "two Sects which, at this moment, divide . . . the British People, and agitate that ever-vexed country"(SR 216). After representing in his usual deadpan ethnographic manner the costumes of the "Dandiacal Sect" and that of the "Irish Poor-Slave," Teufelsdröckh turns to the domestic establishments of both. The dandy's household, whose description is quoted from Edward Bulwer-Lytton's *The Disowned*, consists in an empty, "splendidly furnished" dressing room.[39] This sect consists only in untenanted forms. The Irish household, however, quoted from John Bernard's *Retrospections of the Stage*, contains what has been emphatically absent throughout these pages: "On entering the house we discovered the family, eleven in number, at dinner; the father sitting at the top, the mother at bottom, the children on each side of a large oaken Board which was scooped out in the middle, like a Trough" (SR 215). The labor, the hunger, and the feelings of these previously invisible bodies, barely clothed and housed, inspire Carlyle to seek something weightier than ironic deference.

Legitimation, Consensus, and the Amnesic Labor of Reading

Carlyle's project of national reform, which is emphatically different from parliamentary reform, begins with the resuscitation of the "bodily man." Carlyle diagnoses Britain's problem as a legitimation crisis: the failure of the political order to provide its subjects with an ideological "arena" in which to act as embodied beings. Carlyle does not propose to restore legitimacy simply by bringing hitherto excluded bodies into the public sphere, either directly or through political representation. Rather, he turns to literature to provide a new kind of justification, as well as a new means. Taking historical writing as exemplary, Carlyle makes the recovery of the bodily man the goal of writing and reading. Reading, in particular, is seen as a kind of labor whose goal is to arrive at a rapt collective belief in the embodied, material existence of the historical subject. This is true whether the history in question is that of eighteenth-century France or medieval England. The labor is arduous and involves the overcoming of historical alterity and distance; it is often figured as the dissolution of the text. Soon, however, Carlyle becomes more interested in the act of reading itself than in its goal of recovering a lost historical body. The forgetful and self-forgetful labor of reading comes to figure, for Carlyle, the force that can ultimately restore legitimacy to Britain's fractured state.

In his essay "Characteristics," published in 1831 in the *Edinburgh Review*, Carlyle defines a political order as "that in which, and by virtue of which, all [man's] other attainments and attempts find their arena, and have their value" (CH 354). The task of a legitimate polity is to provide a coherent, widely accepted and even unchallengeable discourse, within which knowl-

edge can be produced and recognizable moral and aesthetic actions performed. It needs to provide the conditions for productive bodily and mental
expenditures of energy. Even the "spontaneous devotedness to the object"
(CH 365) that Carlyle praises, whether in literature or in religion, arises only
in polities that can give undisputed ideological guidance in the form of a clear
scale of values. A legitimate political order produces clear feelings for "what
is heroic" (CH 371), true, and valuable. In a mythical order whose image Carlyle invokes, "[a]ction . . . was easy, was voluntary, for the divine worth of human things lay acknowledged" (CH 371). Nations need to suffuse the material environment with emotional worth, even desirability. They also need to
provide a discourse within which truth claims can be made and tested.[40] Carlyle asserts that "every Polity . . . is the embodiment . . . of an Idea: all its tendencies of endeavour, specialities of custom, its laws, politics, and whole procedure . . . are prescribed by an Idea" (CH 356). As his references to "custom
. . . laws, politics, and whole procedure" suggest, Carlyle's "Idea" resembles
what a recent social theorist has called the social "imaginary": that which
grounds, defines, delimits, and gives meaningfulness to those networks of
signs that Carlyle had explored in *Sartor Resartus*.[41] It is his contention that
Britain is failing to do just that: "Action is paralysed; for what worth now remains unquestionable?" (CH 371).

The central thesis of "Characteristics" is that "the worth and authenticity of all things seems dubitable or deniable" (CH 369). It shares much with
essays by John Stuart Mill and others on the "spirit of the age." Mill writes,
for example, that "[a]t all other periods there exists a large body of received
doctrine, covering nearly the whole field of the moral relations of man, and
which no one thinks of questioning, backed as it is by the authority of all.
. . . This state of things does not now exist."[42] Mill ultimately finds a solution
to the present crisis in a transfer of power from a class defined by birth and
wealth to one defined by professional and intellectual training. Carlyle's diagnosis, however, is peculiarly concerned with the problem of how a sense
of legitimacy can be restored to any social arrangement. As Carlyle wrote to
Emerson, "we have lived to see all manner of Poetics and Rhetorics and Ser-
monics, and . . . all manner of Pulpits for addressing mankind from, as good
as broken and abolished."[43] Despite his arch tone, his figures anticipate later
theoretical analyses of "legitimation problems." As the social theorist Jürgen
Habermas explains, there is a need to distinguish between legitimacy as an
ideal, legitimations as types of arguments, and the criteria that validate those
arguments. Legitimacy means "the worthiness of a political order to be recognized," while *"[l]egitimations . . .* show how and why existing (or recommended) institutions are fit to employ political power." Legitimations, in
turn, need to be distinguished from "the *grounds or reasons*, that can be mo-
bilized. What are accepted as reasons and have the power to produce consensus . . . depends on the *level of justification* required in a given situation."[44]

Carlyle analyzes the problem similarly. His metaphor of "poetics" refers to the codified rules that would guide the production of particular legitimating arguments. His choice of a controlling metaphor already suggests the importance Carlyle attaches to literature as a form of legitimation. The crisis of "Poetics and Rhetorics" points to uncertainty at a fundamental level that Habermas calls the "level of justification." Essays such as "Characteristics" describe the crisis as occurring precisely at this level. "[T]his is . . . the era when all manner of Inquiries into what was once the unfelt, involuntary sphere of man's existence . . . occupy the whole domain of thought. . . . Our whole relations to the Universe and to our fellow-man have become an Inquiry, a Doubt" (CH 360–61). Carlyle is at pains to convey the radical nature of the crisis: each inquiry, itself a symptom of malaise, seems to reveal deeper and more fundamental levels of enquiry that must be undertaken. Unlike Habermas, Carlyle suspects that there is no agreement about what it would take to agree, no shared second-order beliefs about what it means to believe. Habermas argues that the earliest level of justification took the form of myths of origin that justified the rule of particular individuals or families; in modernity, "the formal principle of reason replaced material principles like Nature or God in . . . questions concerning the justification of norms or actions."[45] Legitimacy can be claimed by a modern political order, according to Habermas, if it originates under and continues to respect the conditions of open, fair, rational argument. It is probably unnecessary to point out Carlyle's hostility to reason's "sceptical, suicidal cavillings" (CH 371) and to the democratic institutions that encourage such debate. However, Carlyle would agree that material principles are now defunct: norms need to be justified with reference to the manner in which agreement is reached. It seems more appropriate to refer to manner rather than conditions, for Carlyle's notion of agreement or consensus is always highly concrete. For Carlyle, legitimacy arises from local, specific, and radical convergences of feeling: moments of consensus powerful enough to blur individual identities and distinctions. While Carlyle sometimes treats consensus as an occult phenomenon, an empirical social riddle, his is not a pure conservative mysticism either. He makes it clear that this social convergence of feeling can be openly mediated through a person, occasion, or text, though they rarely occur through reasoned debate or argumentation. This is where literature takes up its crucial role.

Literature becomes important to Carlyle for the particular type of consensus it can produce, the means it has at its disposal, and the labor it both displays and elicits from the reader. It is not an obvious, or even a first choice for Carlyle, as he suggests in an early notebook: "Political Philosophy should be a scientific revelation of the whole secret mechanism whereby men cohere together in society; should tell us what is meant by 'country' (patria), by what causes men are happy, moral . . . instead of all which, it tells us how 'flannel jackets' are exchanged for 'pork hams.'"[46] Carlyle identifies the phenomenon of consensus as specifically "political" and assumes that the end of any deliberate association lies in this domain. "I have strange glimpses," he continues, "of the power of spiritual Union, of Association among men of like object. . . . *Society* is a wonder of wonders; and Politics (in the right sense, far, very far from the common one) *is* the noblest Science."[47] But political economy as practiced makes the mistake, in Carlyle's eyes, of assuming the primary importance of commerce and exchange in the private sphere. In the pages of political economy written by Adam Smith and David Ricardo, the role of consensus is largely replaced by that of exchange. It thus falls to literature to create, as well as to examine critically, shared feelings about "what is meant by 'country'," and "by what causes men are happy." Carlyle's turn to literature, while not entirely voluntary, proves fortuitous since his vision of consensus differs significantly from the models of earlier political theorists.

The idea that collective consent defines the realm of legitimate politics grounds Britain's post-1688 constitutional order. Locke, for example, argues in his *Second Treatise* that "[t]hat which begins and actually *constitutes any political society*, is nothing but the consent of any number of freemen."[48] Mill also uses the notion of "free, voluntary, and undeceived consent" to define the limits of the state's power over individuals; "that portion of a person's life and conduct," which intersects with another's conduct under such conditions, has a right to be excluded from the interference of law, politics, or public opinion.[49] Consent in these cases derives its primary meaning as the conceptual opposite of compulsion or force. As Locke states, "no one can . . . be subjected to the political power of another, without his own consent."[50] In keeping with his hostility to methodological individualism, however, Carlyle tries to elide the distinctions between consent, consensus, and external power, even as he implicitly relies on those differences. Convergence of feeling, for Carlyle, amounts to a kind of consent that may even be recognized only after the fact. It may defy the distinction between voluntary and involuntary. Even when unacknowledged, the institution of literature serves as a critical example of how this blurring might be possible, and how consent can be both voluntary and involuntary, rational and irrational, private and public. This is most curiously illustrated in some of Carlyle's descriptions of hero-worship. Carlyle's favorite evidence for the reality of such a phenomenon consists in literary celebrity or "Lionism." One suspects that it is his most or perhaps only compelling proof. In *Sartor Resartus*, we are shown Voltaire: "the aged, withered man . . . could drag mankind at his chariot-wheels, so that princes coveted a smile from him, and the loveliest of France would have laid their hair beneath his feet" (SR 190). The lectures on hero-worship depict the scene of Voltaire's apotheosis even more extensively: "The old man of Ferney comes up to Paris . . . all persons from Queen Antoinette to the Douanier at the Porte Ste. Denis, do they not worship him?"

(HW 14). The celebrity of the Scottish poet Robert Burns becomes an equally familiar topos to Carlyle's readers: "Witty duchesses celebrate him as a man whose speech 'led them off their feet.' This is beautiful: but still more beautiful that . . . the waiters and ostlers at inns would get out of bed, and come crowding to hear this man speak!" (HW 191). The worship is theatrical, and the consensus in question little more than a momentary, irresistible contagion of superficial interest, as Carlyle himself points out, and yet he turns to it repeatedly as his best example. Carlyle emphasizes the convergence of feeling across class boundaries and interests; he also stresses how this contagion of curiosity exerts a social pressure different from that of external political force. The fact that both Voltaire and Burns are both men of letters is not accidental, for Carlyle favors the metaphor of literary speech in his accounts of true hero-worship's inner movement: "[i]t is ever the way with the Thinker, the spiritual Hero. What he says, all men were not far from saying, were longing to say. The Thoughts of all start up . . . round his Thought; answering to it, Yes, even so!" (HW 21) If the follower's consent was based on either deception or coercion, the scenario would fall into the category of what Carlyle condemns as "Charlatanism."[51] It is not even through a deliberate project of persuasion that the hero gains converts; confluence of thought has to be spontaneous rather than engineered. The hero's discourse resembles what the literary theorist Mikhail Bakhtin calls "internally persuasive discourse": "the internally persuasive word is half-ours and half-someone else's."[52] As Carlyle puts it, "A man can believe, and make his own . . . what he has received from another" (HW 126). Carlyle would say that the act of consent, in fact, collapses rather than reinforces the distinction between one's own power and that of another. Most interestingly, given Carlyle's reputation as a worshipper of physical force, his description of this moment of consensus echoes Pope's definition of "true wit" in his "Essay on Criticism": "What oft was Thought but ne'er so well Exprest."[53]

As Carlyle sees it, the social institution of literature can bring about a type of consensus that incorporates features of both consent and compulsion, private feeling and public expression. When properly embodied in a text, Carlyle suggests, literature can also induce a mediated and stabilized consensus that contrasts with the fickle popular consensus that he saw as a characteristic feature of the French Revolution. Carlyle's *French Revolution* gives prominent attention to two narratives, in which highly vaunted scenes of formal public consent end up disintegrating. The first narrative begins on the first anniversary of the taking of the Bastille with the Feast of the Federation, an elaborate ceremony in which the people as of one accord swear loyalty "to the King, to the Law, to the constitution which the National Assembly *shall* make" (FR 1:314). It ends a year later with angry petitions to depose the King, an attempt to impose martial law, and violence on the Champ de Mars: "Precisely after one year and three days, our sublime Federation Field is wetted, in this manner, with French blood" (FR 2:45). The second narrative comes perilously close to Carlyle's model of consensus: the apotheosis of Mirabeau, who becomes by unanimous consent "the first tenant of that Fatherland's Pantheon," dedicated "Aux Grands Hommes de la Patrie Reconnaissante": "Tenant, alas, who inhabits but at will," Carlyle notes, "and shall be cast out" (FR 1:417). Carlyle reminds his readers, "Witness long scenes of the French Revolution, in these late times," as evidence for the powerful volatility of social consensus:

> there is still a real magic in the action and reaction of minds on one another. The casual deliration of a few becomes, by this mysterious reverberation, the frenzy of many; men lose the use, not only of their understandings, but of their bodily senses . . . this noble omnipotence of Sympathy has been so rarely the Aaron's-rod of Truth and Virtue, and so often the Enchanter's-rod of Wickedness and Folly! No solitary miscreant . . . would venture on such actions and imaginations, as large communities of sane men have . . . entertained as sound wisdom. (ST 462–63)

Without the mediating interposition of literary texts as the locus of common labor and common feeling, sympathy works not as a force of cohesion but as the sinister essence of unreason, even depriving its victims of their own "bodily senses." How safely common feeling or consensus can function as a valid legitimating principle seems to depend on the mediation of literature.

Literature's mediating role depends paradoxically on how well it poses initial obstacles to sympathy between writer, text, and reader. Literature is valuable for the particular kinds of labor it elicits from each party. The reader's task, for example, is to dissolve creatively the text's opacity, to imbue it with a furtive significance. This labor bears the features of fetishism as Carlyle comes to employ that trope. In his essay on the French philosopher Diderot, written for the *Foreign Quarterly Review* in 1833, Carlyle makes a proclamation concerning the "proper task of Literature": "Day after day looking at the high destinies which yet await Literature . . . it grows clearer to us that the proper task of Literature lies in the domain of BELIEF" (Did 84). If the tone is confident, the content of the proclamation is strikingly vague: "in the domain of belief" only suggests that literature is related in some way to the production of that "indubitable" sense of worth or legitimacy that grounds action. It turns out that literature's task is not to produce belief in the truth-value of certain propositions. Indeed, such a task is the opposite of what literature should do. Carlyle condemns Diderot's biographer Naigeon for providing little more in his work than "a dull, sulky, snuffling, droning, interminable lecture on Atheistic Philosophy . . . how true it is, how inexpressibly important . . . with the vehemence of some pulpit-drumming

'Gowkthrapple' or 'precious Mr. Jabesh Rentowel'" (Did 89). The problem
with such writing is that it is overly theatrical, in the sense in which Michael
Fried uses the term to describe some genres of art in Diderot's time. Literature with something to prove is too suffused with the "consciousness of being beheld"; it acknowledges and even invites the reader's gaze.[54] What Carlyle wants the literary text to do is to turn away while offering the reader the
chance to peer inside. The true task that Naigeon neglects is to allow the
reader to envision, simply, "the bodily man, the clothed, boarded, bedded,
working and warfaring Denis Diderot, in that Paris of his; how he looked and
lived, what he did . . . what color his stockings were!" (Did 89) The type of
belief that falls to literature to produce carries no content or creed, and yet
it is more than simply a matter of verisimilitude or a sense of probability. Indeed, Carlyle expressly wishes to exclude "Novel-writers and such like"
from the domain of literature as producing matter fit only "for children, mi-
nors, and semifatuous persons of both sexes" (Did 84). Nor is this belief a
type of aesthetic contemplation of the absolute revealed in an apprehensible
form "consubstantial" with what it symbolizes.[55] Nor is it simply a belief in
the factual accuracy of the events represented, though this is crucial. Rather,
Carlyle suggests that literature's function is to produce a negative belief, an
ability to disregard discursive claims about "how true [a proposition] is, how
inexpressibly important." The reader's labor finds its proper end in a vision
of the "bodily man," "how he looked and lived, what he did." This stands as
an answer to the body's absence in *Sartor Resartus*.

Carlyle values literature most of all for the forgetfulness and self-forgetfulness of the labor that it elicits. The recovered vision of the "bodily man"
is useful in practical terms because it eclipses the reader's self-consciousness.
Ideally, the reader forgets his own role in producing this vision and assents to
the autonomous, even necessary existence of that particular thing or body
which he contemplates. Literature should both demonstrate and produce
what Fried calls absorption, a rich obliviousness to being beheld. But this absorption is far from simple or spontaneous. It involves a complex disavowal,
an effortful negation of the materiality of the text and the social institutions
that bring it into existence. To Naigeon's biography of Diderot, Carlyle
prefers what he calls Diderot's "Preternuptial" correspondence with Sophie
Volland. The latter offers merely a naïve historical record, unmediated by any
tendentious interpretation of the period.

> these light Letters . . . again unveiling and *showing* Parisian Life, are
> worth more to us than many a heavy tome laboriously struggling to
> explain it. . . . The curtain . . . is again drawn up; the scene is alive
> and busy. Figures grown historical are here seen face to face, and live
> before us. . . . Hovering in the distance . . . comes Rousseau. Poor
> Jean-Jacques! (Did 111–12, original emphasis)

The figure of the theater returns, becoming an imaginary crossing of the boundary between stage and audience. But this crossing is possible on the condition of what Burke and Reynolds thought of as "making allowances." Carlyle praises deep sympathetic absorption when he sees it performed by a text or by a reader, but this is possible only if those involved disavow those other modalities of literature that Carlyle himself, more than anyone, emphasized: literature as industry, literary text as commodity, author and reader as workers. In this essay on Diderot and elsewhere, Carlyle likes to trace how the institution of literature "emerged out of Cloisters into the open Marketplace," as patronage gave way to "the Laws of Copyright . . . the Calamities of Authors," and as the economic role of booksellers and the capital they could provide evolved into the dominance of "our present Periodical existence" (Did 107–9). Most of all, though, Carlyle emphasizes the role of the printing press: "Printing . . . comes necessarily out of Writing" (HW 164). Carlyle frequently uses the printing press as a figure for the institution of literature: "the Printing Press, with its Printer's Devils, with its Editors, Contributors, Booksellers, Billstickers!"[56] The literature thus produced is in the first instance a commodity measurable as such: "are there not forty-eight longitudinal feet of small-printed History in thy Daily Newspaper?" (OH 77). The work of the author is subject to the same forces of reification: "a Literary Contributor, if in good heart and urged by hunger, will many times . . . accomplish his two Magazine sheets within the four-and-twenty hours" (OH 77). "Strange state of literature!" Carlyle had written in an early private notebook: "A man must just lay out his manufacture in one of those Old-Clothes shops and see whether any one will buy it."[57] And the reader, as Carlyle often likes to assert, performs a labor different only in degree but not in kind from what the author does in creating a work (HW 82). Both are in the business of manipulating "Old Clothes"; Carlyle's trope for the literary text points us again to the context of industrial production. But literature's peculiar force to create what Carlyle calls "belief" only comes about when these productive forces and contingencies are misrecognized. Carlyle praises Diderot's art criticism in the *Salons* for its pure mimetic force, "painting the picture over again for us, so that we too *see* it" (Did 147). Most of all, he admires the "fervor, inventiveness" with which Diderot enters into the paintings he describes, as though the complex social institution of art production and exhibition did not exist. His own absorption in the paintings carries the reader along to deny, for the moment, the very mechanisms on which this experience depends.[58]

Literature's ideal, for Carlyle, has less to do with transparency than with a certain opacity that it enables. Its "task" is to create the conditions for shared feeling and common action while guarding against the possibility of mass "deliration." Defending the principle of enlightenment in the context of hero-worship, Carlyle asserts, "the exercise of private judgment . . . does by no means necessarily end in selfish independence, isolation; but rather ends necessarily in the opposite of that" (HW 125). This statement applies equally well to his vision of reading as an exercise of private judgment that brings about a legitimating "communion" of feeling with others. This consensus hinges on the reader's disavowal of his active role in producing these feelings. But this misrecognition is not to be confused with total unawareness. The task of literature overlaps with the mandate of the fetish.

French Revolutions, British Empire, and the Code of Fetishism

Carlyle's summary of the French Revolution is well known: "those two words, French Revolution . . . mean the open violent Rebellion, and Victory, of disimprisoned Anarchy against corrupt worn-out Authority" (FR 1:204). In this definition, Carlyle ominously invokes terms (anarchy, authority) that can be applied to describe political problems in Britain as well. But in his 1837 history, Carlyle invents another more colorful code with which to link France's ancien régime political culture and its revolution with the British nation and the problems that Britain must overcome in order to fulfill its imperial destiny. The code is fetishism. Carlyle's history of the French Revolution both begins and ends with surprisingly positive references to "African" fetish-worship. The narrative opens by discussing Louis XV as an idol worshiped by those who constructed him; at the end, Carlyle closes with an account of Robespierre's Feast of the Supreme Being as a poorly managed, unsuccessful attempt at fetish-worship. Carlyle comes to name fetishism explicitly when he takes up the question of national self-regeneration. Through its associations, the theme of fetishism brings up the context of British empire. Yet rather than simply treating it as an atavistic practice, Carlyle decides to trace fetishism's resemblance to Kantian idealism. In both cases, he argues, the mind constitutes what it contemplates. By bringing together these disparate discourses, Carlyle manages to suggest an alternative route to enlightened political practice: rather than French ideas leading to French-style revolution, German metaphysics point the way toward the expansion of empire. The hope is that Britain will be able to accomplish its regeneration by means of empire rather than revolution. And British empire will be based not on theatrical spectacle but on private reading, figured in the terms of a successful fetishism.

In part, Carlyle's turn to the discourse of the fetish is overdetermined by his interpretation of the French Revolution. One recent historical analysis of Jacobin politics argues that the revolution was driven by a pervasive fear of institutionalizing authority: "the Jacobins . . . suspected *all* political power:

not just that of hereditary monarchs and titled aristocrats, but that of . . . anyone who had any power at all. . . . The only individuals above suspicion were
those without any power or public ambition, persons who had rights and
nothing more."[59] Carlyle views the revolution similarly, though with a more
sympathetic emphasis on the practical challenge of constructing some institution of effective authority. Robespierre's attempt to create a new rational
state religion appears to Carlyle a bad-faith attempt to address this challenge.
Carlyle's narrative of the revolution structures itself around the succession
of failed attempts to institutionalize authority in a publicly recognized symbolic form. It shows repeated attempts to create a form acknowledged as legitimate by enough people to operate politically. The life span of each is brief,
as Carlyle emphasizes: authority passes from the Estates General to the National Assembly to the Constituent Assembly and from thence to the Jacobin
Club. Of the latter he remarks initially, "[t]his is the true Constitution . . .
grown, unconsciously, out of the wants and efforts of these Twenty-five Millions of men . . . this power is *it*" (FR 2:94). Carlyle uses the trope of the
"sceptre" to indicate the ironic tensions between official and demotic embodiments of power: "the sceptre has departed from this Legislative [As-
sembly] once and always" (FR 2:160). Power passes to and through a number of different bodies, communes, and factions until finally it passes away
from the Jacobin "Mighty Mother" after Robespierre's execution: "the
strength could not be restored her; the strength had departed forever" (FR
2:430).

The problem of embodying legitimate authority in a concrete symbol
most vividly shapes Carlyle's account of the October Days of 1789—the
same episode that had provoked such different emotions in Richard Price
and Edmund Burke. Carlyle sees this "spontaneous" march as arguably the
high point of the revolution. Of the Feast of the Federation and other revolutionary spectacles he remarks, "in comparison with unpremeditated out-
bursts of Nature, such as an Insurrection of Women, how foisonless, unedi-
fying, undelightful" (FR 1:326). Carlyle's narrative of October 5 follows the
actors from one location to the next as they seek to appropriate the practically
effective symbol or embodiment of authority: "Grand it was . . . to see so
many Judiths, from eight to ten thousand of them in all, rushing out to search
into the root of the matter!" (FR 1:244). Carlyle's description of the procession back to Paris with the king is memorable for its tone of irony: "The wet
day draggles the tricolor, but the joy is unextinguishable. Is not all well now
. . . ? Finally, the King is shown on an upper balcony, by torchlight, with
a huge tricolor in his hat: 'and all the people . . . grasped one another's
hand;'—thinking *now* surely the New Era was born" (FR 1:279). Political
authority had already, in Carlyle's words, departed not only from the monarchy but also from all social institutions. Residing only within the private individual, it cannot be incarnated in a stable form or even publicly repre-

sented. That the king "is shown . . . by torchlight" suggests that he has come to be seen not merely as a man, as Burke had worried, but as a defunct emblem or cheap puppet-show: as a fetish that fails to command any but the most deluded reverence.

But Carlyle's explicit references to the topos of fetish-worship serve another purpose as well: of linking and simultaneously differentiating the French nation and the British empire.[60] He begins his history with the ancien régime, evoking Louis XV at the height of his power:

> Time was when men could (so to speak) of a given man, by nourish-
> ing and decorating him with fit appliances, to the due pitch, *make*
> themselves a King, almost as the Bees do; and what was still more to
> the purpose, loyally obey him when made. The man so nourished
> and decorated, thenceforth named royal, does verily bear rule; and is
> said, and even thought, to be, for example, "prosecuting conquests in
> Flanders," when he lets himself like luggage be carried thither: and
> no light luggage; covering miles of road. For he has . . . his very
> Troop of Players, with their pasteboard coulisses, thunder-barrels,
> their kettles, fiddles, stage-wardrobes . . . all mounted in wagons,
> tumbrils, second-hand chaises. (FR 1:7; original emphasis)

Perversely, Carlyle feigns ignorance of legitimist ideology. Legitimism was grounded, as a later historian points out, on the "recognition of the right to rule inherent in a particular family and, at any particular moment, in a particular individual."[61] Its emotional energies were overwhelmingly directed at "the embodiments of royalty themselves—the royal line and its individual representatives."[62] But Carlyle describes the absolutist monarch as an inert body, contingently selected, whose legitimacy proceeds from nothing but the strange, busy fetishism of the nation.[63] Both the king's natural and political bodies have been "nourished and decorated" by the people, and his agency appears to be merely a matter of honorific speech. Rather than stressing some particular Gallic tendency toward such behavior, Carlyle posits a "time" when subjects were either unconscious of their own fetishism, performing it innocently and instinctively, "almost as the Bees do," or else more cynical about it, willing to accept that authority comes into being as one among "the productions of the human brain," in Marx's paraphrase of Feuerbach.[64] The equivocation is important. But the lengthy catalogue of the theatrical machinery that accompanies Louis XV suggests that this fetishism was more theatrical than instinctive. The long description of "appliances," reminiscent of Burke at his most ironic, hints that ancien régime deference was an elaborate open delusion. There is no secret about the "pasteboard coulisses, thunder-barrels . . . kettles . . . stage-wardrobes," and the analogous mental props that generated the monarch's power and magnificence. Far from being believed to inhere in a natural sovereign, Carlyle implies, legitimate authority was produced through a knowing complicity between subject and spectacle.

A theatrical, even cynical public fetishism is linked with the idea of the French nation yet more strongly in a scene that corresponds to this earlier description: Robespierre's final public act in June 1794, as he presides over the Feast of the Supreme Being. Given toward the very end of his history, this episode frames the revolution in scenes of fetish-making. Carlyle suggests that little has changed as a result of the revolution, except that fetishes are now not collectively produced but self-appointed instead.

> Incorruptible Robespierre . . . will now also be Priest and Prophet.
> He has donned his sky-blue coat, made for the occasion; white silk
> waistcoat broidered with silver, black silk breeches, white stockings,
> shoe-buckles of gold . . . he has made the Convention *decree* . . . the
> "Existence of the Supreme Being" . . . sets his torch to Atheism and
> Company, which are but made of pasteboard steeped in turpentine
> . . . from within, there rises "by machinery," an incombustible Statue
> of Wisdom. . . . Look at it one moment, O Reader, not two . . .
> Mumbo-Jumbo of the African Woods seems to me venerable beside
> this new Deity of Robespierre; for this is a *conscious* Mumbo-Jumbo,
> and *knows* that he is machinery. (FR 2:407–8, original emphasis)

The detailed description of Robespierre's clothes links this scene with the earlier discussion of Louis XV's fabricated authority; yet these clothes, as befitting the novelty of this invented religion, are "made for the occasion," deliberately ordered, self-consciously worn, and lacking even the authority of the old. Robespierre plays a dual role in Carlyle's description of this event: as the ambiguous genitive, "this new Deity of Robespierre," suggests he is both maker and idol, worshiper and worshiped. Even more saliently, he is a performer on a theatrical stage, surrounded by newer versions of the machinery that Louis XV had carried along with him. This is not the only moment in which Carlyle applies the trope of theater to the French Revolution, but it is among the most important. Even more than the props and machinery being used on the stage, it is the public setting, the gaze of the assembled citizens that constitutes the theatricality of the moment. It is this gaze that seems to constitute Robespierre's theatrical self-consciousness.[65] And it is this dimension, rather than the fetishism of the "African Woods," that Carlyle repudiates. His address to the reader anticipates the moment in Carlyle's lectures on hero-worship. There Carlyle exhorts the reader to respect and even to defer to the fetish-worshiper's unself-conscious absorption. The reader in both cases is clearly the British reader, whose panoramic, global view can encompass France "beside" Africa. Carlyle also hopes that this reader will possess an even more useful selective blindness. A nation's knowing complicity with its own fictions, its cherished personifications, should take place not in this public setting but in another type of situation. Carlyle rejects the public, theatrical irony of this scene, with its "incombustible" clichés, as unfit for the British. A private form of irony is in order—one more closely linked with the absorption of private reading than with the theatrical stage.

At the beginning of his history of the French Revolution, Carlyle had already discussed the subject of "Mumbo-Jumbo," to whom he compares Robespierre so unfavorably. Alluding to Britain's imperial ambitions, both official and unofficial, Carlyle does not argue on behalf of repudiating "African" fetish-worship or subjecting it to enlightened reform. Rather, his goal is to make it private and to link it to the political challenges faced by the British nation. An important mediating link is provided by Kantian "Metaphysic." Carlyle starts by establishing a parallel between "outward Sense" and "inward Sense":

> if the very Rocks and Rivers (as Metaphysic teaches) are . . . *made* by
> these outward Sense of ours, how much more, by the inward Sense, are
> all Phenomena of the spiritual kind: Dignities, Authorities, Holies, Un-
> holies! Which inward sense, moreover, is not permanent like the outward
> ones, but forever growing and changing. (FR 1:8; original emphasis)

Carlyle's allusion to "Metaphysics" dissolves the substantiality of the nation in its material existence, "the very Rocks and Rivers" that give it a physical extension. Carlyle is not primarily concerned with the problem of knowledge and of what these objects might be in themselves; he even takes for granted as common knowledge this simplified version of the tenets of transcendental idealism. Carlyle wants to present the moral, political, and affective "Phenomena" of the nation as not epistemological but historical problems. He thus alludes to several problems that had been treated in *Sartor Resartus*. On the one hand, he points to a persistent tendency to regard both inner and outer phenomena as reified, as given rather than made. On the other hand, there is the problem of mediation or the need for sensuous representations of abstract ideas. Finally, there is the problem of historicity, emphasized more heavily in the later work: how to reconcile the shifting claims and expanding knowledge of the present with the need for continuously legitimate social institutions. Carlyle finds in the fetish-worshiper a resourceful, and only partially ironic, answer to these problems. The "Black African" provides the bridge between the absolutism of the past and some future, regenerated "European" political form.[66] Carlyle continues:

> Does not the Black African take of Sticks and Old Clothes (say, ex-
> ported Monmouth-Street cast-offs) what will suffice, and, of these,

cunningly combining them, fabricate for himself an Eidolon . . . and
name it Mumbo-Jumbo; which he can thenceforth pray to, with up-
turned awe-struck eye, not without hope? The white European
mocks; but ought rather to consider; and see whether he, at home,
could not do the like a little more wisely. (FR 1:8)

It goes without saying that the figure of the African functions as a mirror for
the European subject; indeed, Carlyle enjoins precisely this reflexive exercise
on the "white European."[67] In the context of Carlyle's argument, this moment illustrates the vaguely Hegelian proposition that the "inward sense" is
"growing and changing." Thus, it could be taken as proof of British progress
that such operations can no longer be performed on its territory.[68] But this
figure of "Africa" also appears to offer a subtle solution to the philosophical
problems that Carlyle has just evoked: by reifying that which he has himself
made in order to give concrete embodiment to an inward idea, the "black
African" seems at once to satisfy the senses' demand for things to perceive,
and also to acknowledge that primary capacity of these senses to create, to
make rather than to passively receive. Even more important, Carlyle's "African" presents a powerful counterforce to a British empire founded on commerce. Using "cast-offs," he rebukes the frenzied production and consumption of the British. Instead of the boundless appetite of the British consumer,
he takes only "what will suffice." Finally, Carlyle's imagination replaces the
actual global circuit of British commerce with a strange trade: exporting
"Monmouth-Street cast-offs" in exchange for a potential principle of social
revitalization.

Carlyle's allusion reminds his readers of the extension of British empire
on the African continent and elsewhere; he stresses with anxiety the superior
virtue of the culture of the colonies. By revising his probable source and re-
inflecting the nature of the scene, he suggests how Britain can bring fetishism
"home."[69] The key lies in the familiar metaphor of old clothes: a Carlylean
figure for the text. While "Mumbo-Jumbo" is mentioned along with other
fetishes by Helvétius in his articles on African religion for the *Encyclopédie*,
it is likelier that Carlyle associates this particular name with a British writer
who played an important role in gathering and consolidating imperial knowledge: Mungo Park, who helped to "open" Western Sudan and inaugurated
the first phase of European exploration of Western Africa. Park introduces
this purported African deity in his popular *Travels in the Interior District of
Africa* (1799), an episode of which is discussed in *Past and Present*.[70] In the
scene most relevant to Carlyle's history, Mungo Park writes:

near the entrance [to the town] I observed, hanging upon a tree, a
sort of masquerate [*sic*] habit, made of the bark of trees, which I was
told on enquiry belonged to Mumbo Jumbo. This is a strange bug-

bear, common to all the Mandingo towns, and much employed by the
Pagan natives in keeping their women in subjection. . . . This strange
minister of justice (who is supposed to be either the husband himself,
or some person instructed by him) . . . disguised in the dress that has
been mentioned . . . begins the pantomime at the approach of night
. . . and the ceremony commences with songs and dances, which continue till midnight, about which time Mumbo fixes on the offender.
This unfortunate victim being thereupon immediately seized . . . is
scourged with Mumbo's rod.[71]

In Park's account, "Mumbo-Jumbo," which he refers to as a "masquerate
habit," is "hanging upon a tree" only in anticipation of its nocturnal use. The
costume is a means of exerting agency, an instrument of justice used "amidst
the shouts and derision of the crowd."[72] Park describes the scene in theatrical terms, as a "pantomime," but also in political terms: "[t]his strange minister of justice" imposes discipline on his female subjects. He leaves it uncertain whether "the women" are kept in subjection through genuine belief
and fear or merely through the physical violence inflicted by the man in disguise. Equally ambiguous in Park's account is the degree of complicity with
the political "pantomime." Are the derisive shouts of the crowd directed toward the women or toward the man disguised as something greater than himself? In its concern with the administration of justice, particularly with regard to unruly women, Park's scene is unexpectedly well suited to its new
context. Carlyle's history largely revolves around scenes of insurrectionary
women as well as men engaged in "pantomime." But as Carlyle redacts this
scene, he removes the costume from this context of public activity and struggle. Instead of a costume worn for performance, "Mumbo Jumbo" becomes
a construction of "sticks and old clothes." Most significantly, it is no longer
the occasion of a lively theatrical action but becomes instead an object of solitary contemplation, an event in the domain of belief. The "African" with "up-
turned . . . eye" is the very picture of absorption, a strong contrast with the
theatrical Robespierre, in his "white silk waistcoat," who self-consciously parades before his assembled nation.

As the reference to "Monmouth Street" hints, this portrait reveals, in
thinly disguised form, Carlyle's own self-portrait in Sartor Resartus. The
construction of old clothes slyly recycles and represents Carlyle's own texts.
It is no African but Carlyle's textual alter-ego, Teufelsdröckh, who proclaims
his eagerness "to do reverence . . . to Empty, or even to Cast Clothes." "What
still dignity dwells in a suit of Cast Clothes! . . . often have I turned into [Lon-
don's] Old-Clothes Market to worship. With awe-struck heart I walk through
that Monmouth Street, with its empty Suits" (SR 182–83). It is Carlyle who
professes to be "awe-struck" before Monmouth-Street cast-offs. The relation of Carlyle's African to "the imperialist self" is a complicated one: he is

a disguise for a disguise.[73] Unlike Teufelsdröckh, he is unfamiliar to Carlyle's readers and hence likely to evoke prejudices that are, at least, different. But it seems that Carlyle values his "African" scene most for its pure absorption and its capacity to evoke the same state in its viewer. As Michael Fried has argued, Diderot's French audience came to dislike portraits because they forced the beholder to become too self-conscious about his own position in front of the painting. As we have seen, Carlyle disparages argumentative, polemical literature for the same reason. *Sartor Resartus* ironically (in a technical sense and in a more colloquial sense) exhibits such theatricality in exaggerated form, openly addressing and most probably alienating the reader, as Carlyle constantly worries. Carlyle praises the type of literature that, transparent in appearance, invites the reader to feel as though he could move around within its represented world. Such a literature would be analogous to paintings of absorptive states: people sleeping, reading, or otherwise absorbed in their own activity and unaware that they are being beheld. By beholding such absorption, the reader is pulled inside what he sees and invited to forget his own creative participation.[74] Carlyle's figure of the "African" thus sets up the alignment of reading with fetishism. Both concern the contemplation of an object possessed of an illusory autonomy. Carlyle will now turn squarely to the British nation's need to find an effective fetish, to find something that it can forget that it has made. This is the challenge, Carlyle suggests, that must be met if Britain is not to disintegrate like France.

Covering and Recovering the Antiquarian Object

While to some extent Carlyle interprets the theatricality of the French Revolution as the result of French national character, he also sees it as a structural feature of social revolutions that begin from below. Carlyle's history stresses the pervasiveness of crowds, mobs, and assemblies: a national audience, boldly and bodily present, that demands self-display and constant self-justification from every participant in the revolution.[75] In Britain in 1842, already prepared by Chartism to expect "*our* French Revolution," Carlyle sees the most telling symptoms of this revolution's imminence in the nearly pure theatricality of the Manchester mobs: "A million of hungry operative men . . . rose all up, came out into the streets, and——stood there" (PP 20).[76] Placing oneself on the public stage to be beheld is the first step toward revolution. Compounding this tendency is what Carlyle sees as the pervasive theatricality of Britain's dominant public culture: a theatricality driven by commerce. While the public sphere in Carlyle's eyes includes the work of the state and the institutions that supposedly criticize it, the domain of economic activity exerts its influence over the public sphere's ends and means, as *Past and Pres-*

ent suggests. Both civil society and the public sphere rely on engineered spectacles, empty proclamations, and "puffery": "What sight is more pathetic than that of poor multitudes of persons met to gaze at King's Progresses, Lord Mayor's Shews, and other gilt-gingerbread phenomena" (PP 60). The symbol of this public theatrical-commercial culture is the "great Hat seven-feet high, which now perambulates the London Streets . . . upon wheels" (PP 144). The public sphere separates sign from meaning, object from use, production from consumption, and nation from history. It creates empty, inflated values and promotes the random movement of bodies and minds, a movement that could accelerate into revolution.[77]

Past and Present addresses itself to a nation on the verge of dissolution in 1843: Carlyle sees in the Corn Laws and the new Poor Laws a struggle pitting landed and manufacturing interests against each other, at the expense of the actual laboring classes. Though the problem manifests itself as social disunity, the real problem is not difference but Britain's ideological unity, Carlyle argues: all Britain's classes are "girt in with a cold universal Laissez-faire," paradoxically related through this universal unrelatedness (PP 210). In the marketplace, too, all values are uniform in a sense because they are infinitely commensurable. Any one thing can be exchanged for practically any other through the universal equivalent of money, as Carlyle emphasizes. *Past and Present* tries to replace this false ideological unity with a true practical one. It hopes to find in labor a force that will forestall revolution, unify the nation, and clarify its relation to past and future history. Landed aristocracy, industrial aristocracy, factory operatives, poets——each class, Carlyle argues, has its own distinct type of work to perform, and the nation's task is to provide an arena within which all these types of labor can be performed. Even as Carlyle attempts to overcome social divisions through the notion of labor, however, he runs up against some critical uncertainties in his concept. It is not clear how far its definition can be stretched before work separates into a mere trope on the one hand and actual labor on the other. Moreover, Carlyle would like to define labor primarily in terms of the internal effects it has on the worker: composure, discipline, and development are some aspects of this internal transformation. Yet the mensurable, material effects of labor, its transformation of the external world, also prove crucial to *Past and Present*. The latter is not inherently at odds with the idea of labor as bildung. But the status of the thing produced by labor is the problem with which *Past and Present* sets out and to which it returns repeatedly. Commodity-producing labor itself has produced Britain's current crisis, in the eyes of the political economists whose views Carlyle parodies here:

> Ye miscellaneous, ignoble manufacturing individuals, ye have produced too much! . . . the Commercial Bazaar and multitudinous Howel-and-Jameses cannot contain you. You have produced, pro-

duced;—he that seeks your indictment, let him look around. Millions of shirts . . . hang there in judgment against you. . . . you are
criminally guilty of producing shirts, breeches, hats, shoes and commodities, in a frightful over-abundance. (PP 172)

Unlike the empty clothes hung up for contemplation in Carlyle's imagined
scene of fetish-worship, or the benign emptiness of Park's bark-costume,
these commodities in their very "over-abundance" seem to pronounce a theatrical public indictment against their producers. Carlyle would like to avoid
the question of ownership, and, in part, the theme of dynamic labor does allow him to sidestep the question of property. But he cannot avoid it entirely:
if, as he argues, work is to be valued for its way of augmenting and stabilizing
the self, then surely the products of that labor can be claimed for the same
purposes.

   In *Past and Present*, fetishism appears not as a visible code, but as a way
to configure a problem: how to diminish and defer the claims that could be
made by "those who do labour" against "those who produce nothing" and
yet own the property. Fetishism's features are evoked not through references
to idols or to "African woods" but rather through a reading of the nation's
history. *Past and Present* treats history as a text that tells a story about the
"forgotten work" of generations. In its turn, reading this history is a process
that embodies both labor and oblivion. It is represented as an effortful creation that produces nothing tangible. Even more important, the state of absorption brought about through reading is here linked again with questions
of power and misrecognition. Generally, reading in *Past and Present* confers
a fetishlike autonomy on the object it imagines and the meanings it discovers. It is as much a denial and forgetting of inwardness as a deepening of it.
Carlyle's choice of exemplary text clarifies how the nation and its history can
crystalize as fetishes through the creatively misrecognized labor of reading.
He embeds in his text a twelfth-century Latin manuscript recently printed
by the antiquarian Camden Society. The manuscript is a classic antiquarian
object: strange, barely legible, yet native and possessed of national significance. This antiquarian manuscript also bears the features of the fetish. The
laborious encounter with this text is illustrated with the familiar tropes of
veiling and transparency, of clothes that arrest the view. The text is produced
by the author, whose labor under particular historical circumstances is strongly
emphasized. Carlyle attaches as much pathos to the work of trying to decipher it in the present day. Yet Jocelin's *Chronicle* seems autonomous, not
merely self-sufficient but even able to dissolve the reader back into the flux
of contingency. It stands in a double relation to the reader: created, deriva-
tive, inferior, but at the same time, primary, superior, almost transfixing in its
power. Significantly, Carlyle's antiquarian curiosity, a chronicle of medieval
monastery life that would have been cherished by Jonathan Oldbuck, con-

tains a story of peculiar relevance to his larger project. It not only presents an account of institutional reform, as many readers have noted, but also displays as central to that process a particular action: the refurbishing of a sacred fetish, a saint's body. The scene acquires an allegorical significance for Carlyle: taking its cue from this scene, *Past and Present* comes to figure the reading of national history as the recovery of a sacred corpus. The nation's identity, and its ability to sustain and inspire the "bodily men" of the present, come to depend on a reading of history that coincides with a self-forgetting. And for this discovery Carlyle is indebted to the antiquarian object: a fetish that finesses the ironic problem of part and whole by being at once dependent and independent, unfinished and complete, worthless and incommensurable.

Past and Present both raises and evades important questions about the role of individual agency in shaping history or in reading it. Carlyle plays, for example, on the range of meanings possessed by the word *discern*. On the one hand, he stresses the need to discern in the sense of distinguishing or separating. The function of moral conscience is to discern simply "the quite *infinite* difference there is between a Good man and a Bad" (PP 225). The goal of political arrangement, likewise, is to teach subjects to distinguish "those . . . better than himself, wiser, braver" (PP 241). It is this sense of qualitative discernment that Carlyle has in mind when he enjoins his reader to "become a faithful discerning soul. . . . Then shall we discern, not one thing, but . . . a whole endless host of things that can be done" (PP 30–31). The trope of discerning marks out the field of necessary work. History, however, seems to take over for the individual subject this important task of discriminating between better and worse, lesser and greater. Carlyle begins by figuring history as the true "high and highest Court . . . the Court of Courts . . . where the universal soul of Fact and very Truth sits President" (PP 15). Carlyle uses the external apparatus of English law, "horse-hair wigs and learned-sergeant gowns . . . parchment records" (PP 15–16), to develop this trope of history as court of justice.[78] History pronounces judgment on words, deeds, and the value of national institutions such as Parliament. But history's sentence is curiously equivocal. Its essence to be delayed: "Judgment for an evil thing is many times delayed some day or two, some century or two" (PP 14). In fact, delay and deferral seem to be its very essence: "[an unjust institution] will continue standing, for its day, for its year, for its century, doing evil all the while; but . . . dissolution, explosion . . . incessantly advance towards it. . . . Await the issue" (PP 16–17). At some point, no matter how delayed, the invisible hand of history will abolish unjust institutions, perhaps in the form of a social revolution. But obsolescence comes to all things regardless of their virtue, as Carlyle has repeatedly argued. Carlyle's emphasis on the need for patient waiting, "some day or two, some century or two," suggests that history is nothing but the period of indefinite deferral, and that waiting and watching are all that can be done. The figure of history as judge merges into that of the spectator of a trial by combat. "Await the issue. In all battles . . . each fighter has prospered according to his right. . . . His very death is no victory over him. He dies indeed, but his work lives, very truly lives. A heroic Wallace . . . cannot hinder that his Scotland become, one day, a part of England: but he does hinder that it become, on tyrannous unfair terms, a part of it" (PP 17). The trope of judicial combat, as well as the reference to Scotland's anti-imperial past, recall Walter Scott, and, in particular, the famous ending of Scott's *Ivanhoe*, a novel Carlyle mentions in *Past and Present*. But history does not participate in the battle; it merely watches. History is almost personified in a way that recalls the idle crowds assembled to watch Ivanhoe and Bois-Guilbert do battle—or the even more idle reader of Waverley Novels. History seems to diminish in status from supreme judge to mere spectator, then dwindles further to become a mere semifatuous novel-reader. In its capacity as judge or court, history was to account for what endures and gets handed down and what does not, but its role weakens into that of a spectator watching a contingent spectacle, even when that spectacle is nothing less than the formation of British empire.

The notion of discerning softens: instead of a decisive separation made on the basis of unquestioned criteria, discerning becomes a matter of simply perceiving, of making or marking out with the eyes. "As through a glass darkly, we with our own eyes and appliances, intensely looking, discern at most: A . . . human figure" (PP 50). Thus, Carlyle describes the reading of history. In this way, he imbues the simple attempt to envision the past with the moral prestige offered by the tougher sense of discernment. In most cases, what the spectator of history beholds is unlikely to bolster his own sense of agency. As Carlyle looks back on the making of Britain, deliberately choosing here to focus on the formation of British literature, here too he perceives a characteristically chaotic welter, with little or no conscious agency:

> The great *Iliad* in Greece, and the small *Robin Hood's Garland* in England, are each, as I understand, the well-edited "Select Beauties" of an immeasurable waste imbroglio of Heroic Ballads in their respective centuries and countries. Think what strumming of the seven-stringed heroic lyre, torturing of the less heroic fiddle-catgut, in Hellenic Kings' Courts, and English wayside Public Houses; and beating of the studious Poetic brain, and gasping here too in the semi-articulate windpipe of Poetic men, before the Wrath of a Divine Achilles, the Prowess of a Will Scarlet . . . could be adequately sung! Honour to you, ye nameless great and greatest ones! (PP 133)

Leaping into mock-epic, Carlyle represents the progress of literature as a jumble of dullness. Kings' courts and public houses, Homer and squalling ballad-singers rub shoulders in this odd description. The antithesis of great and small gives way to a sense that these are all on the same level as "Literature"—"that huge froth-ocean . . . we loosely call Literature" (HW 163–64). While in other works Carlyle can praise, for example, "the sphere-harmony of a Shakespeare . . . the cathedral-music of a Milton" (HW 163), in this picture England's literary achievements depend on a highly contingent process of historical obsolescence. The English literary canon is determined by fashion and ignorance, taking shape as the equivalent of polite anthologies and crude chapbooks. Despite its resemblance to a process of natural selection, Carlyle's picture of history appears to be a far more contingent jumble. Some achievements endure because of their merit, while others endure because of their lack of merit. This is Carlyle's version of Burkean inheritance. It is closer, as we can see, to the antiquarian attitude toward history.

Not only nations but individual subjects also take on distinct forms through a process of contingent whirling observed from outside. *Past and Present* praises labor, above all, as a restorative reshaping. But Carlyle's celebrated work is an act performed by no one, least of all by the worker. Although the political aspirations of the working classes were based on the claim that labor is an exertion of agency, Carlyle's most famous depiction of work takes away the basis of that claim.[79] He describes labor not as the active exercise of one's own force but rather as a passive submission to a composing, harmonizing force: a force that seems to emanate from the created object or its means of production.

> Destiny, on the whole, has no other way of cultivating us. A formless Chaos, once set it *revolving*, grows round and ever rounder; ranges itself, by mere force of gravity, into strata, spherical courses; is no longer a Chaos, but a round compacted World. . . . Hast thou looked on the Potter's wheel,—one of the venerablest objects, old as the Prophet Ezechiel and far older? Rude lumps of clay, how they spin themselves up, by mere quick whirling, into beautiful circular dishes. And fancy the most assiduous Potter, but without his wheel; reduced to make dishes, or rather amorphous botches, by mere kneading and baking! (PP 197)

Offering labor the highest praise, Carlyle removes every trace of "assiduous" agency from it. The worker's role is merely to be present at the spectacle of his self-formation. Even personified Destiny is helpless without its tool, the potter's wheel that does the work. This wheel also performs ideological work. It rehabilitates the notion of revolution, though not by restoring it directly to its original astronomical context, where revolutions are vast, impersonal, and immune to human interference. Instead, it links the image to the potter's wheel, an archaic figure for "the work of our hands"—except that the hands are missing.[80] The rude materiality of the clay seems to give itself form: "lumps of clay, how they spin themselves up, by mere quick whirling." The worker's hands are replaced by a strange simulacrum of agency; the "assiduous Potter" is even derided as producing only "amorphous botches." Here, work is meant to feel like a being-worked, as the autonomous force of labor itself transforms the worker from "chaos" to creation.

Carlyle praises labor for the ethical and even affective composure that it can bring about. Contending that labor should be understood as an ethical rather than simply economic act, Carlyle insists that work produces clarity as opposed to jumble: "[E]ven in the meanest sorts of labour, the whole soul of a man is composed into a kind of real harmony, the instant he sets himself to work!" (PP 196) He also values what he describes as its essentially poetic character: "[h]e that works, whatsoever his work, he bodies forth the form of Things Unseen" (PP 205). This description applies to the worker—"a small Poet every Worker is"—and perhaps more truly to the reader, who produces determinate images in his mind. Both are figured by "the poet's pen," which is itself a trope for "Imagination," in the original passage from Shakespeare's *A Midsummer Night's Dream*.[81] But the work of reading, the type of labor that Carlyle is most concerned to demonstrate, to perform, and to encourage in *Past and Present*, does not appear to produce these effects. At best, it can be said to do so only ironically. It seems prone to misrecognize objects and relationships and to dissolve the self. As Carlyle prepares the reader to encounter the medieval text that forms the centerpiece of his work, the *Chronica Jocelini de Brakelonda*, he provides his most vivid rendering of the act of reading.[82]

> Through the thin watery gossip of our Jocelin, we do get some glimpses of that deep-buried Time; discern veritably, though in a fitful intermittent manner, these antique figures and their life-method, face to face! Beautifully, in our earnest loving glance, the old centuries melt from opaque to partially translucent, transparent here and there. . . . Readers who please to go along with us . . . shall wander inconveniently enough . . . through some poor stript hazel-grove, rustling with foolish noises, and perpetually hindering the eyesight; but across which, here and there, some real human figure is moving: very strange, whom we could hail if he would answer;—and we look into a pair of eyes deep as our own, *imaging* our own, but all unconscious of us; to whom we for the time are become . . . invisible!
> (PP 54–55, original emphasis)

The use of "glance" rather than "gaze" recalls the same passage from *Midsummer Night's Dream* alluded to previously: "The poet's eye . . . Doth glance from heaven to earth, from earth to heaven." But here the role of the reader's shaping imagination is ambiguous. What gives history its peculiar virtue is its resistance to the fashionings of imagination. As Carlyle's phrase "discern veritably" suggests, reading history should be a matter of optical acuity. Carlyle purports to describe a process of making out through an obscure medium what is really and objectively there. He figures this process as a dissolution or melting "from opaque to partially translucent"—a redaction of the familiar trope of looking through habits until they become transparent. Punning on the trope of the text's "leaves," Carlyle's allegory describes how the reader moves through the dissolving pages into the represented world: the "poor stript hazel-grove" of the thin unfinished manuscript. But here the dissolution appears to extend to the reader's sense of self as well. The effect described at the end of the passage is uncanny, unsettling rather than composing. The "pair of eyes . . . *imaging* our own, but all unconscious of us" seems to dissolve the reader's solidity back into the flux of historical contingency. Carlyle highlights his own equivocal term, "imaging." It suggests both imagination, in the sense of bodying forth "the form of things unseen," and optical reflection. In either sense, the term suggests that the reader receives himself at the hands of what he reads. He does more than contemplate his nonexistence in the twelfth century or witness the deep "unconscious" absorption of the past in its own concerns. The reader sees himself as the belated reflection of the image that he has himself created, illustrating the dynamic of the fetish.

The *Chronica Jocelini* provides a chastening mirror for the British nation in some obvious ways. Though written by and about the activities of "Ancient Monk[s]," the Chronicle is characterized, as Carlyle notes, by a surprising "secularity" (PP 65). Describing the reform of the St. Edmundsbury monastery in twelfth-century England, the Chronicle offers both an allegory and a concrete example of institutional restructuring, led by a singular individual. Abbot Samson, the newly elected leader, is a classic Carlylean hero, and his "incessant toil and tribulation" (PP 104) rebuke do-nothing aristocrats and laissez-faire economists.[83] But in the history's "culminating moment" (PP 122), Samson's role is far less active. Samson's crowning act is to "reedif[y]" the shrine that contains the body of St. Edmund, the monastery's patron saint, who had died three centuries earlier. In this scene, driven by a desire "to look once upon the Body of his Patron," Samson opens the "Loculus, chest or sacred Coffin" (PP 122–23). He presides over a scene of reading. Carlyle claims to translate the following directly from the Latin original:

The Loculus was filled with the Sacred Body. . . . But the Abbot, looking close, found now a silk cloth veiling the whole Body, and then a linen cloth of wondrous whiteness; and upon the head was spread a small linen cloth, and then another small and most fine silk cloth. . . .

These coverings being lifted off, they found now the Sacred Body all wrapt in linen; and so at length the lineaments of the same appeared. But here the Abbot stopped; saying he durst not proceed farther . . . proceeding, he touched the eyes; and the nose, which was very massive and prominent . . . and then he touched the breast and arms; and raising the left arm he touched the fingers, and placed his own fingers between the sacred fingers . . . and he touched the toes and counted them. (PP 124)

Samson's spectatorial role is echoed and emphasized by the presence of others who are looking closely at him: "one of our Brethren . . . sitting on the roof of the Church, with the servants of the Vestry, and looking through, clearly saw all these things" (PP 125). The Abbot performs a readerly discernment, looking closely at the "Sacred Body." This act is performed secretly, at midnight. Jocelin, the writer of the Chronicle, notes, "We all thought that the Abbot would shew the Loculus to the People; and bring out the Sacred Body again, at a certain period of the Festival. But in this we were wofully mistaken" (PP 123). Instead of theatricality, Carlyle gives us a scene of absorption, as Samson works to decipher the object, giving it the "intensest . . . inspection" that the Chronicle itself demands from its readers, in turn.

Abbot Samson is certainly more fortunate than readers of Carlyle's histories or of any historical text. Through his reading he comes into contact with the very material body of the past. The "bodily man" here is not the reader's rapt inward representation but rather a tangible, miraculously intact presence. Emphasizing the body's features and parts, this passage evokes the other bodies, past and present, docile and threatening, adorned and unadorned, that populate Carlyle's texts. The fullness of the Loculus seems to quell the irony in Carlyle's earlier reverence for the "hollow cloth garment." But the martyr's body is also a text, evocative of other texts about revolution and counterrevolution. The "sacred body" is a figure, most obviously, for Jocelin's Chronicle in its material existence: "the *Chronicle of Jocelin* is . . . unwrapped from its thick cerements" (PP 48). It also figures more generally what Carlyle posits as the redeeming otherness of history: the autonomous, self-absorbed rather than theatrical life of the past that it is literature's task to render believable. In "The Diamond Necklace," for example, Carlyle had lamented, "Instead of looking fixedly at the *Thing*, and . . . endeavouring to *see* it, and fashion a living Picture of it . . . [the historian] has now quite other matters to look to. The thing lies shrouded, invisible, in thousand-fold hallucinations" (DN 228, original emphasis). But in Samson's case, the covering folds are what make it readable. In Carlyle's earlier works, transparency or translucence had been presented as the goal; but here opacity becomes central to the meaning of reading. The perusal of each layer of linen and silk is dramatically described. Though the body is uncovered, it is not a scene of revolutionary stripping of the type that Burke had feared. Part of the scene's power arises from the way in which it rewrites the meaning of the act of stripping away. Particularly after the revolution controversy provoked by Burke's *Reflections*, unveiling had become the trope of choice for radical, skeptical, and demystifying enquiry; here it carries a different sense altogether. Meaning accrues in and through these encounters with successive layers of covering. When Samson arrives at the saint's body, he touches and numbers its parts. But he does not actually touch the body itself. At the last layer, "the Abbot stopped." The final veil is what enables Samson's reading. It allows the "lineaments" to be visible, but it still makes active surmise necessary. This scene illustrates reading as the misrecognized work of the imagination, as a paradigmatic alliance between knowledge and willed ignorance.

Like the historical and literary texts that Carlyle sees as vital to the nation, the martyr's body is a locus of common feeling, a source of legitimacy for a community. But its features appear to be projected onto it by the beholder. The description of the martyr's nose as "massive and prominent," in fact, echoes an earlier description of Samson's face as "massive . . . with 'a very eminent nose'" (PP 74). This act of imaginary mirroring depends also on the veil's presence; the veil is the condition of possibility for the reader to "fashion a living Picture" for himself and of himself. "To predict the Future, to manage the Present, would not be so impossible, had not the Past been so sacrilegiously mishandled; effaced, and what is worse, defaced! The Past cannot be seen . . . cannot even be *not* seen"(PP 239). Not seeing the past, paradoxically, makes it readable. Its usefulness is enhanced by selective blindness about one's own manipulation of it. The veil functions as the sign of this forgetting. Like Walter Scott's antiquarian-patriotic piety, it hints at a discrepancy between what is there and what is imagined to be there. Samson, after all, takes or mistakes as objective truth the image he has created for himself through conspicuously imperfect sight and mediated touch.

By means of this veiling, history can be regarded as a "thing" to be read, either metaphorically or literally. In this way, history can instill in the nation a regard for permanence, productivity, and earnest disavowal of one's own labor: in short, for masculinity. Notable throughout, the gendered quality of this project becomes most striking in Carlyle's personification of "Fame" as the antithesis of the history he reveres. Fame is conspicuously feminized: "she is and will be very noisy, this 'Fame' . . . but if you will consider it, what is she?" (PP 135). Not only is Fame "noisiest, inarticulately babbling, hissing, screaming," but she is also inconstant, inconsistent, equivocal in a stereotypically feminine-infantile way:

Scarcely two hundred years back can Fame recollect articulately at all; and there she but maunders and mumbles. She manages to recollect a Shakspeare or so; and prate, considerably like a goose, about him; . . . with regard to a Wodan, even a Moses . . . [s]he begins to be uncertain as to what they were. . . . *She* is transitory, futile, a goose-goddess . . . she forgets us all (PP 135–36, original emphasis)

Fame is simply another name for the historical record, one of Carlyle's favorite themes. In other works, Carlyle discusses the relative paucity of the historical record in rather different terms. In the essay "On History Again," written for *Fraser's Magazine*, for instance, Carlyle offers a mathematical description of the same phenomenon as "*Hyperbolic-Asymptotic*; ever of *infinite* breadth around us: soon shrinking within narrow limits; ever narrowing more and more into the infinite depth around us."[84] In that essay, the metaphor of perspective, borrowed from painting, seems to work equally well: "Look back from end to beginning, over any History; over our own England: how, in rapidest law of perspective, it dwindles from the canvas!" (OH 81). But in *Past and Present*, a work far more concerned with building a nation, this aspect of the historical record is represented as History's feminized other. She is pure orality; mumbling and prating, she neither writes down nor tries to read.[85] Thus, her forgetting, unlike the nation's deliberate and constitutive forgetting, is unproductive, "futile." She exemplifies transitoriness. Most deplorably, Fame refuses to inscribe onto the blankness of the past the existence of heroic, mute male poets; in Fame's eyes, "no work from the inspired heart of a Man [was] needed there" (PP 135). Through this personification it becomes clear how reading the text of history can be virtuous: in and through that act, forgetting, passivity, and disavowal become productive, permanent, and masculine. Carlyle seems to perceive a particular need to assign a gender-identity to the type of reading he prescribes to the nation. But Carlyle is concerned with more than masculinity alone.

Carlyle poses as the condition of national existence what he calls "forgotten work." He extends the idea of amnesic labor to all the disparate efforts that constitute empire.

It is all work and forgotten work, this peopled, clothed, articulate-speaking, high-towered, wide-acred World. The hands of forgotten brave men have made it a World for us. . . . Our English Speech is speakable because there were Hero-Poets of our blood and lineage. . . . This Land of England has its conquerors, its possessors, which change from epoch to epoch, but its real conquerors, creators, and eternal proprietors are these following, and their representatives . . . all the men that ever cut a thistle, drained a puddle out of England, contrived a wise scheme in England, did or said a true or valiant thing in England. . . . The quantity of done and forgotten work that lies silent under my feet in this world, and escorts and attends me,

and supports and keeps me alive, wheresoever I walk or stand, whatsoever I think or do, gives rise to reflections! (PP 134–35)

Carlyle figures Britain in the present, and, in particular, the state of its cultural institutions, "Satanic-School, Cockney-School and other Literatures,"
as "a waste imbroglio, and world-wide jungle and jumble" (PP 134). This is
the "jumble" that calls out for imperial ordering through heroic labor performed by men. But what is crucial is that those bodily men be dimly recol-
lected but not recognized or remembered by name. Rather, Carlyle sees the
task of reading the nation as the confident recovery of anonymity. It is essential that Britain's work, and especially its literature, be thought of as
anonymous, for this namelessness gives it a certain independence, a lack of
indebtedness to any determinate creator or audience. This goes beyond the
autonomous self-absorption of a text that can draw a reader within its world.
Rather, anonymity is the ground or condition that enables the labor of reading to be itself heroic. The work of literature, whether writing or reading, is
to surmise the existence and even the features of a "somebody": "Between
that day and this . . . there has been a pretty space of time; a pretty space of
work, which *somebody* has done!" (PP 131). A rich anonymity has to be there
for the reader to be able to imagine a name, surmise features, give a quasi-
determinate form to this paradoxically full absence. Freed by the gaps in the
historical record or by his own erasures to imagine the familiar features of the
nation's "real conquerors, creators, and eternal proprietors," the reader can
perform an imaginary atonement with the past. In some ways Carlyle returns
to Burke's original notion of inheritance. He removes the complacent security that came to accompany the notion of inheritance as it was simplified and
popularized. Instead of a nation bequeathing itself to itself and thus rein-
forcing its identity, here the nation's identity and the legitimacy of its past labor depend on the reader's deliberate self-investment in the artificial activity
of reading. Burke had written, "the people of England know;" Carlyle suggests that the readers of England can imagine the nation to be an anonymous
inheritance passed down to them from "Hero-Poets." In this way, the reader's
work can be self-forgetful in a way that mirrors the earlier labor of surmised
ancestors. As for the reader's relation to the nation thus realized, it is one of
almost pure fetishism.

   Britain's national virtue, according to Carlyle, seems essentially dependent on material fetishes—on the mediation of things regarded as tangible—
rather than verbal communication. "The Spoken Word of England turns out
to have been trivial, of short endurance; not valuable. . . . The grim inartic-
ulate veracity of the English People, unable to speak its meaning in words,
has turned itself silently on things" (PP 169). The literary text also counts
as a silent material thing, "poor bits of rag paper with black ink on them"
(HW 164). Words, things, paper and cloth become indistinguishable for

these purposes. It is possible to see Carlyle as making an exception of Scotland here; praising Wallace for having in effect said to England, "ye must not tread us down like slaves" (PP 18), Carlyle tends to represent Scotland in terms of voice and vocal dissent, rather than the muteness consistently associated with every English class and with Irish suffering. But from *Past and Present*, nevertheless, we can construct two different models of the dynamic relation between Britain's men, or at least English men, and the objects they produce. In one model, the worker or reader discovers his own powers through the mediation of the thing he makes: "thou hast no other knowledge but what thou hast got by working; the rest is yet all a hypothesis of knowledge" (PP 197). The created object is instrumentally useful as a means of attaining self-knowledge. But in the dominant model, the worker or reader produces an object, disavows or forgets his own act, and stands lost in rapt contemplation before what he has made, hoping to receive his own identity from it. Here the object, like Jocelin's "sacred body," belongs to the order of ends rather than means. In both scenarios, the marketplace is completely eclipsed; neither exchange nor consumption appear to exist. But the two are significantly different. Britain's virtue seems to be active, ever-expanding, and contemplative, retiring, at the same moment. The alliance between these two characterizations is an ironic one. But here the irony cannot be so readily seen through, to use Carlyle's own metaphor from *Sartor Resartus*. Indeed, irony provides the conditions for not-seeing. The particular types of blindness recommended in *Past and Present* point toward the great modern theories of fetishism elaborated by Marx and Freud. In *Capital*, Marx would use fetishism as a trope for the degradation and alienation of labor in the form of the commodity.[86] Freud, in his essay on sexual fetishism, would, in turn, offer a remarkable allegory of conservatism: "the fetish is precisely designed to preserve [a belief] from extinction"—a belief in something which "should normally have been given up": the female phallus or, as Freud himself gleefully suggests, "throne and altar."[87] Carlyle would agree with Freud that "[t]his way of dealing with reality . . . almost deserves to be described as artful," another example of the poiesis inherent in labor.[88] Where those later thinkers analyze fetishism in relation to capitalist economies and psychic economies, respectively, Carlyle places the hidden resourcefulness of fetishism at the center of another problematic achievement of modernity: British empire. Like Burke and Scott, but with different feelings, Carlyle saw the alienation, the satisfaction, and the peculiar conservative longevity that national fetishes can possess and confer.[89] Blurring the boundaries between demystifying critique and conservative apologia, these writers publicly rested their hopes for the nation's future on a selective and bold forgetfulness about the present, a lucid forgetfulness that resembles what a postmodern critic has described as the "formula of fetishistic disavowal: "'I know very well, but still . . . '"[90]

Notes

Chapter One

1. Maria Edgeworth, *Castle Rackrent*, ed. George Watson (Oxford: Oxford University Press, 1995) 5.

2. *Ibid.* 7–8.

3. See Edgeworth's essay on Irish "bulls" for a discussion of this type of logical contradiction (Richard Lovell Edgeworth and Maria Edgeworth, *Essay on Irish Bulls* [London: J. Johnson, 1802]). On this essay and its relation to *Castle Rackrent* and others of Edgeworth's works, see Catherine Gallagher, *Nobody's Story: The Vanishing Acts of Women Writers in the Marketplace, 1670–1820* (Berkeley: University of California Press, 1994). See also Mitzi Myers, "Goring John Bull: Maria Edgeworth's Hibernian High Jinks versus the Imperialist Imaginary," in *Cutting Edges*, ed. James Gill (Knoxville: University of Tennessee Press, 1995) 367–94; and Michael Neill, "Mantles, Quirks, and Irish Bulls: Ironic Guise and Colonial Subjectivity in Maria Edgeworth's *Castle Rackrent*," *Review of English Studies* 52, 205 (2001): 76–90.

4. Edgeworth, *Castle Rackrent*, 7–8. As the following chapters will demonstrate, the metaphor of "habit" becomes crucial in the formulation of British nationalism. An important study, James Chandler's *Wordsworth's Second Nature* (Chicago: University of Chicago Press, 1984), focuses on this trope of habit or second nature. It should be noted here that Spenser here uses "nation" in the older sense of the word as referring not to politically organized, self-governing bodies, but as something closer to ethnic groups. For a brief overview of the history of the word's different meanings, see Michael Hechter, *Containing Nationalism* (Oxford: Oxford University Press, 2000) 10–11.

5. In his praise of prejudice, Burke writes that Britons refuse "to cast away the coat of prejudice. . . . Prejudice renders a man's virtue his habit" (*Reflections on the Revolution in France*, ed. L. G. Mitchell, vol. 8 of *The Writings and Speeches of Edmund Burke*, ed. Paul Langford [Oxford: Clarendon, 1989] 138). See the useful explanations of "liberal" and "cultural nationalism" in David Aram Kaiser, *Romanticism, Aesthetics, and Nationalism* (Cambridge: Cambridge University Press, 1999) 18–25. I see cultural nationalism in Kaiser's sense as somewhat different from, though obviously not entirely separate from, the dis-

course of national character explored in David Simpson's *Romanticism, Nationalism, and the Revolt Against Theory* (Chicago: University of Chicago Press, 1993). Burke clearly participates in this latter discourse, as Simpson shows, but I would argue that his motives and manner of doing so go beyond the project of establishing an English national character.

6. See, for example, John Barrell, "'An Entire Change of Performances?' The Politicisation of Theatre and the Theatricalisation of Politics in the mid-1790s," *Lumen* 17 (1998): 11–50; Betsy Bolton, *Women, Nationalism, and the Romantic Stage: Theatre and Politics in Britain, 1780–1800* (Cambridge: Cambridge University Press, 2001); Miranda Burgess, *British Fiction and the Production of Social Order, 1740–1830* (Cambridge: Cambridge University Press, 2000); Marilyn Butler, *Jane Austen and the War of Ideas* (Oxford: Clarendon, 1975), and *Romantics, Rebels, and Reactionaries* (Oxford: Oxford University Press, 1981); Linda Colley, *Britons: Forging the Nation, 1707–1837* (New Haven: Yale University Press, 1992); Seamus Deane, *The French Revolution and Enlightenment in England, 1789–1832* (Cambridge: Harvard University Press, 1988); Kevin Gilmartin, *Print Politics; The Press and Radical Opposition in Early Nineteenth-Century England* (Cambridge: Cambridge University Press, 1996); Albert Goodwin, *The Friends of Liberty* (Cambridge: Harvard University Press, 1979); Angela Keane, *Women Writers and the English Nation in the 1790s: Romantic Belongings* (Cambridge: Cambridge University Press, 2000); Paul Keen, *The Crisis of Literature in the 1790s* (Cambridge: Cambridge University Press, 1999); Gary Kelly, *Women, Writing, and Revolution, 1790–1827* (Oxford: Clarendon, 1993); Iain McCalman, *Radical Underworld* (Cambridge: Cambridge University Press, 1988); J.G.A. Pocock, *Virtue, Commerce, and History* (Cambridge: Cambridge University Press, 1985); Alan Richardson, *Literature, Education, and Romanticism: Reading as Social Practice, 1780–1832* (Cambridge: Cambridge University Press, 1994); Nicola Watson, *Revolution and the Form of the British Novel, 1790–1825* (Oxford: Oxford University Press, 1994).

7. On Tory satire, see James Noggle, *The Skeptical Sublime: Aesthetic Ideology in Pope and the Tory Satirists* (Oxford: Oxford University Press, 2001); Claude Rawson, *Order from Confusion Sprung* (London: Allen and Unwin, 1985).

8. I am indebted for the idea of "pacts" between different or "adjacent discourses" to Deidre Lynch's study, *The Economy of Character: Novels, Market Culture, and the Business of Inner Meaning* (Chicago: University of Chicago Press, 1998) 11.

9. For recent discussions of the United Kingdom as a problematic nation-state, see *National Identities: The Constitution of the United Kingdom*, ed. Bernard Crick (Oxford: Blackwell, 1991).

10. This view of deference contrasts but is not wholly incompatible with the description offered by Jonathan Clark in his *English Society, 1688–1832* (Cambridge: Cambridge University Press, 1985): "it involved sympathetic involvement, expectations of reciprocity, common outlook, identification of interest, and sheer coercion in the name of a social ideal far more than weak submission" (78).

In keeping with his larger aims, Clark represents it as overall a fruitful social symbiosis.

11. "the cradle of our people," *Reflections* 131. Review of "Dépêches et lettres interceptés, etc. Copies of the original letters and dispatches . . . to the Emperor Napoleon, at Dresden; intercepted by the advanced troops of the Allies in the North of Germany," *Quarterly Review* 20 (January 1814): 493.

12. *Paul's Letters to his Kinsfolk, Miscellaneous Prose Works of Sir Walter Scott* (Edinburgh: A. and C. Black, 1852) 5: 329–30. On the politics of crowds in the nineteenth century, see John Plotz, *The Crowd* (Berkeley: University of California Press, 2000).

13. Scott recounts many scenes from 1813 to 1815 that appear to reaffirm the edict of absolute monarchy that "the whole state is in the person of the prince" (Jacques-Bénigne Bossuet, *Politique tirée des propres paroles de l'Ecriture sainte,* cited in Keith Baker, *Inventing the French Revolution* [Cambridge: Cambridge University Press, 1990] 226).

14. Ernest Gellner, *Nations and Nationalism* (Ithaca: Cornell University Press, 1983) 1.

15. Hechter, *Containing Nationalism* 7.

16. Walker Connor, *Ethnonationalism* (Princeton: Princeton University Press, 1994) 204, 197. The distinction between "civic" (e.g., British, American, and French) and "ethnic" (eastern European) nationalisms derives from Hans Kohn, *The Idea of Nationalism* (Toronto: Collier-Macmillan, 1969).

17. Ross Poole, *Nation and Identity* (London: Routledge, 1999) 27.

18. Homi Bhabha, *The Location of Culture* (London: Routledge, 1994) 161, 145.

19. Eric Hobsbawm and Terence Ranger, eds., *The Invention of Tradition* (Cambridge: Cambridge University Press, 1983); Benedict Anderson, *Imagined Communities* (London: Verso, 1991).

20. Craig Calhoun, *Nationalism* (Minneapolis: University of Minnesota Press, 1997) 34. See also David Miller, *On Nationality* (Oxford: Clarendon, 1995).

21. The most important example of this gradual assimilation of irony to nationalism is to be found in Benedict Anderson's work. In *Imagined Communities'* discussion of the "cultural roots" of nationalism, two of Anderson's most important literary examples of national imagining make striking use of irony. In one example, the Indonesian novel *Semarang Hitam*, Mas Marco Kartodikromo uses classic verbal irony: "he came upon an article entitled, PROSPERITY [:] A destitute vagrant became ill and died on the side of the road from exposure" (31). At the opening of José Rizal's *Noli Me Tangere*, also quoted by Anderson, the narrator not only employs this type of verbal irony ("the community of parasites, spongers, and gatecrashers whom God, in his infinite goodness, created, and so tenderly multiplies in Manila" [27]) but also directly addresses the reader in a classic illustration of ironic parabasis or breaking of the frame. Anderson cites these examples to show how they imagine "a single community . . . moving on-

wards through calendrical time" (27); but it seems more than coincidence that he chose passages so clearly illustrative of irony. His recent book, *The Spectre of Comparisons* (London: Verso, 1998) makes central a notion of irony as divided consciousness and suggests that such consciousness is fundamental to the formation of modern nationalism. For a useful overview of Anderson's oeuvre, see *Diacritics* 29, 4 (Winter 1999). Another notable convergence of nationalism and irony can be found in *Nationalism, Colonialism, and Literature* (Minneapolis: University of Minnesota Press, 1990), edited by Terry Eagleton, Fredric Jameson, and Edward Said, in which Eagleton sees both nationalism and class struggle as "involv[ing] an impossible irony" ("Nationalism: Irony and Commitment," 23). This irony, though, exists at the level of considering these projects theoretically or abstractly—not at the everyday level of practice. Seamus Deane also articulates a classic ironic position in his description of the *Field-Day Anthology of Irish Writing* project: "to engage in the action of establishing a system . . . While remaining aware that all such systems . . . are fictions" (in Eagleton et al., 15).

22. Neil MacCormick, "Nation and Nationalism," in *Theorizing Nationalism*, ed. Ronald Beiner (Albany: SUNY Press, 1999) 189–204, 196. See, for example, Janet Sorenson's claim that the "rhetoric and practice" of cultural nationalism—even "resistant" or peripheral ones—"obscure the pressing distinctions of class and gender in the claims of a culture (and language) shared by all its members" (*The Grammar of Empire in Eighteenth-Century British Writing* [Cambridge: Cambridge University Press, 2000] 25).

23. For example, Angela Keane writes in a recent study that this "Romantic national idea, with its emphasis on the organic relationship between nation and state, allied to a localist attention to the folkloric connection between people and place . . . becomes hegemonic" (*Women Writers and the English Nation in the 1790s* 9). Burke's *Reflections*, she argues, shows "the extent to which the discourse of citizenship and the social contract had become 'biologised,' absorbed into the Romantic national idea, by the 1790s" (5).

24. Marlon Ross, "Romancing the Nation State," in *Macropolitics of Nineteenth-Century Literature: Nationalism, Exoticism, Imperialism*, ed. Jonathan Arac and Harriet Ritvo (Philadelphia: University of Pennsylvania Press, 1991) 58.

25. Butler, *Romantics, Rebels, and Reactionaries*. See also Claudia Johnson, *Equivocal Beings* (Princeton: Princeton University Press, 1995); Deidre Lynch, "Domesticating Fictions and Nationalizing Women: Edmund Burke, Property, and the Reproduction of Englishness," in *Romanticism, Race and Imperial Culture, 1780–1834*, ed. Alan Richardson and Sonia Hofkosh (Bloomington: Indiana University Press, 1996) 40–71; Angela Keane, *Women Writers*.

26. Katie Trumpener, *Bardic Nationalism* (Princeton: Princeton University Press, 1997). Romantic (particularly German Romantic) stress on the unique particularity of individual nations is discussed by Friedrich Meinecke in *Historism*, trans. J. E. Anderson (New York: Herder, 1972).

27. On the connection between modernization and imperialism, see also Saree Makdisi, *Romantic Imperialism: Universal Empire and the Culture of Modernity* (Cambridge: Cambridge University Press, 1998).

28. Mikhail Bakhtin, *The Dialogic Imagination*, trans. Caryl Emerson and Michael Holquist (Austin: University of Texas Press, 1981) 232, 225. Bakhtin is here describing the chronotope he calls the "idyll."

29. *Sartor Resartus*, ed. Kerry McSweeney and Peter Sabor (Oxford: Oxford University Press, 1987) 182.

30. Edgeworth, *Castle Rackrent* 124 (original emphasis). There is some confusion in the story as given between the names of Mr E. and Mr M. (the two landowners), but the only way that the story makes sense is if the tenant stands on the piece of his landlord's ground that has been inserted into the other man's territory.

31. *Ibid.* These two anecdotes were the only new material added in the 1810 edition.

32. Calhoun argues in *Nationalism* that nationalism "does not completely explain any specific . . . activity or event, but it helps to constitute each through cultural framing" (22).

33. Linda Colley, *Britons: Forging the Nation, 1707–1837* (New Haven: Yale University Press, 1992), Marilyn Morris, *The British Monarchy and the French Revolution* (New Haven: Yale University Press, 1992). On the theatricality of the Georgian public sphere, see Gillian Russell, *The Theatres of War: Performance, Politics, and Society, 1793–1815* (Oxford: Clarendon, 1995). As Clifford Siskin points out, "The problem specific to British nationalism was . . . how to form a group—how to address disparate elements as a totality" (*The Work of Writing* [Baltimore: Johns Hopkins University Press, 1998] 85). While Siskin sees culture, particularly in the Scottish context, as what provides the assumption of a wholeness or plenitude that underlies and holds together surface differences, my study explores the role of irony in negotiating between these surface contradictions.

34. Colley's analysis gives many examples of how underprivileged or marginalized social groups used patriotic claims in just this fashion. See also Marc W. Steinberg, "Citizenship Claims in Early Nineteenth-Century England," in *Citizenship, Identity and Social History*, ed. Charles Tilly (International Review of Social History Supplement 3) (Cambridge: Cambridge University Press, 1995): 19–50. Steinberg notes that English silk weavers "seized upon the notion of Englishness to validate their class claims for a secure livelihood," as well as to bolster their particular conception of masculine gender identity (41). See also the essays in Raphael Samuel, *Patriotism: The Making and Unmaking of British National Identity*, 3 vols. (London: Routledge, 1989). The contradiction here is similar to the ones that arise in contemporary "identity politics" in a multicultural democracy like the United States, contradictions described by Charles Taylor in "The Politics of Recognition," in *Multiculturalism*, ed. Amy Gutmann (Princeton: Princeton University Press, 1994): 25–74.

35. *The Anti-Jacobin or Weekly Examiner*, 2 vols., 5th ed. (London: Hatchard, 1803) 2:53–54.

36. Thomas Harpley to John Reeves, 25 December 1792, cited in Morris, *British Monarchy* 153.

37. There is also the variant of dramatic irony, in which the protagonist's limited knowledge or understanding contrasts with the broader apprehension offered by the play to the spectators.

38. For a full discussion of New Critical and many other approaches to irony, see Linda Hutcheon's important study, *Irony's Edge: The Theory and Politics of Irony* (New York: Routledge, 1995).

39. *Ibid.* 46, 89.

40. Benjamin Constant, *The Spirit of Conquest and Usurpation*, trans. Biancamaria Fontana (Cambridge: Cambridge University Press, 1988) 55.

41. *Ibid.* 95—96. Bracketed words appeared in the first edition.

42. *Paul's Letters* 328. "This appetite for glory has of late been fed with such insubstantial food, as has apparently rendered the French indifferent to the distinction betwixt what is unreal and what is solid" (328—29).

43. Constant, *The Spirit of Conquest* 54. See Adam Ferguson, *An Essay on the History of Civil Society*, ed. Fania Oz-Salzberger (Cambridge: Cambridge University Press, 1995).

44. Constant, *The Spirit of Conquest* 141, 55.

45. *Ibid.* 53.

46. *Ibid.* 76—77.

47. *Ibid.* 54. On the idea of the spirit of the age, see James Chandler, *England in 1819* (Chicago: University of Chicago Press, 1998).

48. Constant, *The Spirit of Conquest* 100.

49. *Ibid.* 55.

50. Anne Mellor, *English Romantic Irony* (Cambridge: Harvard University Press, 1980) 11.

51. Though with the deconstructive treatment of the intentionality of irony as a rhetorical figure the way is opened up to explore a rich range of attendant psychological phenomena. See, for example, Paul de Man, *Blindness and Insight* (Minneapolis: University of Minnesota Press, 1983) and Tilottama Rajan, *Dark Interpreter* (Ithaca: Cornell University Press, 1980).

52. This tendency within Romanticism has famously been christened "Romantic ideology" by Jerome McGann's book of that title (Chicago: University of Chicago Press, 1983).

53. Jameson, *The Political Unconscious* (Ithaca: Cornell University Press, 1983) 41.

54. The discourse overlaps significantly with that of the Romantic symbol, which also focuses on the relationship between the part and the whole, the particular and the universal. But it explores this problem from a different perspective and reaches a different conclusion. Theories of the symbol as articulated by Coleridge and others tend to locate the problem in the limitation of the particular—a limitation that has to be overcome to create a genuine symbol. See the lucid discussion provided by Kaiser, *Romanticism, Aesthetics, and Nationalism* 28—38. While I have benefited from the ways in which he aligns his discussion of the symbol with the political philosophies of liberalism and cultural nationalism, I see his "logic of the symbol," that is, a "simultaneous standing for and standing

apart" (35) as closer to irony than to the symbol. On the mediating or linking force of the Romantic imagination, particularly in relation to the ideology of nationalism, see Forest Pyle, *The Ideology of Imagination: Subject and Society in the Discourse of Romanticism* (Stanford: Stanford University Press, 1995). It should also be noted that the relation between part and whole is the domain of the trope of synecdoche, according to traditional rhetoric. In this sense Romantic irony, as a rhetorical figure, could be seen as a self-conscious, skeptical extension of this particular trope, in the way that the extension of metaphor gives rise to the figure of allegory.

55. As Paul de Man has argued in *Blindness and Insight*. For a fascinating discussion of Romantic irony as actually performing the opposite of what it professes, see Paul Hamilton, "*Waverley*: Scott's Romantic Narrative and Revolutionary Historiography" (*Studies in Romanticism* 33 [1994]: 611–34).

56. Friedrich Schlegel, *Philosophical Fragments*, trans. Peter Firchow, foreword by Rodolphe Gasché (Minneapolis: University of Minnesota Press, 1991) 74.

57. Schlegel's discussion of the necessity of self-restriction in *Critical Fragment* 37 is also frequently cited in connection to Romantic irony.

58. "Irony is the clear consciousness of eternal agility, of an infinitely teeming chaos" (*Ideas* 69, in *Philosophical Fragments* 100).

59. *Lyceum* fragment 37, cited in Mellor, *English Romantic Irony* 14.

60. *Athenaeum* fragment 428, in *Philosophical Fragments* 88–89.

61. Eric Hobsbawm, *Nations and Nationalism since 1780: Programme, Myth, Reality* (Cambridge: Cambridge University Press, 1990) 22.

62. Anticipating later theorists like Adam Smith, Bernard Mandeville, for example, had argued that the individual parts of society were afflicted by a notably false consciousness; though they complain of the vicious behavior of others, they can be brought to see and to appreciate how "the skilful management" of politicians, or "the state's craft," orchestrates the vices of the individual parts into a prosperous and progressive social whole: "Thus ev'ry part was full of vice, / Yet the whole mass a paradise." Bernard Mandeville, *The Fable of the Bees: or, Private Vices, Publick Benefits*, ed. F. B. Kaye (Oxford: Clarendon, 1924) 1:24, 1:7.

63. Mellor provides an excellent discussion of the Romantic irony of *Sartor Resartus* (109–34). Note also that Carlyle's well-known "Characteristics" is a review of Schlegel's *Philosophical Lectures* (Vienna, 1830) together with Thomas Hope's *Essay on the Origin and Prospects of Man* (London: 1831).

64. "Jean Paul Friedrich Richter," (*Critical and Miscellaneous Essays in Four Volumes* [Boston: Dana Estes, 1895] 1:3–25) 13.

65. In his *Literary Notebooks, 1797–1801*, Schlegel works out this distinction between classical unity and ethical totality, the latter being achieved when a work "mixes and weaves together extremely heterogeneous components" (cited in Rodolphe Gasché, "Foreword: Ideality in Fragmentation," in Schlegel, *Philosophical Fragments* xxviii).

66. "Richter" 1:22 (original emphasis).

67. *Ibid.* 21.

68. *Critical Fragment* 103, in *Philosophical Fragments* 12.

69. Gary Handwerk provides an important exposition of what he calls "ethical irony" in his study, *Irony and Ethics in Narrative: From Schlegel to Lacan* (New Haven: Yale University Press, 1985); he argues that irony ensues in a recognition of how "identity" in fact inheres in what he calls "intersubjectivity" (3). See also, for a discussion of Schlegel's Romantic irony as a metaphor for an ideal liberal politics, Adam Carter's "'Insurgent Government': Romantic Irony and the Theory of the State," *Irony and Clerisy*, Romantic Circles Praxis Series, *Romantic Circles* (1999): 38 pars., online, available: *http://www.rc.umd.edu/praxis/irony/carter/schelegel.html*, December 1999. An important late theory of Romantic irony, Georg Lukács's *Theory of the Novel* (trans. Anna Bostock [Cambridge: MIT Press, 1971]) also illustrates in fascinating ways how irony mediates as a discourse between literature and politics. By contrasting it with the "world situation" of the epic, Lukács attempts to define the "world situation" of the novel or modernity. The novel faces unique challenges as a literary form, he argues, because it arises from a world without either organic unity or immanent meaning. The genre reflects this situation in its compositional challenges; the novel tends to be "heterogeneously contingent and discrete . . . the relatively independent parts are more independent, more self-contained than those of the epic" (75). Just like the parts of modern experience, the parts of the novel resist their harmonious integration into a whole; they continue, rather, to pull away toward a state of independence. Irony is the subject's mode of accepting this situation. In it the subject, to put it rather simply, occupies two positions. On the one hand, there is "subjectivity as interiority, which opposes power complexes that are alien to it" (75) interiority as its own law. But on the other hand, the subject sees itself from elsewhere as simply another "part of the outside world, confined in its own interiority" (81) —one object of irony among others. In his extraordinary preface, written almost fifty years later (in Budapest, July 1962), Lukács historicizes his own argument about the characteristic irony of modernity. He writes that the motive for *The Theory of the Novel*, written in 1914–15, was a "vehement, global . . . scarcely articulate rejection of the war [World War I] and especially of enthusiasm for the war." Describing his "emotional attitude" toward the war as indecipherable, he nevertheless tries to adumbrate it in the following way:

> The Central Powers would probably defeat Russia; this might lead to the downfall of Tsarism; I had no objection to that. There was also some probability that the West would defeat Germany; if this led to the downfall of the Hohenzollerns and the Hapsburgs, I was once again in favour. But then the question arose: who was to save us from Western civilisation? (11)

His preface not only invites but virtually commands us to view his theory as an allegory of its historical moment. From this point of view, the "parts" he refers to as continually threatening to spin off into a state of pseudo-independence can be imagined on two levels. On the literal level, there is the unstable heterogeneity of the novel—the strange digressions in Goethe's *Wilhelm Meister's Apprenticeship*, for example. Such digressions have to be tied artificially to the novel through thematic linkages and other means. But on another level there are also the cultural and political "parts" that make up the unstable, "heterogeneously contingent" whole of the Hapsburg empire. Or the yoking together of heterogeneous parts that, in 1707 and 1800, framed the United Kingdom geographically and framed temporally the eighteenth-century novel praised by the later Lukács. These national or subnational "parts" likewise resist easy integration into a larger whole or the larger narrative that is empire. We should also note, finally, that Carlyle was the first English translator of *Wilhelm Meister*.

70. "Burns," *Critical and Miscellaneous Essays in Four Volumes* (Boston: Dana Estes, 1895) 1: 256–314, 286.

71. *Ibid.* 263.

72. *Ibid.* 283–84.

73. *Ibid.* 260, 270.

74. *Ibid.* 260.

75. *Ibid.* 297.

76. *Ibid.* 285.

77. *Ibid.* 284.

78. *Ibid.* 260. For a very different reading of this essay, see Leith Davis, *Acts of Union* (Stanford: Stanford University Press, 1999).

79. Quoted in Walt Whitman, "Death of Thomas Carlyle," *The Critic*, 12 February 1881, reprinted in *Thomas Carlyle: The Critical Heritage*, ed. Jules Paul Seigel (London: Routledge, 1971) 461–62.

80. "Burns," *Critical and Miscellaneous Essays* 286.

81. "Sir Walter Scott," *Critical and Miscellaneous Essays in Four Volumes* (Boston: Dana Estes, 1895) 3:433.

82. *Ibid.* 437, 445.

83. These two ideas—nation and authenticity—have been importantly linked by modern Scottish nationalists who have seen Scott, as did Edwin Muir, as the chief purveyor of a fake, sentimentalized vision of Scotland. See Ian Duncan, "North Britain, Inc.," *Victorian Literature and Culture* 23 (1995): 339–50, for a discussion of these and other attitudes toward Scott and Scotland.

84. Scott has recently come to attain a more canonical stature in the study of British Romanticism. The increasingly pervasive acknowledgment of Scott's importance can be linked to what is again a relatively recent flowering of critical interest in eighteenth-century Scotland's cultural and historical significance; and this interest in the specifically Scottish Enlightenment, I believe, grows out of the dramatic development of postcolonial studies, on the one hand, and, on the other hand, post-Marxist commitment to examining the discourses of politics rather than the struggles of social classes against each other. On the new canonicity of Scott, see the introduction to *Scott, Scotland, and Romanticism*, ed. Ian Duncan, Ann Rowland, and Charles Snodgrass (*Studies in Romanticism* 40, 1 [Spring 2001]: 3–12). Recent critical attention to Scott has often focused on his relationship to the nation. Besides Trumpener (*Bardic Nationalism*) and Burgess

(*British Fiction*), see also Robert Crawford, *Devolving English Literature* (Oxford: Clarendon, 1992); Leith Davis, *Acts of Union*; Penny Fielding, *Writing and Orality: Nationality, Culture, and Nineteenth-Century Scottish Fiction* (Oxford: Clarendon, 1996), Janet Sorenson, *Grammar of Empire*.

85. A different view of the Union of 1707 as marking a clear boundary between political and commercial Scotland underlies, for example, the discussion of Scott by Alexander Welsh, *The Hero of the Waverley Novels* (Princeton: Princeton University Press, 1992), and provides the starting point of Ian Duncan's important work on Scott's use of romance. The latter contends that in Scott's novels, "political struggle was to be confined to the past, enabling in the present a purely economic progress of agricultural and commercial 'improvement'" (*Modern Romance and Transformations of the Novel* [Cambridge: Cambridge University Press, 1992] 53).

86. Virtually every critic of Scott has noticed his obsessive tendency to frame his novels in layers of editorial and supereditorial voices. See, for example, Kathryn Sutherland, "Fictional Economies: Adam Smith, Walter Scott, and the Nineteenth-Century Novel," *ELH* 54 (1987): 97-127. For a striking recent discussion of this topic, see Chandler, *England in 1819* 320-47. On framing as it applies particularly to *Waverley*, see P. D. Garside, "*Waverley*'s Pictures of the Past," *ELH* 44 (1977): 659-82.

87. *Waverley*, ed. Andrew Hook (London: Penguin, 1985) 163.

88. Cairns Craig points out that the "marginal characters of this scene, in the background . . . become an audience to the events of Fergus' feast," in the context of arguing that the scene's theatricality figures Scott's faith in the ability of the imagination to actively shape a nation's future; see "Scott's Staging of the Nation," in *Scott, Scotland, and Romanticism*, ed. Ian Duncan, Ann Rowland, and Charles Snodgrass (*Studies in Romanticism* 40, 1 [Spring 2001]: 13-28).

89. *Waverley* 163.

90. *Ibid.* 165.

91. *Ibid.* 164.

92. A classical ideological reading of this scene would take the following approach: these dependents believe they have a choice when in reality they have none. Though they believe that they prefer the cheaper liquor, their taste simply reflects their subordinate social position. This belief would be understood as a case of false consciousness: "consciousness that benefits some social entity or structure and has been formed according to a poor [i.e., insufficiently reflective] mechanism" (Michael Rosen, *On Voluntary Servitude: False Consciousness and the Theory of Ideology* [Cambridge: Harvard University Press, 1996] 47). Pierre Bourdieu would read this scene as evidence of the way that social practice is generated not by consciousness but by "the socially informed body, with its tastes and distastes, its compulsions and repulsions, with . . . all its *senses*" (Pierre Bourdieu, *Outline of a Theory of Practice*, trans. Richard Nice [Cambridge: Cambridge University Press, 1977] 124).

93. Bourdieu, *Outline of a Theory of Practice* 94, emphasis added.

94. Bourdieu writes, "nothing suits the [subaltern] better than to play his

part in an interested fiction which offers him an honourable representation of his condition" (196). The subaltern's deference is calculated objectively to raise his own status within the existing rules of the game.

95. Christopher Harvie, *Scotland and Nationalism* (London: Allen and Unwin, 1977) 69, 67. See also Michael Fry, *The Dundas Despotism* (Edinburgh: Edinburgh University Press, 1992); and Keith Robbins, *Nineteenth-Century Britain: Integration and Diversity* (Oxford: Clarendon, 1988).

96. On eighteenth-century Scotland's redefinition of the public sphere, see J.G.A. Pocock, *Virtue, Commerce, and History* (Cambridge: Cambridge University Press, 1985); also the essays in *Wealth and Virtue*, ed. Istvan Hont and Michael Ignatieff (Cambridge: Cambridge University Press, 1983); Nicholas Phillipson, "Towards a Definition of the Scottish Enlightenment," in *City and Society in the Eighteenth Century*, ed. P. Fritz and D. Williams (Toronto: University of Toronto Press, 1973). Phillipson and others have shown how political impulses were displaced onto other social forms.

97. *Waverley* 492.

98. The concluding chapter foregrounds thematically an economy of substitution. Lady Emily is the "representative of Mrs Edward Waverley" (489) and Colonel Talbot the unwilling proxy of the estate's new master. Claiming credit for the whole complex transaction, Bailie Macwheeble points out that he has been Waverley's proxy throughout the process of purchasing the estate: "wha cookit the parritch for him? . . . young Mr Wauverley, put it a' into my hand frae the beginning . . . I circumvented them . . . I cajoled them" (487). And Macwheeble boasts of having used, instead of Waverley's name, other spectral representatives: "I didna gae slapdash to them wi' our young bra' bridegroom . . . I scared them wi' . . . the Mac-Ivors . . . I beflumm'd them wi' Colonel Talbot— wad they offer to keep up the price again' the Duke's friend?" (487–88). The description of Waverley in the portrait as well, "contemplative, fanciful, and enthusiastic," functions as the substitute for the character whose actual memories might derange the calibrated comedic harmony of the final scene.

99. *Waverley* 489.

100. *Ibid.* 484.

101. Michael Fried, *Absorption and Theatricality: Painting and Beholder in the Age of Diderot* (Berkeley: University of California Press, 1980) 99. The earlier Tully-Veolan that Waverley sees is characterized by its overwhelming absorption, in the sense that Fried uses that term. The estate seems to demonstrate that "suspension of activity and fixing of attention" that Fried sees as characteristic of this state in French painting of the 1750s (Fried 56). The description of the exterior of the house ends with the note, "the whole scene still maintained the monastic illusion . . . " (79). Unlike Monkbarns in *The Antiquary*, Tully-Veolan was never an actual monastery; the "monastic" character refers to this quality of rapt inward concentration that Waverley detects. The figures, too, who populate this estate are too occupied in their activities—singing or working—to notice Waverley's presence until after he watches them; they are caught off-guard.

102. The phrase was coined by Gregory Smith and developed into a full-

blown reading of Scott and Scottish literature by Edwin Muir, David Craig, and others; for a succinct recapitulation of this history see Duncan, "North Britain, Inc." (339–40). While this notion of dualism, particularly when understood as psychological ambivalence, has resulted in a fatalistic view of history and an essentializing view of Scotland, its venerable history and persistence are worth remarking. For one version of it, see Charles Macklin's 1781 play, *The Man of the World*, in which the Scottish anti-hero, Sir Pertinax MacSycophant, asserts that all men in public life have a "releegious" and a "poleetical" conscience. MacSycophant, as his name suggests, has built his successful career on a complete division between public behavior and private thoughts.

103. See, for example, Johnson (*Equivocal Beings*), Keane (*Women Writers*), Bolton (*Women, Nationalism, and the Romantic Stage*), as well as Carol Kay, *Political Constructions* (Ithaca: Cornell University Press, 1988).

104. For a very different, and extremely compelling reading of the "sense of difference" or doubleness of Burke's rhetoric, see John Whale, *Imagination Under Pressure* (Cambridge: Cambridge University Press, 2000). Whale sees this doubling or oscillation in Burke as precisely what gives it socially "hegemonic potential" (38).

105. *Correspondence of Edmund Burke*, vol. 8, ed. R. B. McDowell (Cambridge: Cambridge University Press and Chicago: Chicago University Press, 1969) 254.

106. To Richard Burke, 23 March 1792, *Correspondence of Edmund Burke*, ed. P. J. Marshall and John A. Woods (Chicago: University of Chicago Press, 1968), 7:118.

107. *Ibid.*

108. "Letter to Sir Hercules Langrishe," *Writings and Speeches* 9:598.

109. I refer here to the extraordinary biography of Burke by Conor Cruise O'Brien, *The Great Melody* (Chicago: University of Chicago Press, 1992).

110. "Langrishe," *Writings and Speeches* 9:615.

111. See O'Brien, *The Great Melody*, for a detailed discussion of Burke's relation to Ireland; see also Marianne Elliot's biography, *Wolfe Tone: Prophet of Irish Independence* (New Haven: Yale University Press, 1989), for a contrasting viewpoint on the politics of this period.

112. Cited in Tim Fulford, "Romanticism and colonialism: races, places, peoples, 1800–30," in *Romanticism and Colonialism: Writing and Empire, 1780–1830*, ed. Tim Fulford and Peter J. Kitson (Cambridge: Cambridge University Press, 1998) 38.

113. *Correspondence* 7:300.

114. Johnson, *Equivocal Beings* 3.

115. Mary Wollstonecraft, for example, memorably voices this suspicion in her denunciation of Burke's theatrical sentimentality in her *Vindication of the Rights of Men; and, A Vindication of the Rights of Women*, ed. D. C. Macdonald and Kathleen Scherf (Ont., Canada: Broadview, 1997). On Burke's theatricality, see Gillian Russell, "Burke's dagger: theatricality, politics and print culture in

the 1790s," *British Journal of Eighteenth-Century Studies* 20 (1997): 1–16.

116. See Nicholas Robinson, *Edmund Burke: A Life in Caricature* (New Haven: Yale University Press, 1996).

117. Kevin Whelan, *The Tree of Liberty: Radicalism, Catholicism, and the Construction of Irish Identity 1760-1830* (Notre Dame: University of Notre Dame Press, 1996).

118. Burke's mother's family, the Nagles, as shown by Kevin Whelan, "The regional impact of Irish Catholicism, 1700–1850," in *Common Ground: Essays on the Historical Geography of Ireland presented to T. Jones Hughes*, ed. W. Smyth and L. K. Whelan (Cork, Cork University Press, 1988), cited in O'Brien, *The Great Melody* 15.

119. "The Axe Laid to the Root or Reasons humbly offered for Putting the Popish Clergy in Ireland under some Better Regulations," cited in Whelan, *The Tree of Liberty* 33.

120. "A Description of the Conditions and Manners, as well as the Moral and Political Character, Education, etc. of the Peasantry of Ireland between 1780 and 1790" (London: 1804), cited in Whelan, *The Tree of Liberty* 42. Edgeworth's *Castle Rackrent* provides one of the best literary examples of this type of deference.

121. *Ibid.*

122. On consent and force as adding up to hegemony, see Antonio Gramsci, *Selections from the Prison Notebooks*, ed. and trans. Quintin Hoare and Geoffrey Nowell (New York: International Publishers, 1971).

123. Burke, *Letter to a Noble Lord, Writings and Speeches of Edmund Burke*, vol. 9, ed. R. B. McDowell (Oxford: Clarendon, 1991) 162.

124. See M. O. Grenby, *The Anti-Jacobin Novel* (Cambridge: Cambridge University Press, 2001) 126–40.

125. Thomas Nowell, *A Sermon Preached before the Honourable House of Commons . . .* (1772), quoted in J.C.D. Clark, *English Society 1688–1832: Ideology, Social Structure and Political Practice during the Ancien Regime* (Cambridge: Cambridge Univ. Press, 1985) 213.

126. *Reflections* 209–10.

127. See, besides Grenby (*The Anti-Jacobin Novel*), Robert Hole, *Pulpits, Politics, and Public Order in England, 1760–1832* (Cambridge: Cambridge University Press, 1989); A.M.C. Waterman, *Revolution, Economics and Religion: Christian Political Economy, 1798–1833* (Cambridge: Cambridge University Press, 1991).

128. See Grenby's discussion of *Such Follies Are* and Smith's novel *Marchmont* in *The Anti-Jacobin Novel* (164).

129. The aristocratic Clarence Hervey creates "a diversion in . . . favour" of the duelling women, Lady Delacour and Harriet Freke, a Wollstonecraft figure, shouting, "Huzza, my boys! Old England for ever!" (*Belinda*, ed. Kathryn J. Kirkpatrick [Oxford: Oxford University Press, 1994] 58).

130. On the cultural authority of Scott, see Ina Ferris, *The Achievement of Literary Authority: Gender, History, and the Waverley Novels* (Ithaca: Cornell

University Press, 1981); and Fiona Robertson, *Legal Histories: Scott, Gothic, and the Authorities of Fiction* (Oxford: Clarendon, 1994). On Carlyle's authority as a "sage," see John Holloway, *The Victorian Sage* (Hamden, Conn.: Archon, 1962); George P. Landow, *Elegant Jeremiahs: The Sage from Carlyle to Mailer* (Ithaca: Cornell University Press, 1986); and *Victorian Sages and Cultural Discourse: Renegotiating Gender and Power*, ed. Thais E. Morgan (New Brunswick: Rutgers University Press, 1990). On the conservatism of Scott and Carlyle, see also John P. Farrell, *Revolution as Tragedy: The Dilemma of the Moderate from Scott to Arnold* (Ithaca: Cornell University Press, 1980).

131. See Seamus Deane, *Strange Country: Modernity and Nationhood in Irish Writing since 1790* (Oxford: Clarendon, 1997).

132. *Waverley* 33. On Scott's relationship to existing hierarchies of literary genres, see Ferris, *Achievement of Literary Authority*, Duncan, *Modern Romance*, and Burgess, *British Fiction*. Of course, the claim to be doing something new and unprecedented is an old ploy of the novel, as Scott himself knew as an admirer of Fielding. On the relationship of antiquarianism to enlightenment history, see Ina Ferris, "Pedantry and the Question of Enlightenment History: The Figure of the Antiquary in Scott" (*European Romantic Review* 13, 3 [2002]: 273–83).

133. *The Fortunes of Nigel* (New York: Routledge, n.d.) 260.

134. See Keen, *Crisis of Literature* 3. On the naturalizing service of novels to nation-building, see Siskin, *Work* 172–90.

135. On the novel's relationship to political economy, see Burgess, *British Fiction* 1–24, 73–112.

136. *Reflections* 110. On Burke's idea of nature, see David Bromwich, *A Choice of Inheritance* (Cambridge: Harvard University Press, 1989).

137. *Reflections* 138.

138. Burke to Lord Charlemont, 9 August 1789, *Correspondence of Edmund Burke*, ed. Alfred Cobban and Robert Smith (Chicago: University of Chicago Press, 1967) 6:10.

139. David Williams, *Lessons to a Young Prince by an Old Statesman on the present Disposition in Europe to a general Revolution*, *Select Pamphlets* (Philadelphia: Mathew Carey, 1796) 47, 28.

140. Phyllis Deane, *The First Industrial Revolution* (Cambridge: Cambridge University Press, 1965) 55–56. See also C. A. Bayly, *Imperial Meridian: The British Empire and the World, 1780–1830* (London: Longman, 1989); and Patrick Brantlinger, *Rule of Darkness: British Literature and Imperialism, 1830–1914* (Ithaca: Cornell University Press, 1988).

141. Deane, *First Industrial Revolution* 47.

142. Carlyle, *Past and Present*, ed. Richard Altick (New York: New York University Press, 1965) 255.

143. For a relevant study of the relationships between nation, empire, debt, and fetish, see Patrick Brantlinger's valuable work, *Fictions of State: Culture and Credit in Britain, 1694–1994* (Ithaca: Cornell University Press, 1996). Brantlinger shows how public credit or debt paradoxically holds together the nation and allows it to expand into an empire. The structure of paper money, the struc-

ture of the psychological subject, and the mode of consumption of the novel also reflect the centrality of debt, credit, or lack, that is, fetishism.

144. Carlyle, "Chartism," *Critical and Miscellaneous Essays in Four Volumes* (Boston: Dana Estes, 1895) 4:35–117, 65–66. I am using the term "cynicism" slightly differently from the way it is used by Peter Sloterdijk in his *Critique of Cynical Reason* (trans. Michael Eldred, foreword by Andreas Huyssen [Minneapolis: University of Minnesota Press, 1987]). Sloterdijk defines it as an "unhappy consciousness, on which enlightenment has labored both successfully and in vain" (5). That is, the cynical consciousness is torn between the enlightenment desire to unmask the ruses of power it understands and the "compulsion to survive" by going along with them (7). He uses the term "kynicism" to refer to the subset of cynical consciousness that still retains an anti-authoritarian, anarchic energy (535).

145. Arthur Young, *Travels in France During the Years 1787, 88 and 89*, ed. Constantia Maxwell (Cambridge: Cambridge University Press, 1950) 190. On the trope of circulation in Young, see Jon Klancher, *The Making of English Reading Audiences, 1790–1832* (Madison: University of Wisconsin Press, 1987).

146. Young, *Travels in France* 209–10.

147. According to the absolutist logic of political representation, the nation is embodied solely in the person of its king rather than the people. On changing principles of political representation in this historical moment, see Keith Michael Baker, "Representation," in *The Political Culture of the Old Regime*, ed. Keith Michael Baker (vol. 1 of *The French Revolution and the Creation of Modern Political Culture* [Oxford: Pergamon, 1987–89] 469–72).

148. *Parliamentary Register*, vol. 25 (London: Debrett, 1789) 418. The text continues, "Mr Burke was called to order by the other side of the House."

149. *Ibid.* 127.

150. *Ibid.* 418–20.

151. *Ibid.* 461–62. On Burke's role in the Regency debates, see John Barrell, *Imagining the King's Death* (Oxford: Oxford University Press, 2000) 87–100.

152. *Parliamentary Register* 462.

153. Wollstonecraft, *A Vindication of the Rights of Men* 59–60, original emphasis.

154. *Letter to William Elliott, Writings and Speeches* 9: 39–40. Burke sees this crisis of authority as occurring "in every country" that has either watched or been in contact with revolutionary France.

155. J. S. Mill, "The Spirit of the Age," in *Essays on Politics and Culture*, ed. Gertrude Himmelfarb (Garden City: Doubleday, 1962) 6, 19.

156. See Richard H. Popkin, *The History of Scepticism from Erasmus to Spinoza* (Berkeley: University of California Press, 1979) for a discussion of Pyrrhonian conservatism, or the view, articulated by Montaigne, that it is best simply to "live in the laws and customs of our own society," given the impossibility of rationally demonstrating the truth of any position (49). On the relationship between skepticism and the conservatism of English Restoration culture, see Richard Kroll, *The Material Word* (Baltimore: Johns Hopkins University Press,

1991). See Jürgen Habermas, "Legitimation Problems in the Modern State," in *Communication and the Evolution of Society*, trans. Thomas McCarthy (London: Heinemann, 1976).

157. P. W. Banks, "Of Politicians, Public Opinion, and the Press," *Fraser's Magazine* 12 (July 1835) 36. While the writer, who calls for the Tory party to abandon its aristocratic principles, has in mind narrower political subdivisions, nationalism's logic clearly relies on the principle that spirit emanates from (or is determined by) a particular place. See David Simpson, *Romanticism, Nationalism, and the Revolt Against Theory*.

158. Carlyle, *The French Revolution* (New York: H.M. Caldwell, n.d.) 279.

159. Burke is often seen as a primary architect of this traditionalism. He condemns the despotic institution of revolutionary culture in his first *Letter on a Regicide Peace*: in France, "nothing . . . was left to accident. All has been the result of design; all has been matter of invention" (*Writings and Speeches of Edmund Burke* 9:392–93). See J.G.A. Pocock, *Politics, Language, Time* (New York: Atheneum, 1971), and Chandler, *Wordsworth's Second Nature*.

160. Carlyle, *Past and Present* 132.

161. S. T. Coleridge, *The Friend*, ed. Barbara E. Rooke, 2 vols. (London: Routledge and Kegan Paul/Princeton: Princeton University Press, 1969) 1:106, *Collected Works* vol. 4.

162. *Ibid.* 1:518, 517.

163. *Ibid.* 1:106.

164. See John Barrell, *The Birth of Pandora* (Philadelphia: University of Pennsylvania Press, 1992).

165. *Past and Present* 190, 224, 293. In an important article, Ian Duncan has recently written of Scott's novels that by "appeal[ing] to those who see through the fiction . . . as well as those who do not," they actually lead to a "structural doubling and division of the reader" along these lines ("Authenticity Effects: The Work of Fiction in Romantic Scotland," *South Atlantic Quarterly* 102, 1 [2003]: 107).

166. Sloterdijk, *Critique of Cynical Reason* 7. On how the periodicals of this period constructed for their middle-class readers a "stance of implicit knowingness," see Klancher, *The Making of English Reading Audiences* 47–75.

Chapter Two

1. Anon., "House-Breaking, before Sun-Set," published January 6, 1789, in Nicholas Robinson, *Edmund Burke: A Life in Caricature* (New Haven: Yale University Press, 1996) 127.

2. Burke's tropes have remained a contentious issue, even though Burke criticism has been, with several notable exceptions, relatively uninfluenced by poststructural theory with its typical emphasis on the autonomous intentionality of rhetorical figures. On Burke's imagery, see Paul Fussell, *The Rhetorical World of Augustan Humanism* (Oxford: Clarendon, 1965). Other important studies of Burke's language include J. T. Boulton, *The Language of Politics in the Age of*

Wilkes and Burke (London: Routledge and Kegan Paul, 1963); Olivia Smith, *The Politics of Language, 1791–1819* (Oxford: Clarendon, 1984); Steven Blakemore, *Burke and the Fall of Language* (Hanover: University Press of New England, 1988); and Frans de Bruyn, *The Literary Genres of Edmund Burke: The Political Uses of Literary Form* (Oxford: Clarendon, 1996) among others. Tom Furniss, in *Edmund Burke's Aesthetic Ideology* (Cambridge: Cambridge University Press, 1993), applies the Derridean concept of the supplement to account for Burke's rhetoric. Deidre Lynch remarks that "Burke's statecraft says one thing; his tropes say another" ("Domesticating Fictions and Nationalizing Women: Edmund Burke, Property, and the Reproduction of Englishness," in *Romanticism, Race, and Imperial Culture, 1780–1834*, ed. Alan Richardson and Sonia Hofkosh [Bloomington: Indiana University Press, 1996] 58).

3. On prosopopoeia, see Angus Fletcher, *Allegory: The Theory of a Symbolic Mode* (Ithaca: Cornell University Press, 1964), especially 26 ff.

4. Samuel Taylor Coleridge, *Biographia Literaria*, ed. James Engell and W. Jackson Bate (Princeton: Princeton University Press/London: Routledge and Kegan Paul, 1983) 1:191–92.

5. *Reflections on the Revolution in France*, ed. L. G. Mitchell, vol. 8 of *The Writings and Speeches of Edmund Burke*, ed. Paul Langford (Oxford: Clarendon, 1989) 130. Hereafter cited as RRF parenthetically in the text along with page numbers. The passage is notorious, in particular, because of the final phrase quoted here; it earned Burke the implacable resentment of the working classes and allegedly almost got him a coronet.

6. A certain quantity of highly conventional allegorical embellishment occurs in many forms of philosophical and political (as well as poetical) writing of this time, as in, for example, Adam Smith and Hume. It is also interesting to note that allegorical pageantry, with its representations of darkness and light, fetters and liberty, was a mode particularly esteemed by the makers of the French Revolution for its nonmimetic, transparently fictive character. See Mona Ozouf, *Festivals and the French Revolution*, trans. Alan Sheridan (Cambridge: Harvard University Press, 1988).

7. Hugh Blair, *Lectures on Rhetoric and Belles Lettres*, ed. Harold F. Harding (Carbondale: Southern Illinois Press, 1965) 332. John Lawson, similarly, groups together "apostrophes, hyperboles, and feigning of persons" as "the natural language of the passions," in his *Lectures Concerning Oratory, Delivered in Trinity College, Dublin* (Dublin: George Faulkner, London: W. Bowyer, 1759) 253. On other eighteenth-century views of the relationship between emotion and rhetoric, see Adela Pinch, *Strange Fits of Passion: Epistemologies of Emotion, Hume to Austen* (Stanford: Stanford University Press, 1996), as well as Wilbur Samuel Howell, *Eighteenth-Century British Logic and Rhetoric* (Princeton: Princeton University Press, 1971).

8. Blair, *Lectures on Rhetoric* 319. Blair remarks that often "simple Metaphors . . . escape in a manner unnoticed" (327).

9. "But when there is something striking and unusual . . . it then rises into a figure of speech which draws our attention . . . unless the reader's imagination be

in such a state as disposes it to rise and swell along with [it], he is always hurt and offended by it" (319). Blair is discussing hyperbole in a chapter concerned with hyperbole, personification, and apostrophe.

10. *Ibid.* 332.

11. Wollstonecraft, *A Vindication of the Rights of Men, in a Letter to the Right Honourable Edmund Burke; and, A Vindication of the Rights of Woman,* ed. D. L. Macdonald and Kathleen Scherf (Peterborough, Ontario: Broadview, 1997) 78–79.

12. This picture of Burke is most influentially argued in Marilyn Butler's *Romantics, Rebels, and Reactionaries* (Oxford: Oxford University Press, 1981). See also Deidre Lynch, "Domesticating Fictions," as well as Mary Jean Corbett, *Allegories of Union in Irish and English Writing, 1790–1870: Politics, History, and the Family* (Cambridge: Cambridge University Press, 2000), and Angela Keane, *Women Writers and the English Nation in the 1790s: Romantic Belongings* (Cambridge: Cambridge University Press, 2000).

13. Blair, *Lectures on Rhetoric* 336.

14. *A Philosophical Enquiry into the Origin of Our Ideas of the Sublime and the Beautiful,* ed. James Boulton (Notre Dame: University of Notre Dame Press, 1968) 57.

15. John Barrell, *The Birth of Pandora* (Philadelphia: University of Pennsylvania Press, 1992) 36. See also Clifford Siskin's interesting discussion of personification in *The Historicity of Romantic Discourse* (New York: Oxford University Press, 1988).

16. Bhikhu Parekh, "Discourses on National Identity," *Political Studies* 42 (1994): 492–504, cited in Uday Singh Mehta, *Liberalism and Empire: A Study in Nineteenth-Century British Liberal Thought* (Chicago: University of Chicago Press, 1999) 150.

17. *Ibid.*

18. David Hume, *Treatise of Human Nature,* ed. L. A. Selby-Bigge, rev. P. H. Nidditch (Oxford: Clarendon, 1978) 477–526. On Hume's concept of artifice, see Frederick Whelan, *Order and Artifice in Hume's Political Philosophy* (Princeton: Princeton University Press, 1985).

19. The importance of the concept of naturalization in Hume's thought is emphasized by Carol Kay in *Political Constructions: Defoe, Richardson and Sterne in Relation to Hobbes, Hume and Burke* (Ithaca: Cornell University Press, 1988). Kay points out the significant convergences in the thinking of Hume and Burke, but neglects the skeptical and critical dimension of Burke.

20. Hume, *Treatise* 526.

21. David Miller, *Philosophy and Ideology in Hume's Political Thought* (Oxford: Clarendon, 1994) 194. Carol Kay, Marilyn Butler, and others also emphasize the break constituted by the beginning of the French Revolution, though their analyses differ.

22. The well-known description of the bourgeois public sphere offered by Jürgen Habermas in his *Structural Transformation of the Public Sphere* (trans. Thomas Burger and Frederick Lawrence [Cambridge: MIT Press, 1989]).

23. "Letter to William Elliot," in *Writings and Speeches of Edmund Burke* vol. 9, ed. R. B. McDowell (Oxford: Clarendon, 1991) 42.

24. What Harold Laski later wrote of Burke, that "[h]e denied . . . that the degree to which a purpose is fulfilled is as important as the purpose itself," Burke's *Reflections* offers as an attitude held by English subjects (*Political Thought in England from Locke to Bentham* [London: Thornton Butterworth, 1920] 211). Even when they seek to oppose or curtail power, they are devoted, in his account, to the ideals often imperfectly embodied in political practice; they hold to what Laski sums up as "the splendor of what the facts are trying to be" (211). See also James Chandler's argument in "Poetical Liberties: Burke's France and the 'Adequate Representation' of the English," in *The Transformation of Political Culture*, ed. François Furet and Mona Ozouf (Oxford: Pergamon, 1989) 45–58.

25. They are closer, if anything, to the paradigm of "nobody's story" that a recent critic has seen the novel of Burke's time as offering: an empty space that individuals or groups can try to occupy. See Catherine Gallagher's model of the novel in *Nobody's Story: The Vanishing Acts of Women Writers in the Marketplace, 1670–1820* (Berkeley: University of California Press, 1994).

26. Writers like Eaton and Spence embraced and worked within Burke's personification, often concocting elaborate allegories of swine and swineherds, and seemed to find both freedom and confidence within this artificial construct, as Olivia Smith has suggested in her recent study, *The Politics of Language* (87–88). See also "The Placemen and Pensioners' Address to the Swinish Multitude," in *Paddy's Resource: Being a Collection of Original and Modern Patriotic Songs, Toasts and Sentiments* (Philadelphia: T. Stephens, 1796) 43–44. I am indebted to Carol Flynn for bringing the latter to my attention.

27. "An Entire Change of Performances?" cited in John Barrell, "'An Entire Change of Performances?' The Politicisation of Theatre and the Theatricalisation of Politics in the mid-1790s," *Lumen* 17 (1998): 48.

28. Cited in Smith, *The Politics of Language* 80.

29. On the use of the rhetoric of illusionists' advertisements, see Barrell, "An Entire Change."

30. Burke to Lord Charlemont, 9 August 1789, *Correspondence of Edmund Burke*, ed. Alfred Cobban and Robert Smith (Chicago: University of Chicago Press, 1967) 6:10.

31. Burke to Comtesse de Montrond, 25 January 1791, *Correspondence* 6:210–11. See also his explicit statements in the *Appeal from the New Whigs to the Old* in *The Works of the Right Honourable Edmund Burke*, 12 vols, 1887 (Hildesheim: Georg Olms, 1975), vol. 4:57–216.

32. Burke to Philip Francis, 20 February 1790, *Correspondence* 6:91–92.

33. See David Bromwich, "The Context of Burke's *Reflections*," *Social Research* 58 (1991): 313–54; *The French Revolution and British Culture*, ed. Ceri Crossley and Ian Small (Oxford: Oxford University Press, 1989); *Britain and the French Revolution*, ed. H. T. Dickinson (London: Macmillan, 1989); *Burke and the French Revolution*, ed. Steven Blakemore (Athens: University of Georgia

Press, 1992); F. P. Lock, *Burke's Reflections on the Revolution in France* (London: Allen, 1985); Albert Goodwin, *The Friends of Liberty* (Cambridge: Harvard University Press, 1979). On the political significance of the notion of context itself, see J.G.A. Pocock, "Edmund Burke and the Redefinition of Enthusiasm," *The Transformation of Political Culture, 1789–1848*, ed. François Furet and Mona Ozouf (Oxford: Pergamon, 1989) 19–43.

34. Thomas W. Davies, ed. *Committees for Repeal of the Test and Corporation Acts: Minutes 1786–90 and 1827–8* (London: London Record Society, 1978) 5.

35. See Lock, *Burke's Reflections* 42.

36. See D. O. Thomas, Introduction, *Richard Price: Political Writings* xv–xvi. See also Michael R. Watts, *The Dissenters* (Oxford: Clarendon, 1978) 479–80.

37. Price, *Observations on the Nature of Civil Liberty, the Principles of Government, and the Justice and Policy of the War with America*, in *Political Writings*, ed. D. O. Thomas (Cambridge: Cambridge University Press, 1996) 37.

38. I wish to thank Margery Sabin for pointing out the relevance of this other sense of the word.

39. *Minutes* 60–61.

40. *Minutes* 61.

41. David Williams, *Lessons to a Young Prince by an Old Statesman on the present Disposition in Europe to a general Revolution*, *Select Pamphlets* (Philadelphia: Mathew Carey, 1796) 47.

42. *Ibid.* 28.

43. Hannah Arendt, *The Human Condition* (Chicago: University of Chicago Press, 1958) 177–78.

44. Price, *Discourse on the Love of Our Country*, in *Political Writings* 179.

45. *Ibid.* 181–85.

46. *Ibid.* 185–86; original emphasis.

47. William Godwin, *An Enquiry Concerning Political Justice*, ed. F.E.L. Priestley (Toronto: University of Toronto Press, 1946) 1:230.

48. *Ibid.* 1:236–37.

49. Godwin goes on to deny categorically the possibility of agency. The vaunted critical independence of mind that can be cherished even under extreme political duress turns out not to be an aspect of agency but simply the consequence of the mind's essential passivity: there is no such thing as action.

> Man is in no case . . . the beginner of any event or series of events that takes place in the universe, but only the vehicle through which certain antecedents operate. . . . Two ideas present themselves . . . connected with each other; and a perception of preferableness necessarily follows. An object having certain desirable qualities, is perceived to be within my reach; and my hand is necessarily stretched out with an intention to obtain it. (1:385, 420)

50. Seyla Benhabib, *Critique, Norm, and Utopia* (New York: Columbia University Press, 1986) 136.

51. Cited in Alexander Lord Cockburn, *An Examination of the Trials for*

Sedition which have hitherto occurred in Scotland (Edinburgh: David Douglas, 1888) 54–55.

52. Price, *Discourse on the Love of Our Country* 190.

53. Williams, *Lessons to a Young Prince*, plate III, facing p. 27.

54. *Philosophical Enquiry* 45.

55. Wollstonecraft, *A Vindication of the Rights of Man* 88.

56. J.G.A. Pocock, *Politics, Language, Time* (New York: Atheneum, 1971) 212.

57. See Raymond Williams's interesting remarks on Burke's relationship to his audience in *Writing in Society* (London: Verso, 1983).

58. Angus Fletcher in *The Prophetic Moment* (Chicago: University of Chicago Press, 1971) discusses the two archetypes of the temple and the labyrinth in Edmund Spenser's *Faerie Queene*, ed. A. C. Hamilton (London: Longmans, 1977) 6.

59. Compare, for example, Althusser's late definition of ideology: "Human societies secrete ideology as the very element and atmosphere indispensable to their historical respiration and life" (cited in Raymond Boudon, *The Analysis of Ideology*, trans. Malcolm Slater [Cambridge: Polity Press, 1989] 98). Raymond Geuss gives a useful account of the varieties of neutral or "descriptive" conceptions of ideology in *The Idea of a Critical Theory* (Cambridge: Cambridge University Press, 1981) 4–12.

60. I am led to this reading in part by the emphasis Burke himself places on the notion of the dense medium in the *Reflections*:

These metaphysic rights entering into common life, like rays of light which pierce into a dense medium, are, by the laws of nature, refracted from their straight line. Indeed in the gross and complicated mass of human passions and concerns, the primitive rights of men undergo such a variety of refractions and reflections that it becomes absurd to talk of them as if they continued in the simplicity of their original direction. (RRF 112)

61. Paine, *Rights of Man* (New York: Anchor-Doubleday, 1989) 286. See also Mary Wollstonecraft, *A Vindication of the Rights of Men*; Linda Zerilli, *Signifying Woman: Culture and Chaos in Rousseau, Burke, and Mill* (Ithaca: Cornell University Press, 1994); Furniss, *Edmund Burke's Aesthetic Ideology*; Claudia Johnson, *Equivocal Beings: Politics, Gender, and Sentimentality in the 1790s* (Chicago: University of Chicago Press, 1995); and Ronald Paulson, *Representations of Revolution 1789–1820* (New Haven: Yale University Press, 1983).

62. Godwin, *An Enquiry Concerning Political Justice* 2:134 (book 5, chap. 15). See also James Mackintosh, *Vindiciae Gallicae* (Oxford: Woodstock, 1989).

63. John Millar, *Origin of the Distinction of Ranks* (Edinburgh: Blackwood, 1806) 73, 76.

64. *Ibid.* 78.

65. "[T]he manners introduced by chivalry . . . acquiring stability from custom, may still be observed to have a good deal of influence upon the tastes and sentiments even of the present age" (*Ibid.* 85).

66. Wollstonecraft identifies the latent gendered character of Burke's argument here, linking it to his descriptions of beauty and its paradoxically powerful weakness in his *Philosophical Enquiry*; but she proceeds in her own remarkable analysis to turn the relationship between gender and political relations on its head, arguing that the corrupt forms of power which women and other subalterns do in fact wield stem from precisely the political dynamic that Burke praises in this passage.

67. See Frances Ferguson's argument about Burke's sublime/beautiful dyad, in *Solitude and the Sublime* (New York: Routledge, 1992). Ferguson suggests that Burke ultimately fears the beautiful more than he does the sublime because of the way in which it insidiously undermines the self.

68. Burke seems to have Warren Hastings in mind here, but the position is also more largely that of the Rockingham Whigs, as they worked to curtail the powers of the crown. This is the most common political self-description or self-vindication that Burke offers.

69. The full sentence from the *Philosophical Enquiry* runs as follows: "Indeed so natural is this timidity with regard to power, and so strongly does it inhere in our constitution, that very few are able to conquer it, but by mixing much in the business of the great world, or by using no small violence to their natural dispositions" (67).

70. *Observations on a Late State of the Nation*, in *Writings and Speeches of Edmund Burke*, gen. ed. Paul Langford, vol. 2, ed. Paul Langford (Oxford: Clarendon, 1981) 212.

71. *Thoughts on the Causes of the Present Discontents*, in *Writings and Speeches of Edmund Burke*, vol. 2, 316, 320.

72. Of the "king's men" Burke writes, "Conscious of their independence, they bear themselves with a lofty air to the exterior ministers" (*Ibid.* 274).

73. See Claudia Johnson, *Equivocal Beings* 1–14. Boulton in *The Language of Politics* reads the passage in similar fashion as well.

74. See, for example, Sarah Maza, "The Diamond Necklace Affair Revisited," in *Eroticism and the Body Politic*, ed. Lynn Hunt (Baltimore: Johns Hopkins Univ. Press, 1991) 63–89; Lynn Hunt, *The Family Romance of the French Revolution* (Berkeley: University of California Press, 1992); Iain McCalman, "Mad Lord George and Madame La Motte: Riot and Sexuality in the Genesis of Burke's *Reflections on the Revolution in France*," *Journal of British Studies* 35, 3 (1996): 343–67.

75. Philip Francis to Burke, 19 February 1790, *Correspondence* 6:86.

76. Fletcher, *Allegory* 92, 102.

77. *Ibid.* 96.

78. See, for example, Adam Ferguson's redaction of the familiar anatomy of political forms in his *Essay on the History of Civil Society*, ed. Fania Oz-Salzberger (Cambridge: Cambridge University Press, 1995) 70.

79. Coleridge remarks on this characteristic of Spenser's personification of Grief (cited in Knapp, *Personification and the Sublime: Milton to Coleridge* (Cambridge: Harvard University Press, 1985) 84).

80. *Ibid.* 4.

81. Burke to Philip Francis, *Correspondence* 6:89.

82. *Fourth Letter on a Regicide Peace*, in *Writings and Speeches of Edmund Burke*, vol. 9, ed. R. B. McDowell (Oxford: Clarendon, 1991) 50.

83. Burke almost never condemns any tool as irremediably bad; the *Reflections* is concerned to establish precisely the point that what matters is the use made of instruments.

84. Tom Furniss's argument proceeds along these lines.

85. Except, of course, as a joke—such as Fielding's famous account of Partridge at Garrick's representation of *Hamlet*; as the quotation from Reynolds discussed below suggests, this topos of dramatic criticism has clear application to the social project of redefining class along the lines of cultural literacy. But I see this as a different project in which mystification plays an incidental role.

86. Paine, *Rights of Man* 357.

87. *Ibid.*

88. In her article, "Burke's dagger: theatricality, politics and print culture in the 1790s" (*British Journal of Eighteenth-Century Studies* 20 [1997]: 1–16), Gillian Russell discusses how the theater created and depended on a "visually literate public, capable of decoding a complex set of cultural and political signs" (12–13). On the competence of the eighteenth-century audience, see also William Worthen, *The Idea of the Actor* (Princeton: Princeton University Press, 1984) and Shearer West, *The Image of the Actor: Verbal and Visual Representation in the Age of Garrick and Kemble* (London: Pinter, 1991). West also notes how the "theatre audiences who read journalistic criticism and purchase theatrical prints" could easily decipher and appreciate conventional representational codes (106).

89. On the continuity between theater and street in eighteenth-century English life, see Richard Sennett, *The Fall of Public Man* (New York: Norton, 1976).

90. Thomas Davies, *Memoirs of the Life of David Garrick, Esq. . . .* (Boston: Wells and Lilly, 1818) 2:241–42.

91. Goldsmith's *The Bee*, for example, notes in 1759 that "all Grub Street is preparing its advice to the managers; we shall undoubtedly hear learned disquisitions on the structure of one actor's legs, and another's eyebrows. We shall be told much of enunciations, tones, and attitudes" (cited in West, *The Image of the Actor* 7). Burke's first literary enterprise was the short-lived (1747–48) journal, *The Reformer*, modeled on Addison's *Spectator* and preoccupied with the Dublin theater, the manners of its actors, and its audience (in *The Early Life, Correspondence, and Writings of the Rt. Hon. Edmund Burke*, ed. A.P.I. Samuels [Cambridge: Cambridge University Press, 1923] 297–329).

92. See Howell, *Eighteenth Century British Logic and Rhetoric*, and, for example, Thomas Sheridan, *British Education: or, the Source of the Disorders of Great Britain* (London: 1769).

93. West, *The Image of the Actor* 1 ff.

94. [David Garrick] *An Essay on Acting in which will be consider'd the Mimical Behaviour of a certain fashionable faulty actor* (London, 1744), cited in West, *The Image of the Actor* 4.

95. Davies, *Memoirs of the Life of David Garrick* 45. See Worthen, *The Idea of the Actor* 71 ff.

96. Diderot, *The Paradox of Acting*, trans. William Archer (New York: Hill and Wang, 1957) 19. On how "the actor becomes a metaphor for the ambiguity of all our actions . . . transform[s] the self into an uncomfortable fiction," see Worthen, *The Idea of the Actor* 9.

97. Diderot, *The Paradox of Acting* 71.

98. Lawson, *Lectures Concerning Oratory* 255-56.

99. Aaron Hill, *The Art of Acting; An Essay, in which the Dramatic Passions are properly defined and described* (London: Smeeton, 1801) 9.

100. Hill, 9; original emphasis.

101. *Ibid.* 11.

102. Burke, *Philosophical Enquiry* 132.

103. *Ibid.* 133.

104. Charles Gildon, *The Life of Mr Thomas Betterton* (New York: Augustus Kelley, 1970; London: 1710) 65.

105. *Ibid.* 33, 53, 65.

106. Neal Wood makes this point in "The Aesthetic Dimension of Burke's Political Thought" (*Journal of British Studies* 4, 1 [1964]: 41–64) 45.

107. On the eighteenth-century theater as an important epistemological and ethical paradigm, see David Marshall's study, *The Figure of Theater* (New York: Columbia University Press, 1986).

108. Joshua Reynolds, Discourse XIII (1786), *Discourses on Art* (San Marino: Huntington Library Press, 1959) 239. Reynolds is criticizing as implausible the scene in Fielding's *Tom Jones*, where Partridge mistakes Garrick, playing Hamlet, for an actual person experiencing actual feelings.

109. Burke, *Philosophical Enquiry* 57. See Frances Ferguson's remarks on Burke's conception of beauty in *Solitude and the Sublime*, especially 50–53.

110. Davies, *Memoirs* 2:241.

111. *Ibid.*

112. The playwright Thomas Morton, for example, testified before a Parliamentary committee on the tendency of Georgian audiences to "force passages . . . into political meanings" often unintended by the author (cited in Gillian Russell, *The Theatres of War* [Oxford: Oxford University Press, 1995] 16). Russell describes in more detail how the Georgian theater was an "intensely political place" (16).

113. Burke to William Windham, 24 October 1793, *Correspondence of Edmund Burke* 7:461.

114. See Ozouf's study, *Festivals and the French Revolution,* for a detailed account of the political uses of theatricality in the Revolution.

115. *Letter to a Member of the National Assembly*, in *The Writings and Speeches of Edmund Burke*, ed. L. G. Mitchell (gen. ed. Paul Langford [Oxford: Clarendon, 1989]) 8:315; *Fourth Letter on a Regicide Peace* 9:73.

116. On the assignats and Burke's response to them, see Pocock's "The political economy of Burke's analysis of the French Revolution," *Virtue, Commerce, and History* (Cambridge: Cambridge University Press, 1995) 193–214.

117. It was performed a total of sixty-two times in 1789 — quite a success in spite of what Emmet Kennedy and Marie-Laurence Netter argue was a decided public preference for comedy and nonpoliticized theater. See their conclusion to *Theatre, Opera, and Audiences in Revolutionary Paris*, ed. Kennedy, Netter, et al. (Westport, Conn.: Greenwood Press, 1996) 75-90.

118. On the neoclassical response to allegory, see Theresa Kelley, *Reinventing Allegory* (Cambridge: Cambridge University Press, 1997) 70-83, as well as Knapp, *Personification and the Sublime*, and Pinch, *Strange Fits of Passion*. The best-known locus of allegorical agency is Milton's *Paradise Lost*; Addison and Johnson, among others, found much to censure in the attribution of such material agency to personifications. There is an interesting echo of this passage in Charlotte Smith's *The Emigrants*; Smith's string of allegorical villains has one significant substitution, however: "the hell-born fiends / Of Pride, Oppression, Avarice, and Revenge" (II, 434-44) (*The Poems of Charlotte Smith*, ed. Stuart Curran [New York: Oxford University Press, 1993] 163. This way of conceiving of the role of private moral sentiments in public history is not original to Burke. Vico, for example, argues that "out of ferocity, avarice, and ambition . . . [society] makes national defense, commerce, and politics, and thereby causes the strength, the wealth, and the wisdom of the republics" (Giambattista Vico, *The New Science*, trans. Thomas Goddard Bergin and Max Harold Fisch (Ithaca: Cornell University Press, 1968) pars. 132-33. David Hume, in his *History of England*, also hypostatizes the passions as the real agents of history, as Adam Potkay argues in his paper, "The Cunning of the Passions in Hume's *History of England*" (27th Annual Meeting of the American Society for Eighteenth-Century Studies, March 27-31, 1996, Austin, Texas). According to Potkay, Hume's history can be seen as the history of the passions modifying themselves into interests. Burke's emphasis, as I argue, is different, as is his use of this view of history. Vico and Hume see private feelings or motives as the material that can be transformed through the agency of politicians.

119. Spenser, *The Faerie Queene* II, vii, 22. More personifications inhabit the temple of Philotime, or the love of honor, who holds the "great gold chaine" of Ambition (46).

120. Joanna Baillie, Introductory Discourse, *A Series of Plays in which it is attempted to delineate the Stronger Passions of the Mind* (London: Routledge and Thoemmes, 1996). Baillie is interested in exploring the symptomatology of the passions and in pleading the case for the passions as the true object of aesthetic representation and as the ground of nature itself: "amidst all this decoration and ornament . . . let one . . . expression of passion genuine and true to nature be introduced, and it will stand forth alone in the boldness of reality, whilst the false and unnatural around it, fade away upon every side" (21). The political overtones of her rhetoric are apparent here, as she takes over the metaphor most consistently used to describe the transition from the ancien régime to the era of revolutionary enlightenment.

121. Blair, *Lectures on Rhetoric* 315-17.

122. The phrase "other speech" I borrow from Theresa Kelley, *Reinventing Allegory* (6). It draws on the etymology of "allegory" (*allos agoreuein*).

123. The concept of temperance (which one could argue is another name for prudence but which possesses its own iconographical tradition) is particularly important to Burke's political thought—for example, his description of the legislator's art: "to temper together these opposite elements of liberty and restraint in one consistent work, requires much thought, deep reflection, a sagacious, powerful, and combining mind" (RRF 291).

124. Spenser, *The Faerie Queene* II, x, argument (259).

125. *Ibid.* II, ix, 60, and note to II, x, argument (259).

126. *Ibid.* II, x, 70 ff.

127. This bifurcation can be mapped onto the antinomy that Seamus Deane finds in Irish writing, including Burke's and Edgeworth's: "a tremulous accommodation between two discourses—one dominated by the language of sensibility, feudalized and given to nostalgia for a vanished past—and the other by the language of calculation" (*Strange Country: Modernity and Nationhood in Irish Writing since 1790* [Oxford: Clarendon, 1997] 47).

Chapter Three

1. John Scott, *Paris revisited in 1815 . . . Including a walk over the field of battle at Waterloo* (Boston: Wells and Lilly, 1816) 102.

2. See, for example, James Simpson, *A Visit to Flanders in July, 1815* (New York: Campbell, 1816), 73.

3. Scott, *Paul's Letters to his Kinsfolk*, *Prose Works of Sir Walter Scott* (Edinburgh: Robert Cadell, 1835) 150–52. Further references are hereafter cited parenthetically in the text as PL.

4. Waverley, the hero of Scott's first novel, is well-practiced in viewing a scene with a conditional response—usually, a conditional enthusiasm. Reading the report of a demonstration of feudal loyalty, "'Were it not for the recollection of Fergus's raillery,' thought Waverley to himself, when he had perused this long and grave document, 'how very tolerable would all this sound, and how little should I have thought of connecting it with any ludicrous idea!'" (*Waverley*, ed. Andrew Hook [London: Penguin, 1972] 357).

5. *The Antiquary*, ed. David Hewitt (London: Penguin Books, 1998) 3. Further references to this edition of *The Antiquary* will be cited parenthetically in the text as Ant; other editions will be cited in notes. Hewitt places the novel's action in the summer of 1794 (357); however, I believe that the date as well as the geographical setting betrays a "composite" character (361). In a footnote to the Magnum edition, omitted from Hewitt's, Scott notes that the false invasion scare with which the novel ends occurred on February 2, 1804.

6. Walter Scott, *Ivanhoe*, ed. A. N. Wilson (London: Penguin, 1984) 522.

7. Ina Ferris, *The Achievement of Literary Authority* (Ithaca: Cornell University Press, 1992) 217, 204–5. See also Michael Gamer, "Marketing a Masculine Romance," *Studies in Romanticism* 32 (1994): 523–50, as well as Ian Duncan, *Modern Romance and the Transformation of the Novel* (Cambridge: Cambridge University Press, 1992); Kathryn Sutherland, "Fictional Economies: Adam

Smith, Walter Scott, and the Novel," *ELH* 54 (1987): 97–127; and Katie Trumpener, *Bardic Nationalism* (Princeton: Princeton University Press, 1997).

8. F. R. Hart describes Lovel, the hero, as "an empty significance" in *Scott's Novels: The Plotting of Historic Survival* (Charlottesville: University of Virginia Press, 1966) 255. Alexander Welsh points out that Lovel "might as well have no bodily substance whatever" (*The Hero of the Waverley Novels* [Princeton: Princeton University Press, 1992] 103). Hart complains that "the 'present' is simply a stage for the recovery, the digging up from earth and from memory, of the past . . . all that has force or reality in *The Antiquary* . . . exists in a quasi-legendary past" (248).

9. Coleridge, *Biographia Literaria*, ed. James Engell and W. Jackson Bate, *Collected Works of Samuel Taylor Coleridge*, vol. 7 (Princeton: Princeton University Press, 1983) 1:189. More recent historians have continued to portray the period as one in which social and political differences were laid aside; see, for instance, Hugh Cunningham, "The Language of Patriotism," in *Patriotism: The Making and Unmaking of British National Identity*, ed. Raphael Samuel, 3 vols. (London: Routledge, 1989) 1:62.

10. On the nationalist politics of eighteenth-century antiquarianism, see Trumpener's important study, *Bardic Nationalism*, especially 24. But see also Colin Kidd's discussion of the anti-Buchananism of Scottish antiquarians in *Subverting Scotland's Past* (Cambridge: Cambridge University Press, 1993), as well as Fiona Robertson's study, *Legitimate Histories* (Cambridge: Cambridge University Press, 1994). Some of the political volatility of antiquarianism can be glimpsed from the example of John Leland alone: one of the first great English antiquarians, Leland was commissioned by Henry VIII to purge the monastic libraries and to construct a literary canon, a cultural pedigree of ancestors, that would prove, in Leland's words, "that no particular region may [more] justly be extolled than yours for true nobility and virtues." John Leland, *The Laboriouse Journey and Serche of John Leylande*, *Versions of History from Antiquity to Enlightenment*, ed. Donald Kelley (New Haven: Yale University Press, 1991) 350.

11. John Earle, *Microcosmography*, *Seventeenth-Century Prose and Poetry*, ed. Alexander Witherspoon and Frank Warnke (New York: Harcourt, 1982) 309–10.

12. The Scottish antiquary, Thomas Innes, for example, condemns the "impostures, flatteries, and insolence" of the bards who constructed mythical pedigrees for their patrons (cited in Trumpener, *Bardic Nationalism* 4).

13. Kidd discusses how this Jacobite antiquarian undermined the idea of an ancient "Fergusian constitution" only to try to replace it with his own "exercise in Pictish mythography" in *Subverting Scotland's Past* (101–7).

14. Thomas Carlyle, "Sir Walter Scott," *Critical and Miscellaneous Essays in Four Volumes* (Boston: Dana Estes, 1895), 3:431–32.

15. Trumpener's article, "National Character, Nationalist Plots: National Tale and Historical Novel in the Age of Waverley, 1806–1830" (*ELH* 60 [1993]: 685–731), suggests that even the national tale, by definition concerned with a peripheral fraction of the British nation, relies on the opposition of the figures of

the antiquarian and the bard, the former representing "decorative and scholarly neo-classicism" or ideological detachment even as the latter represents "the 'wild energy' of national feeling" (705). Her examples from Sydney Owenson and Charles Maturin, both contemporaries of Scott, are of particular interest and relevance.

16. See Penny Fielding, *Writing and Orality: Nationality, Culture, and Nineteenth-Century Scottish Fiction* (Oxford: Clarendon, 1996), particularly her enlightening discussion of what she terms the "paradox of orality" in Scott's *Minstrelsy of the Scottish Border* (44–58). David Daiches's discussion in "Scott's Achievement as a Novelist" is also still of interest with regard to the subject of Scott's antiquarianism (repr. in *Scott's Mind and Art*, ed. A. Norman Jeffares [New York: Barnes, 1970] 21–53).

17. David Simpson, *Romanticism, Nationalism, and the Revolt Against Theory* (Chicago: University of Chicago Press, 1993).

18. The work of Welsh, Scottish, and Irish nationalist antiquaries could and did prove embarrassing to the project of creating a greater British nationalism, as Trumpener shows.

19. Alexander Welsh has argued that the cultural authority and popularity of the Waverley Novels must be at least in part attributed to their structural commitment to the narrative of inheritance, *The Hero of the Waverley Novels*, especially 77–85.

20. As Jean-Christophe Agnew has shown, the marketplace, along with its counterpart the theater, was antithetical to notions of essence and authenticity, whether applied to persons or to collective or conventional entities. See *Worlds Apart: The Market and the Theater in Anglo-American Thought, 1550–1750* (Cambridge: Cambridge University Press, 1986).

21. The form and the logic of this argument are indebted to Michael McKeon's scheme of the dialectical development of the novel in *The Origins of the English Novel* (Baltimore: Johns Hopkins University Press, 1987).

22. A good example of the historical novel's investment in this scheme can be found at the end of *Waverley*, when Bradwardine's estate is painstakingly restored in order to be handed down to Waverley and Rose: the signs of rupture are carefully erased. The estate is whole, functional, and its ideological significance is perfectly intelligible to all involved.

23. Edmund Burke, *Reflections on the Revolution in France*, ed. L. G. Mitchell, vol. 8 of *Writings and Speeches of Edmund Burke*, ed. Paul Langford (Oxford: Clarendon, 1989) 83. Further references are hereafter cited in the text as *Reflections*.

24. The Burke-Wordsworth link examined by James Chandler in *Wordsworth's Second Nature* (Chicago: University of Chicago Press, 1984) reinforces this argument; not only does Burke become in Book Seven of the 1850 *Prelude* the personified figure of national tradition, but antiquarianism is explicitly repudiated by Wordsworth as well, in Book Seven of *The Excursion* and elsewhere. In the latter poem, Wordsworth writes that only "the unwritten story fondly traced From father to son" can illuminate the half-effaced inscriptions in

the country churchyard: against this traditionary truth stands "the sagest Antiquarian's eye," ominously blind because of its irreverence and isolation (*The Excursion* 7:921–42, in *Wordsworth: Poetical Works*, ed. Thomas Hutchinson, rev. Ernest de Selincourt [Oxford: Oxford University Press, 1988]).

25. See, for example, Stuart Piggott, *Ancient Britons and the Antiquarian Imagination* (London: Thames and Hudson, 1989), and Philippa Levine, *The Amateur and the Professional* (Cambridge: Cambridge University Press, 1986).

26. J.G.A. Pocock has usefully elucidated Burke's intellectual indebtedness to the tradition of common law, according to which actual statutes were only occasional formalizations of customs that had prevailed from time immemorial; see *Politics, Language, Time* (New York: Atheneum, 1971).

27. Linda Colley, *Britons: Forging the Nation* (New Haven: Yale University Press, 1992); Simpson, *Romanticism, Nationalism, and the Revolt Against Theory*; Seamus Deane, *The French Revolution and Enlightenment in England, 1789–1832* (Cambridge: Harvard University Press, 1988). In these years the visual representation of John Bull makes its first appearance in the caricatures of Gillray, Cruikshank, and others.

28. See Clive Emsley, *British Society and the French Wars* (London: Macmillan, 1979), and Stella Cottrell, "The Devil on Two Sticks: Franco-phobia in 1803," in Samuel, *Patriotism* 1:259–74.

29. Cited in Frank Klingberg and Sigurd Hustvedt, eds., *The Warning Drum: Broadsides of 1803* (Berkeley: University of California Press, 1944) 20.

30. "Bonaparte in Egypt!" *Ibid.* 112.

31. "The Patriot Briton—or England's Invasion," cited in Cottrell, "The Devil on Two Sticks" 263.

32. "Britons' Defiance of France," in Klingberg and Hustvedt, *The Warning Drum* 66.

33. The anxious defensiveness of what appeared to be an impregnable ideology is attested to by the fact that radicals who sought to borrow some of this rhetoric of inheritance were tried and condemned for sedition. In the 1794 trial of one farmer in Scotland, an advertisement was brought in as evidence of his seditiousness; this broadside announced that "all the Rabble—are called upon by the remembrance of their patriotic ancestors, who shed their blood in the cause of freedom" to participate in the British Convention. See Alexander Cockburn, *An Examination of the Trials for Sedition which have hitherto occurred in Scotland* (Edinburgh: David Douglas, 1888) 297–98; also the monumental study by John Barrell, *Imagining the King's Death* (Cambridge: Cambridge University Press, 2000).

34. See Pocock's *Politics, Language, Time* 208 ff., as well as McKeon, *The Origin of the English Novel* 42.

35. William Wordsworth, *The Excursion* 7:942. See Chandler, *Wordsworth's Second Nature*, on the understanding of tradition as essentially oral tradition. Chandler relates the telling anecdote in which Scott offers to send Wordsworth "some very curious letters from a spy" pertaining to the Northern Rebellion, the subject of Wordsworth's "The White Doe of Rylstone," to which the poet re-

sponds, "a plague upon your industrious Antiquarianism that has put my fine story to confusion!" (Chandler 163–64).

36. François Furet, *In the Workshop of History*, trans. Jonathan Mandelbaum (Chicago: University of Chicago Press, 1984), 77. On antiquarian methodology, see also Piggott, *Ancient Britons and the Antiquarian Imagination*.

37. "Brave Soldiers, Defenders of Your Country!" in Klingberg and Hustvedt, *The Warning Drum* 167.

38. "Shakespeare's Ghost," *ibid.* 125. On the pervasive theatricality of the period, particularly in relation to military culture, see Gillian Russell, *The Theatres of War: Performance, Politics, and Society, 1793–1815* (Oxford: Clarendon, 1995).

39. "Publicola's Postscript to the People of England," in Klingberg and Hustvedt, *The Warning Drum* 31–32.

40. [Hannah More], "The Ploughman's Ditty," *ibid.* 188–89.

41. "Declaration of the Merchants . . ." *ibid.* 127.

42. Letter to George Ellis, 27 August 1803, *The Letters of Sir Walter Scott*, ed. H.J.C. Grierson (London: Constable, 1932) 1:196–97.

43. Robert Southey, review of *Life of Wellington* by George Ellis, *Quarterly Review* (July 1815) 522. On the reception of Waterloo in Britain, see Simon Bainbridge, *Napoleon and English Romanticism* (Cambridge: Cambridge University Press, 1995) 153–82.

44. *The Gentleman's Magazine* (January 1815) iv.

45. Scott is particularly keenly aware of the language of commerce and how it can invade other contexts and decisions; in *Rob Roy*, for example, Francis Osbaldistone comments on how, when two causes demand sympathy, "our sympathy, like the funds of a compounding bankrupt, can only be divided between them," and then self-consciously notes, "my reflections . . . already began to have a twang of commerce in them" (*Rob Roy* [New York and London: Signet-Penguin, 1995] 164). Osbaldistone Senior's devoted clerk, Owen, provides a comical example of the use of commercial language to describe military feats, describing "the battle of Almanza, where the total of the British loss was summed up to give thousand men killed and wounded, besides a floating balance of missing" (301).

46. John Scott, *Paris revisited in 1815* 104.

47. For a discussion of the gradual erosion of the bounded marketplace by fairs and other examples of unregulated exchange, see Agnew, *Worlds Apart* 47–53. Agnew's argument that the deficit financing of the state in the eighteenth century placed the state "in the position of a merchant attempting to convert credibility to credit and credit, in turn, to capital" (157) suggests both the ideological necessity of the wartime rhetoric of inheritance and its ideological (in the negative sense) implausibility.

48. On the notion of the curiosity, the role it plays in Scott's fiction, and its relation to the notions of paratext and specie, see Matthew Rowlinson, "Scott Incorporated" (unpublished paper).

49. See Duncan Forbes, "The Rationalism of Sir Walter Scott," *Cambridge Journal* 7 (1953): 20–35; P. D. Garside, "Scott and the 'Philosophical Histori-

ans,'" *Journal of the History of Ideas* 36 (1975): 497–512; and more recently, James Chandler, *England in 1819* (Chicago: University of Chicago Press, 1998). See also Trumpener, *Bardic Nationalism* 72–74, as well as Robert Crawford, *Devolving English Literature* (Oxford: Clarendon, 1992) and *The Scottish Invention of English Literature* (Cambridge: Cambridge University Press, 1998); Fania Oz-Salzberger's introduction to Adam Ferguson, *An Essay on the History of Civil Society*, ed. Fania Oz-Salzberger (Cambridge: Cambridge University Press, 1995); Nicholas Phillipson, "Towards a Definition of the Scottish Enlightenment," *City and Society in the Eighteenth Century*, ed. P. Fritz and D. Williams (Toronto: University of Toronto Press, 1973).

50. Ferguson, *An Essay on the History of Civil Society* 57.

51. *Ibid.* 33. Compare Hannah Arendt, who uses the same classical sources to arrive at a strikingly similar description in *The Human Condition* (Chicago: University of Chicago Press, 1958). The gendered quality of Ferguson's discourse is well noted by Fania Oz-Salzberger in her introduction; I adopt it consciously.

52. Ferguson, *An Essay on the History of Civil Society* 56, 58.

53. *Ibid.* 24. On Ferguson and the discourse of civic virtue, see J.G.A. Pocock, *Virtue, Commerce, and History* (Cambridge: Cambridge University Press, 1985) 230 ff.

54. Cited in Oz-Salzberger, introduction to Ferguson xii. Scott writes that "its purpose was to stir up and encourage the public spirit of Scotland" (*Life and Works of John Home, Miscellaneous Prose Works*, 3 vols. [Edinburgh: Robert Cadell, 1847], 1:839). The friends who formed the core of the club were an intriguing and somewhat implausible mix; they included David Hume, John Home, who had fought on the Hanoverian side in 1745, and Lord Elibank, the head of the Jacobite faction in Scotland and an active correspondent of the exiled Stuarts. Scott describes this club and its social and cultural context in a review of Henry Mackenzie's 1824 edition of Home's works. Ferguson himself exerted his national spirit in numerous forms; for example, as a member of the Select Society, a debating club established in Edinburgh in 1754, together with David Hume, Hugh Blair, Alexander Carlyle, and others, he played an important part in the promotion of the tragedy, *Douglas*, written by their fellow member, John Home, and produced in Edinburgh in 1757 to enormous acclaim. The event was of singular importance in establishing Edinburgh's stature as a cultural rival to London. Alexander Carlyle, writing to defend *Douglas* against both the attacks of the Church and the disdain of the English, portrays Home as undertaking "to raise the reputation of his country higher than ever it was before, for fine writing, which is the first and most excellent of fine arts" and asks triumphantly in mock concern, "Have we not the greatest reason in the world to fear that the English ministry . . . will take it much amiss, that any body here should have the presumption to think he can write the English language as well as they can do in London?" (Alexander Carlyle, *An Argument to prove that the Tragedy of Douglas ought to be Publickly Burnt by the Hands of the Hangman* [Edinburgh: G. Hamilton, 1757] 18–20).

55. Ferguson, *An Essay on the History of Civil Society* 208.

56. *Ibid.* 184, 212.

57. Ernst Renan, "What is a Nation?" in *Nation and Narration*, ed. Homi K. Bhabha (London: Routledge, 1990), 19.

58. Benjamin Constant, *The Spirit of Conquest and Usurpation*, trans. Biancamaria Fontana (Cambridge: Cambridge University Press, 1988) 54–55.

59. On the circumstances surrounding the writing of the novel, see Jane Millgate, *Walter Scott: The Making of the Novelist* (Toronto: University of Toronto Press, 1984) 85–88.

60. In his own anonymous review of the novel for the *Quarterly*, Scott noted that he "has avoided the common language of narrative, and thrown his story, as much as possible into a dramatic shape . . . placing [the reader] . . . in the situation of the audience at a theatre" (review of *Tales of My Landlord*, repr. in *Prose Works* 19:4). The dramatic analogy extends further, however: repeated allusions to Jonsonian city comedy and Greek new comedy sharpen the sense that this is a world in which every object and person has a price rather than a value. For a discussion of this aspect of new comedy, see Harry Levin, *Playboys and Killjoys* (New York: Oxford University Press, 1987).

61. This disparity was brought to my attention by Rowlinson, "Scott Incorporated" (27, n.13). Lovel explains, "It was a quantity of plate which had belonged to my uncle. . . . Some time before his death he had sent orders that it should be melted down. He perhaps did not wish me to see the Glenallan arms upon it" (*The Antiquary* [New York: Lovell, Coryell, n.d.] 376).

62. Antiquarianism functions quite precisely as an ideological superstructure here, as the medium "in which men become conscious of this conflict and fight it out" (Marx, Preface to *A Contribution to the Critique of Political Economy* (1859), *The Marx-Engels Reader*, ed. Robert Tucker [New York: Norton, 1978] 5).

63. It is also important to note the role that gender plays in this scene and throughout the novel. The novel is haunted throughout by the figures of powerful women, who tyranically dominate their families through greater knowledge, economic power, or force of character: Maggie Mucklebackit, Elspeth Cheyne, the Countess of Glenallan. Even Griselda Oldbuck shows herself to be the actual master of the Monkbarns economy. Oldbuck's self-conscious "misogyny" is thus both comically justified (as a type of self-defense) and made a matter of serious reflection. The translation of the familiar topos of feudal loyalty into feminine terms in the Cheyne-Glenallan story is, in my opinion, the most interesting. But the novel plays, rather uncomfortably, with the idea that women are invisibly at the controlling heart of the social and domestic world; the post office scene supports this notion.

64. In his review of the novel, John Wilson Croker remarks, "there are two or three marvellous dreams and apparitions, upon which, we suspect, the author intended to ground some important parts of his denouement; but his taste luckily took fright . . . and they now appear in the work as marks rather of the author's own predilection to such machines, than as any assistance to him in the way of machinery" (Rev. of *The Antiquary, Quarterly Review* (April 1816) 127).

65. For example, the scenes where Elspeth Cheyne is reanimated by the spirit

of the past; the first time before Ochiltree: "she spoke . . . and accompanied her words with an attitude of the hand. . . . She then raised up her form, once tall, and still retaining the appearance of having been so . . . and stood before the beggar like a mummy reanimated by some wandering spirit" (An 218) and gives him a token to present to the Earl of Glenallan. The second time, she combines both the posture of Aldobrand Oldenbuck and Lovel, who seeks to decipher the text: "now, standing upon her feet, and holding [Glenallan] by one hand, peered anxiously on his features . . . holding her long and withered forefinger within a small distance of his face, moved it slowly as if to trace the outlines" (Ant 256). She not only uses his face as a text but also refers to a metaphorical text, where his mother's guilt will have been inscribed: "'It's a sair—sair change—and wha's fault is it?—but that is written down where it will be remembered—it's written on tablets of brass with a pen of steel'" (Ant 256). Here Elspeth offers a genuine knowledge of and from the past, but the knowledge concerns its fraudulence and guilt.

66. Burke, *Reflections* 46.

67. I have been greatly helped in thinking through the relation between money and antiquarian objects by Matthew Rowlinson's discussion, see n. 48 above.

68. J. G. Lockhart, *The Life of Sir Walter Scott* (Edinburgh: Adam and Charles Black, 1871) 1:44.

69. Walter Scott, *Minstrelsy of the Scottish Border* (Edinburgh: James Ballantyne, 1810) 1:xli–ii.

70. *The Antiquary* 384.

71. Sigmund Freud, *The Interpretation of Dreams*, trans. James Strachey (New York: Basic Books, 1965) 600.

72. See J. A. Burrow, *A Liberal Descent* (Cambridge: Cambridge Univ. Press, 1983) and Levine (note 25).

73. P. Levine, *The Amateur and the Professional* 71.

74. Edward A. Freeman, "Address to the historical section of the annual meeting of the Archaeological Institute held at Cardiff," quoted in *ibid.* 81.

75. Lionel Gossman, "History as Decipherment," *New Literary History* 18: (1986) 30.

76. I refer here to Homi Bhabha's discussion of the uncanny, which draws on both Freud's definition and Hannah Arendt's discussion of public and private worlds in *The Human Condition*; see Bhabha's *The Location of Culture* (London: Routledge, 1994).

77. Scott, "Essay on Border Antiquities," *Prose Works* 7:3.

78. *Ibid.* 3–4.

79. *Ivanhoe* 524.

80. *Ibid.* 524–25.

81. *Ibid.* 527. Characteristically, Scott offers two explanations for the existence of this "neutral ground": it may have been "handed down unaltered from [ancestors] to us," or it may reflect a "common nature" that simply subsists unchanged, despite the socioeconomic changes that he alludes to in the

phrase "state of society"—a common nature that has nothing to do with pious transmission.

82. *Ibid.* 530.

83. *Ibid.* 529.

84. Scott, *Letters of Malachi Malagrowther*, ed. P. H. Scott (Edinburgh: Blackwood, 1981) 91–92.

Chapter Four

1. "Sir Walter Scott," *Critical and Miscellaneous Essays in Four Volumes* (Boston: Dana Estes, 1895) 3:452. Further references are hereafter cited parenthetically in the text as WS.

2. "The Diamond Necklace," *Critical and Miscellaneous Essays in Four Volumes* 3:136. Further references are hereafter cited parenthetically in the text as DN.

3. In his Germanic and gendered idiom, Carlyle consistently substitutes "manhood" for the more conventional Latinate "virtue." In "Characteristics," for example, he claims, "the old ideal of Manhood has grown obsolete, and the new is still invisible to us, and we grope after it in darkness, one clutching this phantom, another that" ("Characteristics," *Critical and Miscellaneous Essays in Four Volumes* 2:371). Further references are hereafter cited parenthetically in the text as CH. For fascinating studies of "masculinity" as a problematic in Carlyle's writings, see Herbert Sussman, *Victorian Masculinities* (Cambridge: Cambridge University Press, 1995), and James Eli Adams, *Dandies and Desert Saints: Styles of Victorian Masculinity* (Ithaca: Cornell University Press, 1995). My differences with Sussman's reading of Carlyle will be discussed below. I adopt Carlyle's gendering of the reader in the hopes that this will draw attention to the exclusive and particular, rather than universal, nature of this figure.

4. While it is true that Carlyle came to represent himself as a "sage" or prophet, the "far-off Hebraic utterer" of absolute truths, for much of his career he thought of himself as a historian (Walt Whitman, "Death of Thomas Carlyle," *The Critic*, 12 February 1881, in Jules Paul Seigel, ed., *Thomas Carlyle: The Critical Heritage* [London: Routledge and Kegan Paul, 1961] 462). This tendency to view Carlyle as religious figure, prophet, apostate, or idolater, depending on one's politics, was current from the outset, though Carlyle himself seems to have often used the vatic pose mockingly and with an exaggerated Scottish inflection. Carlyle's reception is surprisingly uniform in this respect. Twentieth-century studies have analyzed Carlyle's rhetoric, as in John Holloway's *The Victorian Sage* (Hamden, Conn.: Archon Books, 1962), or applied a feminist perspective, as in Thais E. Morgan, ed. *Victorian Sages: Renegotiating Gender and Power* (New Brunswick: Rutgers University Press, 1990), or examined Carlyle as religious apostate, as in Frank Turner, *Contesting Cultural Authority* (Cambridge: Cambridge University Press, 1993); but many critics still rely on this understanding of Carlyle as prophet rather than as historian. This also needs to be viewed in light of the professionalization of history in the nineteenth century. On

Carlyle as historian, see John D. Rosenberg, *Carlyle and the Burden of History* (Cambridge: Harvard University Press, 1985); as well as A. Dwight Culler, *The Victorian Mirror of History* (New Haven: Yale University Press, 1985), and Mark Cumming, *A Disimprisoned Epic: Form and Vision in Carlyle's French Revolution* (Philadelphia: University of Pennsylvania Press, 1988).

5. See George Levine, *The Boundaries of Fiction* (Princeton: Princeton University Press, 1968).

6. Both conservatives and radicals had debated the genealogy of the English constitution, or the origins of English liberty, with the intention of using their conclusions to legitimate a particular political right, claim, or privilege. From the position of what J. W. Burrow calls "the Whig compromise," which regarded this constitutional debate as essentially settled, national history could be better used to create a common political memory for the electorate or for the larger collective entity of the nation (*A Liberal Descent* [Cambridge: Cambridge University Press, 1981] 35, 88 ff.).

7. *Ibid.* 106.

8. See Michael Fried, *Theatricality and Absorption: Painting and Beholder in the Age of Diderot* (Berkeley: University of California Press, 1980).

9. *On Heroes, Hero-Worship, and the Heroic in History*, ed. Carl Niemeyer (Lincoln: University of Nebraska Press, 1966) 122. Further references are hereafter cited parenthetically in the text as HW.

10. In his study, *Fetishism and Imagination* (Baltimore: Johns Hopkins University Press, 1982), David Simpson has usefully summed up the nature of the fetishism that seems to afflict Carlyle's texts in their strident adulation of oddly assorted heroes: "fetishism occurs when the mind ceases to realize that it has itself created the outward images or things to which it subsequently posits itself in some sort of subservient relation" (xiii). See also the valuable study by Patrick Brantlinger, *Fictions of State: Culture and Credit in Britain, 1694–1994* (Ithaca: Cornell University Press, 1996). Brantlinger shows how national identity and its corollary, public debt or credit (and indeed the nature of paper money itself), rest on the same dynamic as the fetish: misrecognizing an absence. What interests me about Carlyle's treatment of fetishism, however, is the way Carlyle treats it not as an epistemological problem akin to false consciousness but more as an ethical challenge: to subordinate oneself to one's own production.

11. Nineteenth- and twentieth-century readers, from Ernst Cassirer to Raymond Williams, have expressed embarrassment over what they perceive as Carlyle's personal fetishism and its links to sexuality. The Reverend William Sewell, for example, writing for the *Quarterly Review*, complains: "He has his saints, and martyrs, his religion and priests . . . but they are chosen by himself; and whom has he chosen? Goethe—Richter—Shakspeare —Burns!!! These are his heroes . . . out of whom he would construct a new world. . . . Carlyle . . . has chosen his idols; and of all the objects of worship to which a great and good man might be inclined, he has probably chosen the strangest" (Review of Carlyle's *Works* (1838–40), *Quarterly Review* 66 (1840), reprinted in Seigel, *Thomas Carlyle* 153). See Ernest Cassirer, *The Myth of the State* (Garden City, N.Y.: Doubleday, 1955,

c. 1946), for strong general condemnation of Carlyle; see also Raymond Williams, who, despite his appreciation for Carlyle's ideas, concludes that Carlyle's hero-worship is "impotence projecting itself as power" (*Culture and Society* [New York: Columbia University Press, 1973] 76–77). Several related problems might seem to justify the charge of fetishism: Carlyle's apparent overvaluation (to borrow Freud's term) of arbitrarily chosen objects, figures, or institutions, his failure to recognize his own role, or the mind's role generally, in the canonization of these new idols, and his insistence that these objects or figures be regarded as authoritative, powerful, and worthy of outright obedience. For a more detailed reading of Carlyle's fears about sexuality, see Sussman *Victorian Masculinities* 16–72.

12. *On Heroes, Hero-Worship* 4, 121. Carlyle's interest in fetish-worship is obviously related to his keen interest in iconoclasm.

13. Mungo Park, *Travels in the Interior Districts of Africa* (London: John Murray, 1817) 56–57.

14. Comte defines fetishism as the earliest form of theology, in which "man conceives of all external bodies as animated by a life analogous to his own," and notes that this way of thinking persists even in modernity, when "the production of unknown effects" is in question. Comte's emphasis is on the personification of given natural objects, though he also posits the importance of fetishism to the development of language (in ways quite similar to Carlyle's own accounts of language as the accumulation of dead metaphor), and even to the shift from nomadic to agricultural existence. *The Positive Philosophy of Auguste Comte*, trans. Harriet Martineau (1855; reprint, with an introduction by Abraham S. Blumberg, New York: AMS, 1974) 545–47, 549–56.

15. Hannah Arendt, *On Revolution* (London: Penguin, 1965) 92.

16. William Pietz, "The Problem of the Fetish," part 1, *Res* 9 (Spring 1985): 5–17; 7.

17. Cited in Gareth Stedman Jones, *Languages of Class* (Cambridge: Cambridge University Press, 1983) 131.

18. William Maginn, "The State and Prospects of Toryism," *Fraser's Magazine*, January 1834, 24.

19. *Sartor Resartus*, ed. Kerry McSweeney and Peter Sabor (Oxford: Oxford University Press, 1987) 215–16. Further references are hereafter cited in the text as SR.

20. *The French Revolution* (New York: H.M. Caldwell, n.d.) 351. Further references are hereafter cited in the text as FR.

21. Machiavelli, for example, understood revolution as a "periodic revitalization of civic life that can only come through a return to its original principles; Hobbes and Locke also retain an emphasis on the circularity of revolution. See Steven Smith, "Hegel and the French Revolution: An Epitaph for Republicanism," *Social Research* 56, 1 (1989): 233–61; 221.

22. *Past and Present*, ed. Richard D. Altick (New York: New York University Press, 1965) 172. Further references are hereafter cited in the text as PP.

23. P. W. Banks, "Of Politicians, Public Opinion, and the Press," *Fraser's Magazine*, July 1835, 36.

24. Carlyle practices what Emily Apter has called the "outlaw strategy of dereification" (Introduction, *Fetishism as Cultural Discourse*, ed. Emily Apter and William Pietz [Ithaca: Cornell University Press, 1993] 3). For a contemporaneous discussion of British conservatism, see William Maginn, in "The State and Prospects of Toryism," who sees conservatism as based on opposition to "arbitrary choice" (22).

25. "Signs of the Times," *Critical and Miscellaneous Essays in Four Volumes* (Boston: Dana Estes, 1895), 2:485. Further references are hereafter cited parenthetically in the text as ST. This is what Seyla Benhabib calls "defetishizing critique": "a procedure . . . whereby the given is shown to be not a natural fact but a socially and historically constituted, and thus changeable, reality" (*Critique, Norm, and Utopia* [New York: Columbia University Press, 1986] 47).

26. *Correspondence of Thomas Carlyle and Ralph Waldo Emerson*, ed. Charles Eliot Norton (Boston: Ticknor and Company, 1888) 1:43. For a persuasive and valuable interpretation of Carlyle as political radical, see Philip Rosenberg, *The Seventh Hero: Thomas Carlyle and the Theory of Radical Activism* (Cambridge: Harvard University Press, 1964). On the politics of radicalism and Chartism's relation to earlier languages of radicalism, see Gareth Stedman Jones's important essay, "Rethinking Chartism," in *Languages of Class*.

27. See Levine, *The Boundaries of Fiction* 19–78. Also, Anne Mellor, *English Romantic Irony* (Cambridge: Harvard University Press, 1980) 109–134.

28. Thomas Paine, *The Rights of Man* (Garden City: Anchor-Doubleday, 1989) 364. Further references are hereafter cited parenthetically in the text as RM.

29. The trope can be traced, for instance, back to Jonathan Swift by way of Edmund Burke and Jacobin polemic. See *A Tale of a Tub*, ed. A. C. Guthkelch and D. Nichol Smith (Oxford: Clarendon, 1920).

30. *Reflections on the Revolution in France*, ed. L. G. Mitchell, vol. 8 of *The Writings and Speeches of Edmund Burke*, ed. Paul Langford (Oxford: Clarendon, 1989) 90. Further references are hereafter cited parenthetically in the text as RRF. The phrase "bare life" I borrow from Giorgio Agamben, *Homo Sacer: Sovereign Power and Bare Life*, trans. Daniel Heller-Roazen (Stanford: Stanford University Press, 1998) 9–10.

31. Burke's local point is that socially imposed practices and socially derived beliefs can become second nature to the extent that they cannot be eradicated without a type of violence that shows itself in the end to be impolitic. See David Bromwich, *A Choice of Inheritance* (Cambridge: Harvard University Press, 1989) 45; also James Chandler, *Wordsworth's Second Nature* (Chicago: University of Chicago Press, 1984).

32. Georg Lukács, *History and Class Consciousness*, trans. Rodney Livingstone (Cambridge: MIT Press, 1971) 184.

33. *Le Père Duchesne*, No. 289, *The Press in the French Revolution*, ed. J. Gilchrist and W. J. Murray (New York: St. Martin's Press, 1971) 192. In his *Lettres sur la Législation*, Mirabeau writes, in a passage more stylistically polished but still deeply consistent with Carlyle's demystifying project: "De tout cela il

résulte que dans le fait, l'encens constitue le premier corps de l'état, l'argent le second, et la misère le troisième. Auquel des trois auriez-vous regret, si, soufflant sur toutes ces barrières . . . l'on venoit à faire table rase?" (cited in Keith Michael Baker, "Representation," in *The Political Culture of the Old Regime*, ed. Keith Michael Baker (Oxford: Pergamon Press, 1987) 481).

34. Friedrich Engels, *The Condition of the Working Class in England in 1844*, trans. W. O. Henderson and W. H. Challoner (Stanford: Stanford University Press, 1968) 25.

35. *Sartor Resartus* ponders the very question of ideology itself, as it has been put in a recent study by Michael Rosen: "Why do the many accept the rule of the few, even when it seems to be plainly against their interests to do so?" The usual answer, in Rosen's words, is "consciousness that is, in some way or other, deficient or inadequate (*On Voluntary Servitude* [Cambridge: Harvard University Press, 1996] 1–2).

36. "Diderot," *Critical and Miscellaneous Essays in Four Volumes* 3:141. Further references are hereafter cited parenthetically in the text as Did.

37. See Anne Mellor, *English Romantic Irony*, as well as Levine, *The Boundaries of Fiction*.

38. See Linda Hutcheon on irony and the formation of communities (*Irony's Edge: The Theory and Politics of Irony* [London: Routledge, 1994]).

39. James Eli Adams (*Dandies and Desert Saints*) discusses the "problematics of audience" shared by the dandy and the prophet (27).

40. On the trope of the "spirit of the age" as it eventuates in the overlapping of historical and ethnographic models of explanation, see James Chandler, *England in 1819* (Chicago: University of Chicago Press, 1998). On Carlyle and his relation to Saint-Simonianism, see Richard Pankhurst, *The St. Simonians, Mill and Carlyle* (London: Sidgwick and Jackson, 1957).

41. Cornelius Castoriadis, a thinker with remarkable affinities to Carlyle, defines the "imaginary" thus:

> This element—which gives a specific orientation to every institutional system, which overdetermines the choice and the connections of symbolic networks, which is the creation of each historical period, its singular manner of living, of seeing and of conducting its own existence, its world, and its relations with this world . . . the source of *that which presents itself in every instance as an indisputable and undisputed meaning*, the basis *for articulating what does matter and what does not*, the origin of the surplus of being of the *objects of practical, affective, and intellectual investment, whether individual or collective*—is nothing other than the imaginary of the society or of the period considered (*The Imaginary Institution of Society*, trans. Kathleen Blamey [Cambridge: MIT Press, 1987] 145; emphasis added)

The phrases I have italicized echo Carlyle most closely in thought and even in language. These affinities reveal a good deal, I think, about Carlyle's politics and philosophical orientation.

42. "The Spirit of the Age," in *Essays on Politics and Culture*, ed. Gertrude Himmelfarb (Garden City, N.Y.: Doubleday, 1962) 19.

43. *Correspondence of Thomas Carlyle and Ralph Waldo Emerson* 1:22.

44. Habermas, "Legitimation Problems in the Modern State," *Communication and the Evolution of Society*, trans. Thomas McCarthy (London: Heinemann, 1976) 183.

45. *Ibid.* 183–84.

46. *Two Notebooks of Thomas Carlyle*, ed. Charles Eliot Norton (New York: Grolier, 1898) 144.

47. *Ibid.* 164–65. Carlyle's rhetoric, particularly here, shares many features with the communitarian rhetoric of Owenism; see, for example, Stedman Jones, *Languages of Class* 120–23.

48. *Second Treatise of Government*, ed. C. B. Macpherson (Indianapolis: Hackett, 1980) 53.

49. *On Liberty* (Indianapolis: Hackett, 1978) 11.

50. Locke, *Second Treatise* 52.

51. I have found Philip Rosenberg's discussion in *The Seventh Hero* of hero-worship helpful in seeing this point.

52. Mikhail Bakhtin, *The Dialogic Imagination*, trans. Caryl Emerson and Michael Holquist (Austin: University of Texas Press, 1981) 345.

53. "Essay on Criticism" ll.297–98, in *The Poems of Alexander Pope*, ed. John Butt (New Haven: Yale University Press, 1963) 153.

54. Fried, *Theatricality and Absorption* 100. On the theatricality of both the dandy and the prophet, their shared necessity of presenting themselves "as a spectacle," see Adams, *Dandies and Desert Saints* (35).

55. For a useful summary and exploration of this idea of the symbol as it extends from Coleridge and Blake to high modernism, see Frank Kermode, *Romantic Image* (London: Routledge and Kegan Paul, 1957) 44.

56. "On History Again," *Critical and Miscellaneous Essays in Four Volumes* 3:77. Further references are hereafter cited parenthetically in the text as OH.

57. *Notebooks*, ed. Charles Eliot 231–32.

58. In "Signs of the Times," published in the *Edinburgh Review*, Carlyle draws a contrast between what he calls "mechanism," or institutionalized or bureaucratized methods of producing knowledge, and the unregulated, spontaneous operation of the "primary, unmodified forces and energies of man" (ST 474). Relying on "mechanism" means that attention is given, whether the project be political reform or scientific investigation, to the "circumstances which are without us" instead of to "the mind which is within us" and which is subject to no calculable laws (ST 472).

59. Anne Sa'adah, *The Shaping of Liberal Politics in Revolutionary France* (Princeton: Princeton University Press, 1990) 16.

60. In this regard, Carlyle continues the project of nation-building studied by Linda Colley in *Britons* (New Haven: Yale University Press, 1992); see also the essays in Raphael Samuel, ed., *Patriotism: The Making and Unmaking of British National Identity* (London: Routledge, 1989).

61. Geoffrey Cubitt, "Legitimism and the Cult of Bourbon Royalty," in *The Right in France, 1789–1997*, ed. Nicholas Atkin and Frank Tallett (London: Tauris, 1997) 51.

62. *Ibid.*

63. I am indebted to Ian Duncan for pointing out the georgic character of Carlyle's reference to the bees.

64. *Capital*, trans. Samuel Moore and Edward Aveling, ed. Frederick Engels (New York: Modern Library, 1906) 83.

65. On this dimension of theatricality, see David Marshall's study, *The Figure of Theater* (New York: Columbia University Press, 1986). See also Mona Ozouf's study, *Festivals and the French Revolution*, trans. Alan Sheridan (Cambridge: Harvard University Press, 1988). Ozouf notes that popular spontaneous festivals, as opposed to the officially orchestrated ones, relied on disguise, impersonation, and effigies (88–89); official festivals attempted to bypass mimesis and achieve a total transparency. Carlyle seems to find the latter more objectionable, in part because of the disjuncture between their stated aims and actual theatricalism.

66. Carlyle's rhetorical situating of the topos of the "primitive" other departs boldly from earlier counter-revolutionary use of this subject; Burke's *Reflections*, for example, establishes the pattern of associating "savagery" with revolutionary behavior, comparing the Parisian mob in the October Days to "a procession of American savages . . . leading [their captives] into hovels hung round with scalps" (80). Carlyle reverses the terms in a startling manner, associating the ancien régime with the "primitive" other, and giving an exemplary status, however ironically, to the latter. Carlyle assimilates ancien régime fetishism with "African" fetishism and contemplates both with an equivocal humility akin to what William Empson sees as characteristic of the mode of pastoral. See *Some Versions of Pastoral* (New York: New Directions, 1974). As in Empsonian pastoral, Carlyle situates and defines himself and his sophisticated readers "by imagining the feelings of the simple person. He may be in a better state than [they are] by luck, freshness, or divine grace" (Empson 19).

67. See, for example, Gayatri Spivak's "Three Womens' Texts and a Critique of Imperialism," in *The Feminist Reader*, ed. Catherine Belsey and Jane Moore (New York: Blackwell, 1989), 175–95.

68. Comte, for example, sees fetishism as the earliest stage of social organization; Hegel develops this view as well in *The Philosophy of History*, trans. J. Sibree (Buffalo, NY: Prometheus Books, 1991).

69. See, for example, Patrick Brantlinger's study, *Rule of Darkness: British Literature and Imperialism, 1830–1914* (Ithaca: Cornell University Press, 1988).

70. On the familiarity of fetish-worship to Holbach, Helvétius, and other European Enlightenment thinkers, see William Pietz, "Fetishism and Materialism," in *Fetishism as Cultural Discourse*, ed. Emily Apter and William Pietz (Ithaca: Cornell University Press, 1993) 137. For a useful account of the context of Mungo Park's text, and its reception, see Philip D. Curtin, *The Image of Africa*, 2 vols. (Madison: University of Wisconsin Press, 1964). See also Mary Louise Pratt, *Imperial Eyes: Travel Writing and Transculturation* (London: Routledge,

1992), and Ashton Nichols, "Mumbo Jumbo: Mungo Park and the Rhetoric of Romantic Africa," in *Romanticism, Race, and Imperial Culture, 1780–1834*, ed. Alan Richardson and Sonia Hofkosh (Bloomington: Indiana University Press, 1996) 93–113. Carlyle, who frequently refers to Park, was not alone in being captivated by Park's narrative, parts of which were even set to music by others (Curtin, *Image of Africa* 219).

71. Park, *Travels in the Interior District of Africa* 58–59. Park relates the existence of this institution to the polygamy practiced by the "Kafirs": "every one marries as many as he can conveniently maintain; and as it frequently happens that the ladies disagree among themselves, family quarrels sometimes rise to such a height, that the authority of the husband can no longer preserve peace in his household. In such cases, the interposition of Mumbo Jumbo is called in, and is always decisive" (58–59). Park explicitly interprets "Mumbo Jumbo" as a means of asserting male authority over female chaos; as an analogy to Carlyle's diagnosis of European revolution, this is in itself quite suggestive. It suggests, for example, that Carlyle feminizes the phenomenon of revolution—also a venerable counterrevolutionary maneuver. See, for example, Linda Shires, "Of Maenads, Mothers, and Feminized Males: Victorian Readings of the French Revolution," in *Rewriting the Victorians*, ed. Linda Shires (New York: Routledge, 1992) 147–65.

72. Park, *Travels* 59–60. Nichols points out that Park's text constitutes a transitional moment between a relatively benign Romantic exploratory attitude toward the African continent and the active domination pursued in the Victorian period ("Mumbo Jumbo" 105).

73. Spivak, "Three Womens' Texts" 185–86.

74. Fried, *Theatricality and Absorption* 8–35, 108–109.

75. See Hannah Arendt, *On Revolution*, on the way that the Terror was driven by impossible demands for proofs of sincerity.

76. "These Chartisms . . . are *our* French Revolution: God grant that we, with our better methods, may be able to transact it by argument alone!" ("Chartism," in *Critical and Miscellaneous Essays in Four Volumes* [Boston: Dana Estes, 1895] 4:65–66).

77. Carlyle's criticism of the public sphere accords with the trajectory that Habermas delineates in his *Structural Transformation of the Public Sphere* (trans. Thomas Burger and Frederick Lawrence [Cambridge: MIT Press, 1989]).

78. Carlyle often uses the idiom of natural law to refer to this function of history; however, he uses "the law of nature" somewhat differently from the way it was often used in the relevant historical period. Carlyle does not mean law that can be constructed by the unaided reason, as opposed to divine dispensation or existing positive law; wresting the concept away from rationalism, he defines natural law as the passive selectivity of nature. See Otto Gierke, *Natural Law and the Theory of Society, 1500–1800*, trans. and ed. Ernest Barker (Cambridge: Cambridge University Press, 1958), especially xxxv–li.

79. Stedman Jones's analysis of Chartism in *Languages of Class* stresses the centrality of this demand to the movement.

80. Hannah Arendt, *The Human Condition* (Chicago: University of Chicago Press, 1958) 136.

81. *A Midsummer Night's Dream* V.i.15.

82. For a detailed discussion of Carlyle's use of his antiquarian source, see Grace Calder, *The Writing of Past and Present* (New Haven: Yale University Press, 1949).

83. As Sussman notes, the *Edinburgh Review* praised Jocelin's Chronicle in its 1844 review for precisely this businesslike, masculine character, contrasting it with the effete monasticism of the Tractarian movement (*Victorian Masculinities* 58–59).

84. "On History Again" 82.

85. See Penny Fielding, *Writing and Orality: Nationality, Culture and Nineteenth-Century Scottish Fiction* (Oxford: Clarendon, 1996).

86. Marx's well-known analysis of commodity fetishism exposes this very dynamic as it afflicts capitalist societies, where the "products of men's hands" are perceived as "independent beings endowed with life, and entering into relation both with one another and the human race (*Capital* 83). In comparison with Carlyle, Marx's treatment of the thing is curiously undialectical. For an analysis of Marx's ideas that particularly resonates with Carlyle, see Georg Lukács's essays in *History and Class Consciousness*. On the relation between Marxian and Freudian theories of fetishism, see Laura Mulvey, *Fetishism and Curiosity* (Bloomington: Indiana University Press and London: BFI, 1996), especially 8 ff.; and Emily Apter's introduction to *Fetishism as Cultural Discourse* (1–12).

87. Freud, "Fetishism," in *Standard Edition of the Complete Psychological Works,* trans. and ed. James Strachey et al., 24 vols. (London: Hogarth Press, 1961) 21:152. In Freud's tale, the fetish functions as "a token of triumph over the threat of castration and a protection against it . . . the vehicle both of denying and of asseverating the fact of [female] castration" (154). "In later life a grown man may perhaps experience a similar panic, when the cry goes up that throne and altar are in danger, and similar illogical consequences will ensue" (153). For a development of the latter remark, see Jeffrey Mehlman, "Remy de Gourmont with Freud: Fetishism and Patriotism," in Apter and Pietz, *Fetishism as Cultural Discourse* 84–91.

88. Freud, "Splitting of the Ego in the Defensive Process," in *Standard Edition of the Complete Psychological Works,* trans. and ed. James Strachey et al., 24 vols. (London: Hogarth Press, 1964) 23:277.

89. Social critics after Carlyle have agreed in seeing the revelation of this fact as the starting point of revolution. When brought to bear on the criticism of society, as Marx does in *Capital*, the hope is that merely by revealing the constructed nature of the fetish, its humanly made character and its abject origins, the critic can resurrect this buried or latent knowledge and liberate its transformative energies. Carlyle's practice is most instructive in regard to this desire for social transformation, for his example reveals it to be simply that—a residual desire of Enlightenment rationalism. Rather than assuming that this revelation will bring about "the reappropriation of the alienated wealth of humanity" by its true pro-

ducers (Benhabib, *Critique, Norm, and Utopia* 134), Carlyle seems to hope, rather, that these makers will abase themselves before the objects and values that they have themselves created.

90. Slavoj Žižek, *The Sublime Object of Ideology* (London: Verso, 1989) 18. It is for its curious relation to knowledge or lucidity that fetishism has remained particularly interesting to postmodern critics; as Laura Mulvey has remarked, "fetishism as sign includes . . . a residual knowledge of its origin . . . a potential access to its own historical story" (*Fetishism and Curiosity* 5).

Works Consulted

Abrams, M. H. *Natural Supernaturalism: Tradition and Revolution in Romantic Literature.* New York: Norton, 1971.

Adams, James Eli. *Dandies and Desert Saints: Styles of Victorian Masculinity.* Ithaca: Cornell University Press, 1995.

Addison, Joseph. *The Spectator.* Ed. Gregory Smith. 3 vols. London: Dent, 1973.

Agamben, Giorgio. *Homo Sacer: Sovereign Power and Bare Life.* Trans. Daniel Heller-Roazen. Stanford: Stanford University Press, 1998.

Agnew, Jean-Christophe. *Worlds Apart: The Market and the Theater in Anglo-American Thought, 1550–1750.* Cambridge: Cambridge University Press, 1986.

Alexander, J. H., and David Hewitt, eds. *Scott and His Influence.* Aberdeen: Association for Scottish Literary Studies, 1983.

Alison, Archibald. *History of Europe, from the Fall of Napoleon, in 1815, to the Accession of Louis Napoleon, in 1852.* Edinburgh: Blackwood, 1853–59.

Althusser, Louis. *Lenin and Philosophy and Other Essays.* Trans. Ben Brewster. New York: Monthly Review, 1971.

Anderson, Benedict. *Imagined Communities.* Rev. Ed. London: Verso, 1991.

———. *The Spectre of Comparisons.* London: Verso, 1998.

Anderson, Olive. "The Political Uses of History in Mid-Nineteenth-Century England." *Past and Present* 36 (1967): 87–105.

The Anti-Jacobin or Weekly Examiner, 2 vols. 5th ed. London: Hatchard, 1803.

ApRoberts, Ruth. *The Ancient Dialect: Thomas Carlyle and Comparative Religion.* Berkeley: University of California Press, 1988.

Apter, Emily. Introduction to *Fetishism as Cultural Discourse.* Ed. Emily Apter and William Pietz. Ithaca: Cornell University Press, 1993. 1–9.

Arac, Jonathan, and Harriet Ritvo, eds. *Macropolitics of Nineteenth-Century Literature: Nationalism, Exoticism, Imperialism.* Philadelphia: University of Pennsylvania Press, 1991.

Arendt, Hannah. *The Human Condition.* Chicago: University of Chicago Press, 1958.

———. *On Revolution.* London: Penguin, 1965.

Armstrong, Nancy. *Desire and Domestic Fiction: A Political History of the Novel.* New York: Oxford University Press, 1987.

Ashton, John. *The Dawn of the XIXth Century: A Social Sketch of the Times.* 1886. Reprint, Detroit: Singing Tree, 1968.

Bagehot, Walter. *The English Constitution.* London: Oxford University Press, 1928.

———. "The Waverley Novels." In *Scott's Mind and Art,* ed. A. Norman Jeffares. New York: Barnes, 1970. 132–66.

Baillie, Joanna. Introductory Discourse to *A Series of Plays in which it is attempted to Delineate the Stronger Passions of the Mind.* London: Routledge and Thoemmes, 1996.

Baker, Keith Michael. Introduction to *The Political Culture of the Old Regime,* ed. Keith Michael Baker. Vol. 1 of *The French Revolution and the Creation of Modern Political Culture.* Oxford: Pergamon, 1987–89. xi–xxiv.

———. *Inventing the French Revolution.* Cambridge: Cambridge University Press, 1990.

———, ed. *The Political Culture of the Old Regime.* Vol. 1 of *The French Revolution and the Creation of Modern Political Culture.* Oxford: Pergamon, 1987–89.

———. "Representation." In *The Political Culture of the Old Regime,* ed. Keith Michael Baker, 469–92. Vol. 1 of *The French Revolution and the Creation of Modern Political Culture.* Oxford: Pergamon, 1987–89.

Bakhtin, Mikhail. *The Dialogic Imagination.* Trans. Caryl Emerson and Michael Holquist. Austin: University of Texas Press, 1981.

Banks, P. W. "Of Politicians, Public Opinion, and the Press." *Fraser's Magazine,* July 1835, 32–42.

Bann, Stephen. *The Clothing of Clio.* Cambridge: Cambridge University Press, 1984.

Barish, Jonas. *The Antitheatrical Prejudice.* Berkeley: University of California Press, 1981.

Barrel, John. *The Birth of Pandora.* Philadelphia: University of Pennsylvania Press, 1992.

———. "'An Entire Change of Performances?' The Politicisation of Theatre and the Theatricalisation of Politics in the mid-1790s." *Lumen* 17 (1998): 11–50.

———. *Imagining the King's Death.* Oxford: Oxford University Press, 2000.

Bayly, C. A. *Imperial Meridian: The British Empire and the World, 1780–1830.* London: Longman, 1989.

Beer, Gillian. *Arguing with the Past.* New York: Routledge, 1989.

Beiderwell, Bruce. *Power and Punishment in Scott's Novels.* Athens: University of Georgia Press, 1992.

Beiner, Ronald, ed. *Theorizing Nationalism.* Albany: SUNY Press, 1999.

Bellamy, Liz. *Commerce, Morality and the Eighteenth-Century Novel.* Cambridge: Cambridge University Press, 1998.

Benhabib, Seyla. *Critique, Norm, and Utopia.* New York: Columbia University Press, 1986.

Bentley, Eric. *A Century of Hero-Worship.* Philadelphia: Lippincott, 1944.

Berger, Harry. *The Allegorical Temper*. New Haven: Yale University Press, 1957.

Bermingham, Ann. *Landscape and Ideology: The English Rustic Tradition, 1740–1860*. Berkeley: University of California Press, 1986.

Bhabha, Homi. *The Location of Culture*. London: Routledge, 1994.

———. *Nation and Narration*. London: Routledge, 1990.

Blair, Hugh. *Lectures on Rhetoric and Belles Lettres*. Ed. Harold F. Harding. Carbondale: Southern Illinois University Press, 1965.

Blakemore, Steven, ed. *Burke and the Fall of Language: The French Revolution as Linguistic Event*. Hanover: University Press of New England, 1988.

———. *Burke and the French Revolution*. Athens: University of Georgia Press, 1992.

Boudon, Raymond. *An Analysis of Ideology*. Trans. Malcolm Slater. Cambridge: Polity, 1989.

Boulton, James. *The Language of Politics in the Age of Wilkes and Burke*. London: Routledge, 1963.

Bourdieu, Pierre. *Language and Symbolic Power*. Ed. John B. Thompson. Trans. Gino Raymond and Matthew Adamson. Cambridge: Harvard University Press, 1991.

———. *Outline of a Theory of Practice*. Trans. Richard Nice. Cambridge: Cambridge University Press, 1977.

Bourke, Richard. *Romantic Discourse and Political Modernity*. London: Harvester Wheatsheaf, 1993.

Brantlinger, Patrick. *Fictions of State: Culture and Credit in Britain, 1694–1994*. Ithaca: Cornell University Press, 1996.

———. *Rule of Darkness: British Literature and Imperialism 1830–1914*. Ithaca: Cornell University Press, 1988.

Brewer, John. "Commercialization and Politics." In *The Birth of a Consumer Society: The Commercialization of Eighteenth-Century England*, ed. Neil McKendrick, John Brewer, and J. H. Plumb. Bloomington: Indiana University Press, 1982. 197–262.

———. *Party Ideology and Popular Politics at the Accession of George III*. Cambridge: Cambridge University Press, 1976.

Brinton, Crane. *English Political Thought in the Nineteenth Century*. London: Benn, 1933.

Bromwich, David. *A Choice of Inheritance*. Cambridge: Harvard University Press, 1989.

———. "The Context of Burke's *Reflections*." *Social Research* 58 (1991): 313–54.

———. "Edmund Burke, Revolutionist (1795)." *Yale Journal of Criticism* 4 (1990): 85–107.

———. "Wollstonecraft as a Critic of Burke." *Political Theory* 23, 4 (1995): 617–34.

Bronson, Bertrand. "Personification Reconsidered." *ELH* 14(1947): 163–77.

Bruce, S., and S. Yearley. "The Social Construction of Tradition: The Restoration Portraits and the Kings of Scotland." In *The Making of Scotland: Nation,*

Culture, and Social Change, ed. David McCrone et al. Edinburgh: Edinburgh University Press, 1989.

Bryson, Gladys. *Man and Society: The Scottish Inquiry of the Eighteenth Century*. New York: Augustus Kelley, 1968.

Burchell, Graham, Colin Gordon, and Peter Miller, eds. *The Foucault Effect*. London: Harvester Wheatsheaf, 1991.

Burgess, Miranda. *British Fiction and the Production of Social Order, 1740–1830*. Cambridge: Cambridge University Press, 2000.

Burke, Edmund. *Correspondence of Edmund Burke*. Ed. Thomas Copeland et al. 10 vols. Cambridge: Cambridge University Press; Chicago: University of Chicago Press, 1958–78.

———. *Miscellaneous Works of Edmund Burke*. Vol. 5. Boston: Little, Brown, 1851.

———. *A Philosophical Enquiry into the Origin of Our Ideas of the Sublime and the Beautiful*. Ed. James Boulton. Notre Dame: University of Notre Dame Press, 1968.

———. *The Works of the Right Honourable Edmund Burke*. Vol. 4. 1887. Reprint, Hildesheim: Georg Olms, 1975.

———. *The Writings and Speeches of Edmund Burke*. Gen. ed. Paul Langford. 9 vols. Oxford: Clarendon, 1981–1991.

Burke, Kenneth. *Attitudes Toward History*. 3rd ed. Berkeley: University of California Press, 1984.

———. *On Symbols and Society*. Ed. Joseph P. Grisfield. Chicago: University of Chicago Press, 1989.

Burrow, J. W. *A Liberal Descent*. Cambridge: Cambridge University Press, 1981.

———. *Whigs and Liberals*. Oxford: Clarendon, 1988.

Butler, Marilyn, ed. *Burke, Paine, Godwin and the Revolution Controversy*. Cambridge: Cambridge University Press, 1984.

———. *Romantics, Rebels, and Reactionaries*. Oxford: Oxford University Press, 1981.

Buzard, James. "Translation and Tourism: Scott's *Waverley* and the Rendering of Culture." *Yale Journal of Criticism* 8 (1995): 31–59.

Calder, Grace J. *The Writing of Past and Present*. New Haven: Yale University Press, 1949.

Calhoun, Craig, ed. *Habermas and the Public Sphere*. Cambridge: MIT Press, 1992.

———. *Nationalism*. Minneapolis: University of Minnesota Press, 1997.

Canavan, Francis. *The Political Reason of Edmund Burke*. Durham: Duke University Press, 1960.

Carlyle, Alexander. *An Argument to prove that the Tragedy of Douglas ought to be Publicly Burnt by the Hands of the Hangman*. Edinburgh: G. Hamilton, 1757.

Carlyle, Thomas. *Correspondence of Thomas Carlyle and Ralph Waldo Emerson, 1834–1872*. Ed. Charles Eliot Norton. Boston: Ticknor, 1888.

———. *Critical and Miscellaneous Essays in Four Volumes, Collected and Republished*. 4 vols. Boston: Dana Estes, 1895.

————. *The French Revolution*. 2 vols. New York: H.M. Caldwell, n.d.

————. *On Heroes, Hero-Worship, and the Heroic in History*. Ed. Carl Niemeyer. Lincoln: University of Nebraska Press, 1966.

————. *Past and Present*. Ed. Richard Altick. New York: New York University Press, 1965.

————. *Sartor Resartus*. Ed. Kerry McSweeney and Peter Sabor. Oxford: Oxford University Press, 1987.

————. *Selected Works*. Ed. Julian Symons. Cambridge: Harvard University Press, 1970.

————. *Two Notebooks of Thomas Carlyle, 1822–1832*. Ed. Charles Eliot Norton. New York: Grolier, 1898.

Carter, Adam. "Insurgent Government: Romantic Irony and the Theory of the State." *Irony and Clerisy*, Romantic Circles Praxis Series, *Romantic Circles* (1999): 38 pars., online, available: *http://www.rc.umd.edu/praxis/irony/carter/schlegel.html*, December 1999.

Cascardi, Anthony. *The Subject of Modernity*. Cambridge: Cambridge University Press, 1992.

Cassirer, Ernst. *The Myth of the State*. New Haven: Yale University Press, 1946.

————. *The Question of Jean-Jacques Rousseau*. Trans. Peter Gay. New Haven: Yale University Press, 1989.

Castle, Terry. *Masquerade and Fiction: The Carnivalesque in Eighteenth-Century Culture and Fiction*. Stanford: Stanford University Press, 1986.

Chandler, James. *England in 1819*. Chicago: University of Chicago Press, 1998.

————. "Poetical Liberties: Burke's France and the 'Adequate Representation' of the English." In *The Transformation of Political Culture, 1789–1848*, ed. François Furet and Mona Ozouf, 45–58. Vol. 3 of *The French Revolution and the Creation of Modern Political Culture*. Oxford: Pergamon, 1987–89.

————. *Wordsworth's Second Nature*. Chicago: University of Chicago Press, 1984.

Chapman, Gerald. *Edmund Burke: The Practical Imagination*. Cambridge: Harvard University Press, 1967.

Chartier, Roger. *The Cultural Origins of the French Revolution*. Trans. Lydia G. Cochrane. Durham: Duke University Press, 1991.

Childers, Joseph. "Carlyle's *Past and Present*: History and a Question of Hermeneutics." *CLIO* 13 (1984): 247–58.

Christensen, Jerome. *Lord Byron's Strength: Romantic Writing and Commercial Society*. Baltimore: Johns Hopkins University Press, 1993.

Clark, J. C. D. *English Society, 1688–1832*. Cambridge: Cambridge University Press, 1985.

Clive, John. *Scotch Reviewers*. Cambridge: Harvard University Press, 1957.

Clubbe, John, and Jerome Meckier, eds. *Victorian Perspectives*. Newark: University of Delaware Press, 1989.

Cobban, Alfred. *Edmund Burke and the Revolt Against the Eighteenth Century*. London: Allen, 1929.

————. *A History of Modern France*. Harmondsworth: Penguin, 1957.

Cobbett, William. *Selections*. Ed. A. M. D. Hughes. Oxford: Clarendon, 1925.

Cockburn, Alexander Lord. *An Examination of the Trials for Sedition which have hitherto occurred in Scotland*. Edinburgh: David Douglas, 1888.

Colas, Dominique. *Civil Society and Fanaticism*. Stanford: Stanford University Press, 1997.

Coleridge, Samuel Taylor. *Biographia Literaria*. Ed. James Engell and W. Jackson Bate. Vol. 7 of *Collected Works of Samuel Taylor Coleridge*. Princeton: Princeton University Press, 1983.

———. *The Friend*. Ed. Barbara E. Rooke. Vols. 4 and 5 of *Collected Works of Samuel Taylor Coleridge*. Princeton: Princeton University Press, 1969.

———. *Miscellaneous Criticism*. Ed. T. M. Raysor. London: Constable, 1936.

Colley, Linda. *Britons: Forging the Nation, 1707–1837*. New Haven: Yale University Press, 1992.

Collingwood, R. G. *The Idea of History*. Oxford: Clarendon, 1966.

Collini, Stefan. *Public Moralists: Political Thought and Intellectual Life in Britain, 1850–1930*. Oxford: Clarendon, 1991.

Collini, Stefan, Donald Winch, and John Burrow, eds. *That Noble Science of Politics*. Cambridge: Cambridge University Press, 1983.

Comte, Auguste. *The Positive Philosophy of Auguste Comte*. Trans. Harriet Martineau. 1855. Reprint, with an introduction by Abraham A. Blumberg, New York: AMS, 1974.

Connolly, William. *Appearance and Reality in Politics*. Cambridge: Cambridge University Press, 1981.

Connor, Walker. *Ethnonationalism*. Princeton: Princeton University Press, 1994.

Constant, Benjamin. *Political Writings*. Trans. and ed. Biancamaria Fontana. Cambridge: Cambridge University Press, 1988.

Corbett, Mary Jean. *Allegories of Union in Irish and English Writing, 1790–1870: Politics, History and the Family*. Cambridge: Cambridge University Press, 2000.

———. "Public Affections and Familiar Politics: Burke, Edgeworth and the 'Common Naturalization' of Great Britain." *ELH* 61, 4 (1994): 877–97.

Cottom, Daniel. *The Civilized Imagination*. Cambridge: Cambridge University Press, 1985.

Cottrell, Stella. "The Devil on Two Sticks: Franco-phobia in 1803." In *Patriotism: The Making and Unmaking of British National Identity*, ed. Raphael Samuel. London: Routledge, 1989. 1:259–74.

Court, Franklin. *Institutionalizing English Literature*. Stanford: Stanford University Press, 1992.

Cox, Jeffrey. "Ideology and Genre in the British Antirevolutionary Drama of the 1790s." *ELH* 58 (1991): 579–610.

Craig, Cairns. "Scott's Staging of the Nation." In *Scott, Scotland and Romanticism*, ed. Ian Duncan et al. *Studies in Romanticism* 40, 1 (2001): 13–28.

Crawford, Robert. *Devolving English Literature*. Oxford: Clarendon, 1992.

———. *The Scottish Invention of English Literature*. Cambridge: Cambridge University Press, 1998.

Croker, John Wilson. Review of *The Antiquary*, by Walter Scott. *Quarterly Review* (April 1816): 125–38.

Crossley, Ceri, and Ian Small, eds. *The French Revolution and British Culture*. Oxford: Oxford University Press, 1989.

Cubitt, Geoffrey. "Legitimism and the Cult of Bourbon Royalty." In *The Right in France, 1789–1997*, ed. Nicholas Atkin and Frank Tallett. London: Tauris, 1997. 51–70.

Culler, A. Dwight. *The Victorian Mirror of History*. New Haven: Yale University Press, 1985.

Cullinan, Margaret. "History and Language in Scott's *Redgauntlet*." *SEL* 18 (1978): 659–75.

Cumming, Mark. *A Disimprisoned Epic: Form and Vision in Carlyle's French Revolution*. Philadelphia: University of Pennsylvania Press, 1988.

———. "'Such a Figure Drew Priam's Curtains!': Carlyle's Epic History of the Revolution." In *Representing the French Revolution*, ed. James A. W. Heffernan. Hanover: University Press of New England, 1992. 63–80.

Cunningham, Hugh. "The Language of Patriotism." In *Patriotism: The Making and Unmaking of British National Identity*, ed. Raphael Samuel. London: Routledge, 1989. 57–89.

Curtin, Philip D. *The Image of Africa*. 2 vols. Madison: University of Wisconsin Press, 1964.

Daiches, David. "Scott's Achievement as a Novelist." *Scott's Mind and Art*, ed. A. Norman Jeffares. New York: Barnes, 1970. 21–53.

———. "Scott's *Redgauntlet*." *Essays Collected in Memory of James Hillhouse*, ed. R. C. Rathburn and M. Steinman. Minneapolis: University of Minnesota Press, 1958. 49–59.

Dale, Peter Allan. *In Pursuit of a Scientific Culture: Science, Art, and Society in the Victorian Age*. Madison: University of Wisconsin Press, 1989.

Davies, Thomas. *Memoirs of the Life of David Garrick, Esq . . .* Boston: Wells and Lilly, 1818.

Davies, Thomas W., ed. *Committees for Repeal of the Test and Corporation Acts: Minutes 1786–90 and 1827–28*. London: London Record Society, 1978.

Davis, Leith. *Acts of Union*. Stanford: Stanford University Press, 1998.

Deane, Phyllis. *The First Industrial Revolution*. Cambridge: Cambridge University Press, 1965.

Deane, Seamus. *The French Revolution and Enlightenment in England, 1789–1832*. Cambridge: Harvard University Press, 1988.

———. *Strange Country: Modernity and Nationhood in Irish Writing since 1790*. Oxford: Clarendon, 1997.

De Bruyn, Frans. *The Literary Genres of Edmund Burke: The Political Uses of Literary Form*. Oxford: Clarendon, 1996.

De Maistre, Joseph. *Considerations on France*. Trans. and ed. Richard A. Lebrun. Cambridge: Cambridge University Press, 1994.

DeMan, Paul. *Blindness and Insight*. Minneapolis: University of Minnesota Press, 1983.

Dentith, Simon. *A Rhetoric of the Real*. London: Harvester, 1990.

Dickinson, H.T., ed. *Britain and the French Revolution, 1789–1815*. London: Macmillan, 1989.

———. *Liberty and Property*. London: Weidenfeld, 1977.

Diderot, Denis. *The Paradox of Acting*. Trans. William Archer. New York: Hill and Wang, 1957.

Dirks, Nicholas B., Geoff Eley, and Sherry B. Ortner, eds. *Culture / Power / History*. Princeton: Princeton University Press, 1994.

Doody, Margaret Anne. *A Natural Passion*. Oxford: Clarendon, 1974.

Drescher, Horst, ed. *Thomas Carlyle 1981: Papers Given at theInternational Thomas Carlyle Centenary Symposium*. Frankfurt: Langenscheidt, 1983.

Duncan, Ian. "Adam Smith, Samuel Johnson, and the Institutions of English." In *The Scottish Invention of English Literature*, ed. Robert Crawford. Cambridge: Cambridge University Press,1998. 37–54.

———. "Authenticity Effects: The Work of Fiction in Romantic Scotland." *South Atlantic Quarterly* 102, 1 (2003): 93–116.

———. *Modern Romance and Transformations of the Novel*. Cambridge: Cambridge University Press, 1992.

———. "North Britain, Inc." *Victorian Literature and Culture* 23 (1995): 339–50.

———. "Primitive Inventions: Rob Roy, Nation, and World System." *Eighteenth-Century Fiction* 15, 1 (2002): 81–102.

Duncan, Ian, et al., eds. *Scott, Scotland and Romanticism. Studies in Romanticism* 40, 1 (Spring 2001).

Dunn, John. *The History of Political Theory and Other Essays*. Cambridge: Cambridge University Press, 1996.

———. *Rethinking Modern Political Theory*. Cambridge: Cambridge University Press, 1985.

Eagleton, Terry. *Ideology: An Introduction*. London: Verso, 1995.

———, et al. *Nationalism, Colonialism, and Literature*. Minneapolis: University of Minnesota Press, 1990.

Earle, John. *Microcosmography*. In *Seventeenth Century Prose and Poetry*, ed. Alexander Witherspoon and Frank Warnke. New York: Harcourt, 1982. 309–10.

Edgeworth, Maria. *Castle Rackrent*. Ed. George Watson. New York: Oxford University Press, 1995.

Edgeworth, Richard Lovell, and Maria Edgeworth. *Essay on Irish Bulls*. London: J. Johnson, 1802.

Elbers, Joan. "Isolation and Community in *The Antiquary*." *Nineteenth-Century Fiction* 27 (1973): 405–23.

Eley, Geoff. "Nations, Publics, and Political Cultures." In *Habermas and the Public Sphere*, ed. Craig Calhoun. Cambridge: MIT Press, 1992. 289–339.

Elliott, Marianne. *Wolfe Tone: Prophet of Irish Independence*. New Haven: Yale University Press, 1989.

Empson, William. *Some Versions of Pastoral*. New York: New Directions, 1974.

Emsley, Clive. *British Society and the French Wars, 1793–1815.* London: Macmillan, 1979.

Engell, James. *The Creative Imagination.* Cambridge: Harvard University Press, 1981.

Engels, Friedrich. "The Condition of England: Review of *Past and Present* by Thomas Carlyle." In *Critics of Capitalism,* ed. Elisabeth Jay and Richard Jay. Cambridge: Cambridge University Press, 1986. 85–96.

———. *The Condition of the Working Class in England in 1844.* Trans. and ed. W. O. Henderson and W. H. Challoner. 1958. Reprint, Stanford: Stanford University Press, 1968.

Everest, Kelvin, ed. *Revolution in Writing: British Literary Responses to the French Revolution.* Philadephia: Open University Press, 1991.

Farrell, John P. *Revolution as Tragedy: The Dilemma of the Moderate from Scott to Arnold.* Ithaca: Cornell University Press, 1980.

Féher, Ferenc, ed. *The French Revolution and the Birth of Modernity.* Berkeley: University of California Press, 1990.

Ferguson, Adam. *An Essay on the History of Civil Society.* Ed. Fania Oz-Salzberger. Cambridge: Cambridge University Press, 1995.

Ferguson, Frances. *Solitude and the Sublime.* New York: Routledge, 1992.

Ferris, Ina. *The Achievement of Literary Authority: Gender, History, and the Waverley Novels.* Ithaca: Cornell University Press, 1992.

———. "Pedantry and the Question of Enlightenment History: The Figure of the Antiquary in Scott." *European Romantic Review* 13, 3 (2002): 273–83.

———. "Translation from the Borders: Encounter and Recalcitrance in *Waverley* and *Clan-Albin.*" *Eighteenth-Century Fiction* 9, 2 (1997): 203–22.

———. "Writing on the Border: The National Tale, Female Writing, and the Public Sphere." In *Romanticism, History, and the Possibilities of Genre: Re-Forming Literature, 1789–1837,* ed. Tilottama Rajan and Julia Wright. Cambridge: Cambridge University Press, 1998. 86–106.

Feuerbach, Ludwig. *The Essence of Christianity.* Trans. George Eliot. New York: Harper, 1957.

Fielding, K. J., and Rodger Tarr, eds. *Carlyle: Past and Present.* London: Vision, 1976.

Fielding, Penny. *Writing and Orality: Nationality, Culture, and Nineteenth-Century Scottish Fiction.* Oxford: Clarendon, 1996.

Fleishman, Avrom. *The English Historical Novel.* Baltimore: Johns Hopkins University Press, 1971.

Fletcher, Angus. *Allegory: The Theory of a Symbolic Mode.* Ithaca: Cornell University Press, 1964.

———. *The Prophetic Moment.* Chicago: University of Chicago Press, 1971.

Fontana, Biancamaria. Introduction to *Benjamin Constant: Political Writings,* trans. and ed. Biancamaria Fontana. Cambridge: Cambridge University Press, 1988. 1–42.

Forbes, Duncan. *The Liberal Anglican Idea of History.* Cambridge: Cambridge University Press, 1952.

———. "The Rationalism of Sir Walter Scott." *Cambridge Journal* 7 (1953): 20–35.

Forster, E. M. *Aspects of the Novel*. New York: Harcourt, 1927.

Foucault, Michel. "Two Lectures." In *Culture/Power/History*, ed. Nicholas B. Dirks, Geoff Eley, and Sherry B. Ortner. Princeton: Princeton University Press, 1994. 200–221.

Freeman, Michael. *Edmund Burke and the Critique of Political Radicalism*. Oxford: Blackwell, 1980.

Freud, Sigmund. "Fetishism." In *Standard Edition of the Complete Psychological Works*. Trans. and ed. James Strachey, et al. 24 vols. London: Hogarth Press, 1961. 21: 152–58.

———. *The Interpretation of Dreams*. Trans. James Strachey. New York: Basic Books, 1965.

———. "Splitting of the Ego in the Defensive Process." In *Standard Edition of the Complete Psychological Works*. Trans. and ed. James Strachey, et al. 24 vols. London: Hogarth Press, 1964. 23: 275–78.

Fried, Michael. *Absorption and Theatricality: Painting and Beholder in the Age of Diderot*. Berkeley: University of California Press, 1980.

Friedman, Barton. *Fabricating History: English Writers on the French Revolution*. Princeton: Princeton University Press, 1988.

Fry, Michael. *The Dundas Despotism*. Edinburgh: Edinburgh University Press, 1992.

Fulford, Tim, and Peter J. Kitson, eds. *Romanticism and Colonialism: Writing and Empire, 1780–1830*. Cambridge: Cambridge University Press, 1998.

Furet, François. *In the Workshop of History*. Trans. Jonathan Mandelbaum. Chicago: University of Chicago Press, 1984.

———. *Interpreting the French Revolution*. Trans. Elborg Forster. Cambridge: Cambridge University Press, 1981.

Furet, François, and Mona Ozouf, eds. *The Transformation of Political Culture, 1789–1848*. Vol. 3 of *The French Revolution and the Creation of Modern Political Culture*. Oxford: Pergamon, 1987–89.

Furniss, Tom. *Edmund Burke's Aesthetic Ideology*. Cambridge: Cambridge University Press, 1993.

Fussell, Paul. *The Rhetorical World of Augustan Humanism: Ethics and Imagery from Swift to Burke*. Oxford: Clarendon, 1965.

Gadamer, Hans-Georg. *Truth and Method*. 2nd ed. Trans. Joel Weinsheimer and Donald Marshall. New York: Crossroads, 1989.

Gallagher, Catherine. *The Industrial Reformation of English Fiction*. Chicago: University of Chicago Press, 1985.

———. *Nobody's Story: The Vanishing Acts of Women Writers in the Marketplace, 1670–1820*. Berkeley: University of California Press, 1994.

Gamer, Michael. "Marketing a Masculine Romance." *Studies in Romanticism* 32 (1994): 523–50.

———. *Romanticism and the Gothic: Genre, Reception, and Canon-Formation*. Cambridge: Cambridge University Press, 2000.

Garside, Peter D. "Hidden Origins of *Waverley*." *Nineteenth-Century Literature* 46 (1991): 30–53.

————. "Scott, the Eighteenth Century, and the New Man of Sentiment." *Anglia* 103 (1985): 71–89.

————. "Scott and the 'Philosophical Historians.'" *Journal of the History of Ideas* 36 (1975): 497–512.

————. "*Waverley*'s Pictures of the Past." *ELH* 44 (1977): 659–82.

Gay, Peter. *The Enlightenment: The Rise of Modern Paganism.* New York: Norton, 1977.

Geertz, Clifford. *The Interpretation of Cultures.* New York: Basic, 1973.

Gellner, Ernest. *Nations and Nationalism.* Oxford: Blackwell, 1983.

————. *Reason and Culture.* Cambridge: Blackwell, 1992.

————. *Thought and Change.* Chicago: University of Chicago Press, 1964.

Geuss, Raymond. *The Idea of a Critical Theory.* Cambridge: Cambridge University Press, 1981.

Gierke, Otto. *Natural Law and the Theory of Society, 1500–1800.* Trans. and ed. Ernest Barker. Cambridge: Cambridge University Press, 1958.

Gildon, Charles. *The Life of Mr. Thomas Betterton.* 1710. Reprint, New York: Augustus Kelley, 1970.

Gilmartin, Kevin. *Print Politics: The Press and Radical Opposition in Early Nineteenth-Century England.* Cambridge: Cambridge University Press, 1996.

Godechot, Jacques. *The Counter-Revolution: Doctrine and Action, 1789–1804.* Trans. Salvator Attanasio. New York: Howard Fertig, 1971.

Godwin, William. *An Enquiry Concerning Political Justice.* Ed. F. E. L. Priestley. 3 vols. Toronto: University of Toronto Press, 1946.

Goethe, Johann Wolfgang von. *Wilhelm Meister's Apprenticeship and Travels.* Trans. Thomas Carlyle. 2 vols. London: Chapman, 1824.

Goodman, Dena. *The Republic of Letters.* Ithaca: Cornell University Press, 1994.

Goodwin, Albert. *The Friends of Liberty.* Cambridge: Harvard University Press, 1979.

Gordon, Robert. *Under Which King?* New York: Barnes, 1969.

Gossman, Lionel. *Between History and Literature.* Cambridge: Harvard University Press, 1990.

————. "History as Decipherment: Romantic Historiography and the Discovery of the Other." *New Literary History* 18 (1986): 23–57.

Gramsci, Antonio. *Selections from the Prison Notebooks.* Ed. and trans. Quintin Hoare and Geoffrey Nowell. New York: International Publishers, 1971.

Greenblatt, Stephen. *Renaissance Self-Fashioning.* Chicago: University of Chicago Press, 1980.

Grenby, M. O. *The Anti-Jacobin Novel.* Cambridge: Cambridge University Press, 2001.

Gross, David. *The Past in Ruins: Tradition and the Critique of Modernity.* Amherst: University of Massachusetts Press, 1992.

Habermas, Jürgen. *Communication and the Evolution of Society.* Trans. Thomas McCarthy. London: Heinemann, 1979.

————. *The Philosophical Discourse of Modernity*. Trans. Frederick Lawrence. Cambridge: MIT Press, 1987.

————. *The Structural Transformation of the Public Spheres*. Trans. Thomas Burger and Frederick Lawrence. Cambridge: MIT Press, 1989.

Halévy, Elie. *A History of the English People in 1815*. Trans. E. I. Watkins and D. A. Barber. London: Unwin, 1926.

Hall, John A. and I. C. Jarvie, eds. *Transition to Modernity*. Cambridge: Cambridge University Press, 1992.

Hamilton, Paul. "*Waverley*: Scott's Romantic Narrative and Revolutionary Historiography." *Studies in Romanticism* 33(1994): 611–34.

Handwerk, Gary. *Irony and Ethics in Narrative*. New Haven: Yale University Press, 1985.

Hanley, Keith, and Raman Selden, eds. *Revolution and Romanticism: Politics and Rhetoric*. New York: St. Martin's, 1990.

Harris, Wendell. "Interpretive Historicism: 'Signs of the Times' and *Culture and Anarchy* in their Contexts." *Nineteenth-Century Literature* 44 (1990): 441–64.

Hart, F. R. *Scott's Novels: The Plotting of Survival*. Charlottesville: University of Virginia Press, 1966.

Hartman, Geoffrey. *Beyond Formalism*. New Haven: Yale University Press, 1970.

————. *Criticism in the Wilderness*. New Haven: Yale University Press, 1980.

Harvie, Christopher. *Scotland and Nationalism*. London: Allen and Unwin, 1966.

Hayden, John O., ed. *Scott: The Critical Heritage*. New York: Barnes, 1970.

Hazlitt, William. *The Spirit of the Age*. London: Dent, 1910.

Hébert, Jacques-René. *Le Père Duchesne*, No. 289 (1793). In *The Press in the French Revolution*, ed. J. Gilchrist and W. J. Murray. New York: St Martin's, 1971. 192–93.

Hechter, Michael. *Containing Nationalism*. Oxford: Oxford University Press, 2000.

Heffernan, James A. W., ed. *Representing the French Revolution*. Hanover: University Press of New England, 1992.

Hegel, G.W.F. *Aesthetics*. Trans. T. M. Knox. Oxford: Clarendon, 1975.

Heller, Agnes. *A Theory of History*. London: Routledge, 1982.

Herbert, Christopher. *Culture and Anomie: Ethnographic Imagination in the Nineteenth Century*. Chicago: University of Chicago Press, 1991.

Herder, Johann Gottfried von. *Reflections on the Philosophy of the History of Mankind*. Ed. Frank Manuel. Chicago: University of Chicago Press, 1968.

Higonnet, Patrice. "Cultural Upheaval and Class Formation During the French Revolution." In *The French Revolution and the Birth of Modernity*, ed. Ferenc Féher. Berkeley: University of California Press, 1990. 69–102.

Hill, Aaron. *The Art of Acting: An Essay, in which the Dramatic Passions are properly defined and described*. London: Smeeton, 1801.

Himmelfarb, Gertrude. *The New History and the Old*. Cambridge: Harvard University Press, 1987.

Hirsch, Gordon. "History Writing in Carlyle's *Past and Present*." *Prose Studies* 7, 3 (1984): 225–31.

Hirschman, Albert O. *The Passions and the Interests*. Princeton: Princeton University Press, 1977.

———. *The Rhetoric of Reaction*. Cambridge: Harvard University Press, 1991.

Hobsbawm, Eric, ed. *The Invention of Tradition*. Cambridge: Cambridge University Press, 1983.

———. *Nations and Nationalism since 1780*. Cambridge: Cambridge University Press, 1990.

Hofkosh, Sonia. *Sexual Politics and the Romantic Author*. Cambridge: Cambridge University Press, 1998.

Hole, Robert. *Pulpits, Politics, and Public Order in England, 1760–1832*. Cambridge: Cambridge University Press, 1989.

Holloway, John. *The Victorian Sage*. Hamden: Archon, 1962.

Home, John. *Douglas*. Ed. Hubert J. Tunney. Lawrence, Kansas: University of Kansas Press, 1924.

———. *History of the Rebellion of 1745*. London: Cadell and Davies, 1802.

Honig, Bonnie. *Political Theory and the Displacement of Politics*. Ithaca: Cornell University Press, 1993.

Hont, Istvan, and Michael Ignatieff, eds. *Wealth and Virtue*. Cambridge: Cambridge University Press, 1983.

Hook, Sidney. *From Hegel to Marx*. 1936. Reprint, Ann Arbor: University of Michigan Press, 1962.

Howell, Wilbur Samuel. *Eighteenth-Century British Logic and Rhetoric*. Princeton: Princeton University Press, 1971.

Hoy, David Couzen. "Deconstructing 'Ideology.'" *Philosophy and Literature* 18,1 (1994): 1–17.

Hume, David. *Essays: Moral, Political and Literary*. Ed. Eugene F. Miller. 1889. Reprint, Indianapolis: Liberty Classics, 1987.

———. *A Treatise of Human Nature*. Ed. L. A. Selby-Bigge. 2nd ed. Rev. P. H. Nidditch. Oxford: Clarendon, 1989.

Hunt, Lynn. *The Family Romance of the French Revolution*. Berkeley: University of California Press, 1992.

———. *Politics, Culture, and Class in the French Revolution*. Berkeley: University of California Press, 1984.

Hunter, R.L. *The New Comedy of Greece and Rome*. Cambridge: Cambridge University Press, 1985.

Hutcheon, Linda. *Irony's Edge: The Theory and Politics of Irony*. London: Routledge, 1994.

Iser, Wolfgang. *The Implied Reader*. Baltimore: Johns Hopkins University Press, 1974.

James, William. *Pragmatism and the Meaning of Truth*. Cambridge: Harvard University Press, 1975.

———. *The Will to Believe and Human Immortality*. 1897. Reprint, New York: Dover, 1956.

Jameson, Fredric. *The Political Unconscious*. Ithaca: Cornell University Press, 1981.

Jay, Elisabeth, and Richard Jay, eds. *Critics of Capitalism*. Cambridge: Cambridge University Press, 1986.

Jeffares, A. Norman, ed. *Scott's Mind and Art*. New York: Barnes, 1970.

Johnson, Claudia. *Equivocal Beings: Politics, Gender, and Sentimentality in the 1790s*. Chicago: University of Chicago Press, 1995.

Johnston, Kenneth, and Gene Ruoff, eds. *The Age of William Wordsworth*. New Brunswick: Rutgers University Press, 1987.

Jones, Gareth Stedman. *Languages of Class: Studies in English Working-Class History, 1832–1982*. Cambridge: Cambridge University Press, 1983.

Kaiser, David Aram. *Romanticism, Aesthetics, and Nationalism*. Cambridge: Cambridge University Press, 1999.

Kaufmann, David. *The Business of Common Life*. Baltimore: Johns Hopkins University Press, 1995.

Kay, Carol. *Political Constructions*. Ithaca: Cornell University Press, 1988.

Keane, Angela. *Women Writers and the English Nation in the 1790s: Romantic Belongings*. Cambridge: Cambridge University Press, 2000.

Keen, Paul. *The Crisis of Literature in the 1790s*. Cambridge: Cambridge University Press, 1999.

Kelley, Donald, ed. *Versions of History from Antiquity to Enlightenment*. New Haven: Yale University Press, 1991.

Kelley, Theresa. *Reinventing Allegory*. Cambridge: Cambridge University Press, 1997.

Kennedy, Emmet, and Marie-Laurence Netter. Conclusion to *Theatre, Opera, and Audiences in Revolutionary Paris*, ed. Emmet Kennedy and Marie-Laurence Netter, et al. Westport, Conn.: Greenwood Press, 1996. 87–90.

———. "High Culture and Popular Culture: Paris Theatre Audiences, the Critics, and the Police." In *Theatre Opera, and Audiences in Revolutionary Paris*, ed. Emmet Kennedy, et al. Westport, Conn.: Greenwood Press, 1996. 75–86.

Kidd, Colin. *Subverting Scotland's Past*. Cambridge: Cambridge University Press, 1993.

Klancher, Jon P. *The Making of English Reading Audiences, 1790–1832*. Madison: University of Wisconsin Press, 1987.

Klingberg, Frank, and Sigurd Hustvedt, eds. *The Warning Drum: Broadsides of 1803*. Berkeley: University of California Press, 1944.

Knapp, Steven. *Personification and the Sublime: Milton to Coleridge*. Cambridge: Harvard University Press, 1985.

Koselleck, Reinhart. *Critique and Crisis*. Cambridge: MIT Press, 1988.

Kroll, Richard. *The Material Word*. Baltimore: Johns Hopkins University Press, 1991.

Landes, Joan. *Women and the Public Sphere in the Age of the French Revolution*. Ithaca: Cornell University Press, 1988.

Landow, George P. *Elegant Jeremiahs: The Sage from Carlyle to Mailer*. Ithaca: Cornell University Press, 1986.

Laski, Harold. *Political Thought in England from Locke to Bentham*. London: Thorton Butterworth, 1920.

LaValley, Albert. *Carlyle and the Idea of the Modern.* New Haven: Yale University Press, 1968.

Lawson, John. *Lectures Concerning Oratory, Delivered at Trinity College, Dublin.* London: W. Bowyer, 1759.

Lefebvre, George. *The Coming of the French Revolution.* Trans. R. R. Palmer. Princeton: Princeton University Press, 1947.

Leland, John. *The Laboriouse Journey and Serche of John Leylande.* In *Versions of History from Antiquity to Enlightenment*, ed. Donald Kelley. New Haven: Yale University Press, 1991. 349–54.

Levin, Harry. *Playboys and Killjoys.* New York: Oxford University Press, 1987.

Levine, George. *The Boundaries of Fiction.* Princeton: Princeton University Press, 1968.

———. *The Realistic Imagination.* Chicago: University of Chicago Press, 1981.

Levine, Philippa. *The Amateur and the Professional.* Cambridge: Cambridge University Press, 1986.

Lichtheim, George. *The Concept of Ideology and Other Essays.* New York: Random House, 1967.

Litvak, Joseph. *Caught in the Act: Theatricality in the Nineteenth-Century English Novel.* Berkeley: University of California Press, 1990.

Liu, Alan. *Wordsworth: The Sense of History.* Stanford: Stanford University Press, 1989.

Lock, F. P. *Burke's Reflections on the Revolution in France.* London: Allen, 1985.

Locke, John. *Second Treatise of Government.* Ed. C. B. Macpherson. Indianapolis: Hackett, 1980.

Lockhart, J. G. *The Life of Sir Walter Scott.* Edinburgh: Adam and Charles Black, 1871.

Lukács, Georg. *The Historical Novel.* Trans. Hannah Mitchell and Stanley Mitchell. Lincoln: University of Nebraska Press, 1983.

———. *History and Class Consciousness.* Trans. Rodney Livingstone. Cambridge: MIT Press, 1971.

———. *The Theory of the Novel.* Trans. Anna Bostock. Cambridge: MIT Press, 1971.

Lukes, Steven. *Individualism.* Oxford: Blackwell, 1973.

Lynch, Deidre. *The Economy of Character: Novels, Market Culture, and the Business of Inner Meaning.* Chicago: University of Chicago Press, 1998.

———. "Nationalizing Women and Domesticating Fiction: Edmund Burke, Property, and the Reproduction of Englishness." In *Romanticism, Race, and Imperial Culture, 1780–1834*, ed. Alan Richardson and Sonia Hofkosh. Bloomington: Indiana University Press, 1996. 40–71.

Macaulay, Thomas Babington. *Essays Critical and Miscellaneous.* Philadelphia: Hart, 1951.

———. *The History of England from the Accession of James the Second.* 6 vols. *The Works of Lord Macaulay.* London: Longmans Green, 1898.

———. *Napoleon and the Restoration of the Bourbons.* Ed. Joseph Hamburger. New York: Columbia University Press, 1977.

MacCormick, Neil. "Nation and Nationalism." In *Theorizing Nationalism*, ed. Ronald Beiner. Albany: SUNY Press, 1999. 189–204.

Macherey, Pierre. *A Theory of Literary Production*. Trans. Geoffrey Wall. London: Routledge, 1978.

Machiavelli, Niccolo. *The Prince*. Trans. Harvey C. Mansfield. Chicago: University of Chicago Press, 1985.

Macintyre, Alasdair. *Against the Self-Images of the Age*. New York: Schocken Books, 1971.

Mackintosh, James. *Vindiciae Gallicae*. 1791. Reprint, Oxford: Woodstock, 1989.

Macpherson, C. B. *The Political Theory of Possessive Individualism*. Oxford: Clarendon, 1962.

Maginn, William. "The State and Prospects of Toryism." *Fraser's Magazine*, Jan. 1834, 1–25.

Mahoney, Thomas H. D. *Edmund Burke and Ireland*. Cambridge: Harvard University Press, 1960.

Maine, Henry Sumner. *Ancient Law*. Gloucester: Peter Smith, 1970.

Makdisi, Saree. *Romantic Imperialism: Universal Empire and the Culture of Modernity*. Cambridge: Cambridge University Press, 1998.

Mandell, Laura. "'Those Limbs Disjointed of Gigantic Power': Barbauld's Personifications and the (Mis)Attribution of Political Agency." *Studies in Romanticism* 37 (1998): 27–41.

Mandeville, Bernard. *The Fable of the Bees: or, Private Vices, Public Benefits*. Ed. F. B. Kaye. 2 vols. Oxford: Clarendon, 1924.

Mannheim, Karl. *Ideology and Utopia*. Trans. Louis Wirth and Edward Shils. New York: Harcourt, 1936.

Mansfield, Harvey C. *Statesmanship and Party Government*. Chicago: University of Chicago Press, 1965.

Manuel, Frank. *Freedom from History*. New York: New York University Press, 1971.

Marshall, David. *The Figure of Theater*. New York: Columbia University Press, 1986.

Marx, Karl. *Capital*. Trans. Samuel Moore and Edward Aveling. Ed. Frederick Engels. New York: Modern Library, 1906.

———. *The Economic and Philosophic Manuscripts of 1844*. Ed. Dirk J. Struik. New York: International, 1964.

———. *The Eighteenth Brumaire of Louis Bonaparte*. Trans. Eden Paul and Cedar Paul. London: Allen and Unwin, 1926.

———. Preface to *A Contribution to the Critique of Political Economy*. In *The Marx-Engels Reader*, ed. Robert Tucker. New York: Norton, 1978.

Marx, Karl and Friedrich Engels. *The German Ideology*. Ed. C. J. Arthur. New York: International, 1989.

Maza, Sarah. "The Diamond Necklace Affair Revisited." In *Eroticism and the Body Politic*, ed. Lynn Hunt. Baltimore: Johns Hopkins University Press, 1991. 63–89.

McCalman, Iain. "Mad Lord George and Madame La Motte: Riot and Sexuality in the Genesis of Burke's *Reflections on the Revolution in France*." *Journal of British Studies* 35, 3(1996): 343–67.

————. *Radical Underworld*. Cambridge: Cambridge University Press, 1988.

McCrone, David, et al., eds. *The Making of Scotland*. Edinburgh: Edinburgh University Press, 1989.

McGann, Jerome. *The Romantic Ideology*. Chicago: University of Chicago Press, 1983.

McKendrick, Neil, ed. *Historical Perspectives: Studies in English Thought and Society*. London: Europa, 1974.

McKeon, Michael. *The Origins of the English Novel*. Baltimore: Johns Hopkins University Press, 1987.

McMaster, Graham. *Scott and Society*. Cambridge: Cambridge University Press, 1981.

Mehta, Uday Singh. *Liberalism and Empire: A Study in Nineteenth-Century British Liberal Thought*. Chicago: University of Chicago Press, 1999.

Meinecke, Friedrich. *Historism*. Trans. J. E. Anderson. New York: Herder, 1972.

Mellor, Anne. *English Romantic Irony*. Cambridge: Harvard University Press, 1980.

Michasiw, Kim Ian. "Nine Revisionist Theses on the Picturesque." *Representations* 38 (1992): 76–100.

Mill, John Stuart. *Essays on Politics and Culture*. Ed. Gertrude Himmelfarb. Garden City: Doubleday, 1962.

————. *On Liberty*. Ed. Elizabeth Rappaport. Indianapolis: Hackett, 1978.

Millar, John. *Origin of the Distinction of Ranks*. 1771. Reprint, Edinburgh: Blackwood, 1806.

Miller, David. *On Nationality*. Oxford: Clarendon, 1995.

————. *Philosophy and Ideology in Hume's Political Thought*. Oxford: Clarendon, 1994.

Miller, J. Hillis. "'Hieroglyphical Truth' in *Sartor Resartus*: Carlyle and the Language of Parable." In *Victorian Perspectives*, ed. John Clubbe and Jerome Meckier. Newark: University of Delaware Press, 1989. 1–20.

Millgate, Jane. *Walter Scott: The Making of the Novelist*. Toronto: University of Toronto Press, 1984.

Mitchell, W. J. T. *Iconology*. Chicago: University of Chicago Press, 1986.

Morgan, Thaïs E. *Victorian Sages and Cultural Discourse*. New Brunswick: Rutgers University Press, 1990.

Morris, Marilyn. *The British Monarchy and the French Revolution*. New Haven: Yale University Press, 1998.

Mullan, John. *Sentiment and Sociability*. Oxford: Clarendon, 1988.

Mulvey, Laura. *Fetishism and Curiosity*. Bloomington: Indiana University Press and London: BFI, 1996.

————. "Xala, Ousmane Sembene 1976: The Carapace That Failed." In *Colonial Discourse and Post-Colonial Theory*, ed. Patrick Williams and Laura Chrisman. New York: Columbia University Press, 1994. 517–34.

Myers, Mitzi. "Goring John Bull: Maria Edgeworth's Hibernian High Jinks versus the Imperialist Imaginary." In *Cutting Edges*, ed. James Gill. Knoxville: University of Tennessee Press, 1995. 367–94.

Nairn, Tom. *The Break-up of Britain*. London: New Left Books, 1977.

———. *Faces of Nationalism: Janus Revisited*. London: Verso, 1997.

Neff, Emery. *Carlyle and Mill*. New York: Columbia University Press, 1926.

Neill, Michael. "Mantles, Quirks, and Irish Bulls: Ironic Guise and Colonial Subjectivity in Maria Edgeworth's *Castle Rackrent*." *Review of English Studies* 52, 205 (2001): 76–90.

Newman, Gerald. *The Rise of English Nationalism*. New York: St. Martin's, 1987.

Nichols, Ashton. "Mumbo Jumbo: Mungo Park and the Rhetoric of Romantic Africa." In *Romanticism, Race, and Imperial Culture, 1780–1834*, ed. Alan Richardson and Sonia Hofkosh. Bloomington: Indiana University Press, 1996. 93–113.

Nietzsche, Friedrich. *On the Use and Abuse of History*. Trans. Adrian Collins. Indianapolis: Bobbs-Merrill, 1957.

Nye, Robert. "Medical Origins of Sexual Fetishism." In *Fetishism as Cultural Discourse*, ed. Emily Apter and William Pietz. Ithaca: Cornell University Press, 1993. 13–30.

Oakeshott, Michael. *On History and Other Essays*. Oxford: Blackwell, 1983.

O'Brien, Conor Cruise. *The Great Melody*. Chicago: University of Chicago Press, 1992.

Ogden, C. K. *Bentham's Theory of Fictions*. New York: Harcourt, Brace, 1932.

Orgel, Stephen. *The Illusion of Power*. Berkeley: University of California Press, 1975.

Orr, Linda. "The Revenge of Literature: A History of History." *New Literary History* 18 (1986): 1–22.

Ozouf, Mona. *Festivals and the French Revolution*. Trans. Alan Sheridan. Cambridge: Harvard University Press, 1988.

Oz-Salzberger, Fania. Introduction to *An Essay on the History of Civil Society*, by Adam Ferguson. Ed. Fania Oz-Salzberger. Cambridge: Cambridge University Press, 1995. vi–xxv.

———. *Translating the Enlightenment*. Oxford: Clarendon, 1995.

Paine, Thomas. *The Rights of Man*. 1791. Reprint, Garden City: Anchor-Doubleday, 1989.

Palmer, R. R. *The Improvement of Humanity*. Princeton: Princeton University Press, 1985.

Park, Mungo. *Travels in the Interior Districts of Africa*. London: John Murray, 1817.

Parliamentary Register. Vol. 25. London: Debrett, 1789.

Paulson, Ronald. *Representations of Revolution, 1789–1820*. New Haven: Yale University Press, 1983.

Perkin, Harold. *The Origins of Modern English Society, 1780–1880*. London: Routledge and Kegan Paul, 1969.

Peterson, Linda. *Victorian Autobiography: The Tradition of Self-Interpretation*. New Haven: Yale University Press, 1986.

Phillips, Mark. "Macaulay, Scott, and the Literary Challenge to Historiography." *Journal of the History of Ideas* 50 (1989): 117–33.

Phillipson, Nicholas. "Towards a Definition of the Scottish Enlightenment." In *City and Society in the Eighteenth Century*, ed. P. Fritz and D. Williams. Toronto: University of Toronto Press, 1973.

Pietz, William. "Fetishism and Materialism: The Limits of Theory in Marx." In *Fetishism as Cultural Discourse*, ed. Emily Apter and William Pietz. Ithaca: Cornell University Press, 1993. 119–51.

———. "The Problem of the Fetish," part 1. *Res* 9 (Spring 1985): 5–17.

Piggott, Stuart. *Ancient Britons and the Antiquarian Imagination*. London: Thames and Hudson, 1989.

Pinch, Adela. *Strange Fits of Passion: Epistemologies of Emotion, Hume to Austen*. Stanford: Stanford University Press, 1996.

Plotz, John. *The Crowd: British Literature and Public Politics*. Berkeley: University of California Press, 2000.

Plumb, J. H. *The Origins of Political Stability in England, 1675–1725*. Boston: Houghton Mifflin, 1967.

Pocock, J. G. A. "Edmund Burke and the Redefinition of Enthusiasm." In *The Transformation of Political Culture, 1789–1848*, ed. François Furet and Mona Ozouf. Vol. 3 of *The French Revolution and the Creation of Modern Political Culture*. Oxford: Pergamon, 1987–89. 19–43.

———. *Politics, Language, Time*. New York: Atheneum, 1971.

———. *Virtue, Commerce, and History*. Cambridge: Cambridge University Press, 1985.

Poole, Ross. *Nation and Identity*. London and New York: Routledge, 1990.

Popkin, Richard H. *The History of Scepticism from Erasmus to Spinoza*. Berkeley: University of California Press, 1979.

Poston, Lawrence. "Millites and Millenarians: The Context of Carlyle's 'Signs of the Times.'" *Victorian Studies* 26 (1983): 381–406.

Potkay, Adam. "The Cunning of the Passions in Hume's *History of* England." Paper presented at the 27th annual meeting of the American Society for Eighteenth-Century Studies, Austin, Texas, 27–31 March 1996.

Pratt, Mary Louise. *Imperial Eyes: Travel Writing and Transculturation*. London: Routledge, 1992.

Price, Richard. *Additional Observations on the Nature and Value of Civil Liberty, and the War with America*. In *Political Writings*, ed. D.O. Thomas. Cambridge: Cambridge University Press, 1991. 76–100.

———. "A Discourse on the Love of Country." In *Political Writings*, ed. D. O. Thomas. Cambridge: Cambridge University Press, 1991. 176–96.

———. *Observations on the Nature of Civil Liberty, the Principles of Government, and the Justice and Policy of the War with America*. In *Political Writings*, ed. D. O. Thomas. Cambridge: Cambridge University Press, 1991. 20–75.

Pyle, Forest. *The Ideology of Imagination*. Stanford: Stanford University Press, 1995.

Rajan, Tilottama. *Dark Interpreter*. Ithaca: Cornell University Press, 1980.

Rajan, Tilottama and Julia Wright, eds. *Romanticism, History, and the Possibilities of Genre*. Cambridge: Cambridge University Press, 1998.

Rawson, Claude. *Order from Confusion Sprung: Studies in Eighteenth Century Literature from Swift to Cowper*. London: Allen and Unwin, 1985.

Reid, Christopher. *Edmund Burke and the Practice of Political Writing*. Ireland: Gill and Macmillan, 1985.

Renan, Ernst. "What Is a Nation?" In *Nation and Narration*, ed. Homi K. Bhabha. London: Routledge, 1990.

Reynolds, Joshua. *Discourses on Art*. In *The Literary Works of Sir Joshua Reynolds*. 3 vols. London: T. Cadell, 1819.

Richardson, Alan. *Literature, Education, and Romanticism: Reading as Social Practice, 1780–1832*. Cambridge: Cambridge University Press, 1994.

———, and Sonia Hofkosh, eds. *Romanticism, Race, and Imperial Culture, 1780–1834*. Bloomington: Indiana University Press, 1996.

Ricoeur, Paul. *Lectures on Ideology and Utopia*. Ed. George H. Taylor. New York: Columbia University Press, 1986.

Rigby, Brian. "Radical Spectators of the Revolution: The Case of the *Analytical Review*." In *The French Revolution and British Culture*, ed. Ceri Crossley and Ian Small. Oxford: Oxford University Press, 1989. 63–83.

Robbins, Keith. *Nineteenth-Century Britain: Integration and Diversity*. Oxford: Clarendon, 1988.

Roberts, David. *Paternalism in Early Victorian England*. New Brunswick: Rutgers University Press, 1979.

Robertson, Fiona. *Legitimate Histories*. Cambridge: Cambridge University Press, 1994.

Robinson, Nicholas. *Edmund Burke: A Life in Caricature*. New Haven: Yale University Press, 1996.

Rorty, Richard. *Contingency, Irony, Solidarity*. New York: Cambridge University Press, 1989.

Rosen, Michael. *On Voluntary Servitude: False Consciousness and the Theory of Ideology*. Cambridge: Harvard University Press, 1996.

Rosenberg, John D. *Carlyle and the Burden of History*. Cambridge: Harvard University Press, 1985.

Rosenberg, Philip. *The Seventh Hero: Thomas Carlyle and the Theory of Radical Activism*. Cambridge: Harvard University Press, 1974.

Ross, Marlon. "Romancing the Nation State." In *Macropolitics of Nineteenth-Century Literature: Nationalism, Exoticism, Imperialism*, ed. Jonathan Arac and Harriet Ritvo. Philadelphia: University of Pennsylvania Press, 1991. 56–85.

Rousseau, Jean-Jacques. *Politics and the Arts: Letter to M. d'Alembert on the Theatre*. Trans. Allan Bloom. Glencoe, Ill.: Free Press, 1960.

———. *The Social Contract and Discourses*. Trans. G. D. H. Cole, Rev. J. H. Brumfitt, and John C. Hall. London: Dent, 1973.

Rowlinson, Matthew. "Scott Incorporated" (unpublished paper).

Ruskin, John. *Modern Painters*. Vol. 2. London: Smith, Elder, 1873.

Russell, Gillian. "Burke's Dagger: Theatricality, Politics and Print Culture in the 1790s." *British Journal of Eighteenth Century Studies* 20 (1997): 1–16.

———. *The Theatres of War: Performance, Politics, and Society, 1793–1815*. Oxford: Clarendon, 1995.

Sa'adah, Anne. *The Shaping of Liberal Politics in Revolutionary France*. Princeton: Princeton University Press, 1990.

Said, Edward. *Culture and Imperialism*. New York: Knopf, 1993.

Samuel, Raphael, ed. *Patriotism: The Making and Unmaking of British National Identity*. 3 vols. London: Routledge, 1989.

Schama, Simon. *Citizens*. New York: Knopf, 1989.

Schenk, H. G. *The Aftermath of the Napoleonic Wars*. New York: Oxford University Press, 1947.

Schiller, Friedrich von. *Naive and Sentimental Poetry*. Trans. Julius Elias. New York: Ungar, 1966.

Schlegel, Friedrich. *Philosophical Fragments*. Trans. Peter Firchow. Foreword by Rodolph Gasché. Mineapolis: University of Minnesota Press, 1991.

Schochet, Gordon. *Patriarchalism in Political Thought*. New York: Basic Books, 1975.

Schor, Esther. *Bearing the Dead*. Princeton: Princeton University Press, 1994.

Scott, John. *Paris Revisited in 1815*. Boston: Wells and Lilly, 1816.

Scott, Walter. *The Antiquary*. Ed. David Hewitt. London: Penguin, 1998.

———. *The Bride of Lammermoor*. Ed. Fiona Robertson. Oxford: Oxford University Press, 1991.

———. *The Fortunes of Nigel*. New York: Routledge, n.d.

———. *Heart of Midlothian*. Ed. David Daiches. New York: Rinehart, 1957.

———. *Ivanhoe*. Ed. A. N. Wilson. London: Penguin, 1984.

———. *Letters of Malachi Malagrowther*. Ed. P. H. Scott. Edinburgh: Blackwood, 1981.

———. *Letters of Sir Walter Scott*. Ed. H. J. C. Grierson. 12 vols. London: Constable, 1933.

———. *Minstrelsy of the Scottish Border*. 2 vols. Edinburgh: Ballantyne, 1810.

———. *Miscellaneous Prose Works*. 3 vols. Edinburgh: Robert Cadell, 1847.

———. *Old Mortality*. Ed. Angus Calder. London: Penguin, 1975.

———. *The Prose Works of Sir Walter Scott*. 30 vols. Edinburgh: Robert Cadell, 1835.

———. *Quentin Durward*. New York: Modern Library, n.d.

———. *Redgauntlet*. Ed. Kathryn Sutherland. Oxford: Oxford University Press, 1985.

———. *Rob Roy*. Edinburgh: Black, 1863.

———. *Tales of a Grandfather*. 3rd series. Vols. 1–2. Boston: Parker, 1834.

———. *Waverley*. Ed. Andrew Hook. London: Penguin, 1985.

Seidelman, Steven, ed. *Jürgen Habermas on Society and Politics*. Boston: Beacon, 1989.

Seigel, Jules, ed. *Thomas Carlyle: The Critical Heritage*. London: Routledge, 1971.

Sennett, Richard. *The Fall of Public Man*. New York: Norton, 1976.

Sewell, William. Review of Carlyle's *Works*. *Quarterly Review* 66 (1840). In *Thomas Carlyle: The Critical Heritage*, ed. Jules Paul Seigel. London: Routledge and Kegan Paul, 1971.

Shaw, Harry E. *The Forms of Historical Fiction*. Ithaca: Cornell University Press, 1983.

Shils, Edward. *Tradition*. Chicago: University of Chicago Press, 1981.

Shires, Linda. "Of Maenads, Mothers, and Feminized Males." In *Rewriting the Victorians*, ed. Linda Shires. New York: Routledge, 1992. 147–65.

———, ed. *Rewriting the Victorians*. New York: Routledge, 1992.

Simpson, David. *Fetishism and Imagination*. Baltimore: Johns Hopkins University Press, 1982.

———. *Irony and Authority in Romantic Poetry*. Totowa, N.J.: Rowman and Littlefield, 1979.

———, ed. *The Origins of Modern Critical Thought*. Cambridge: Cambridge University Press, 1988.

———. *Romanticism, Nationalism, and the Revolt Against Theory*. Chicago: University of Chicago Press, 1993.

Simpson, James. *A Visit to Flanders in July, 1815*. New York: Campbell, 1816.

Siskin, Clifford. *The Historicity of Romantic Discourse*. New York: Oxford University Press, 1988.

———. *The Work of Writing*. Baltimore: Johns Hopkins University Press, 1998.

Sloterdijk, Peter. *Critique of Cynical Reason*. Trans. Michael Eldred. Foreword by Andreas Huyssen. Minneapolis: University of Minnesota Press, 1987.

Smith, Adam. *The Theory of Moral Sentiments*. Ed. D. D. Raphael and A. L. Macfie. 1976. Reprint, Indianapolis: Liberty Fund, 1982.

———. *The Wealth of Nations*. Ed. Andrew Skinner. London: Penguin, 1986.

Smith, Charlotte. *The Emigrants*. *The Poems of Charlotte Smith*. Ed. Stuart Curran. New York: Oxford University Press, 1993.

Smith, Olivia. *The Politics of Language, 1791–1819*. Oxford: Clarendon, 1984.

Smith, R. J. *The Gothic Bequest: Medieval Institutions in British Thought, 1688–1863*. Cambridge: Cambridge University Press, 1987.

Smith, Steven. "Hegel and the French Revolution: An Epitaph for Republicanism." *Social Research* 56, 1 (1989): 233–61.

Sorenson, Janet. *The Grammar of Empire in Eighteenth-Century British Writing*. Cambridge: Cambridge University Press, 2000.

Southey, Robert. Rev. of *Life of Wellington*, by George Elliott. *Quarterly Review* (April 1815): 215–75, (July 1815): 448–526.

Spenser, Edmund. *The Faerie Queene*. Ed. A. C. Hamilton. London: Longman, 1977.

Spivak, Gayatri. "Three Womens' Texts and a Critique of Imperialism." In *The Feminist Reader*, ed. Catherine Belsey and Jane Moore. New York: Blackwell, 1989. 175–95.

Stanlis, Peter J. *Edmund Burke and the Natural Law*. Ann Arbor: University of Michigan Press, 1958.

Steinberg, Marc. "Citizenship Claims in Early Nineteenth-Century England." In
    Citizenship, Identity and Social History, ed. Charles Tilly. Cambridge: Cam-
    bridge University Press, 1995. 19–50.
Stephen, Leslie. *A History of English Thought in the Eighteenth Century*. Vol. 2.
    New York: Peter Smith, 1949.
Suleri, Sara. *The Rhetoric of English India*. Chicago: University of Chicago Press,
    1992.
Sussman, Herbert. *Victorian Masculinities*. Cambridge: Cambridge University
    Press, 1995.
Sutherland, Kathryn. "Fictional Economies: Adam Smith, Walter Scott and the
    Nineteenth-Century Novel." *ELH* 54 (1987): 97–127.
Swift, Jonathan. *A Tale of A Tub*. Ed. A. C. Guthkelch and D. Nichol Smith.
    Oxford: Clarendon, 1920.
Taussig, Michael. "*Maleficium*: State Fetishism." In *Fetishism as Cultural Dis-
    course*, ed. Emily Apter and William Pietz. Ithaca: Cornell University Press,
    1993. 217–47.
Taylor, Charles. "The Politics of Recognition." In *Multiculturalism*, ed. Amy
    Gutmann. Princeton: Princeton University Press, 1994. 25–74.
———. *Philosophical Arguments*. Cambridge: Harvard University Press,
    1995.
Thomas, D. O. Introduction to *Richard Price: Political Writings*, ed. D. O.
    Thomas. Cambridge: Cambridge University Press, 1991. vii–xxii.
Thompson, E. P. *The Making of the English Working Class*. New York: Vintage,
    1966.
Thompson, F. M. L., ed. *Cambridge Social History of Britain, 1750–1950*. 3 vols.
    Cambridge: Cambridge University Press, 1990.
Thompson, John B., *Ideology and Modern Culture*. Stanford: Stanford University
    Press, 1990.
Thompson, John B., and David Held, eds. *Habermas: Critical Debates*. London:
    Macmillan, 1982.
Thorslev, Peter. "Post-Waterloo Liberalism: The Second Generation." *Studies in
    Romanticism* 28 (1989): 437–61.
Todd, Janet. *Sensibility: An Introduction*. London: Methuen, 1986.
Trilling, Lionel. *Sincerity and Authenticity*. Cambridge: Harvard University
    Press, 1972.
Trumpener, Katie. *Bardic Nationalism*. Princeton: Princeton University Press,
    1997.
———, "National Character, Nationalist Plots: National Tale and Historical
    Novel in the Age of *Waverley, 1806–1830*." *ELH* 60 (1993): 685–731.
Tucker, Robert, ed. *The Marx-Engels Reader*. New York: Norton, 1978.
Turner, Frank. *Contesting Cultural Authority*. Cambridge: Cambridge University
    Press, 1993.
United Kingdom. *History of the Proceedings and Debates of the House of Commons
    . . . During the Sixth Session of the Sixteenth Parliament of Great Britain*. Vol.
    25. London: Debrett, 1789.

Valente, Joseph. "Upon the Braes: History and Hermeneutics in *Waverley*." *Studies in Romanticism* 25 (Summer 1986): 251–76.

Van Oort, Richard. "Three Models of Fiction: the Logical, the Phenomenological, and the Anthropological (Searle, Ingarden, Gans)." *New Literary History* 29, 3 (1998): 439–66.

Veeser, H. Aram, ed. *The New Historicism*. New York: Routledge, 1989.

Wang, Orrin. "Romancing the Counter-Public Sphere: A Response to *Romanticism and its Publics*." *Studies in Romanticism* 33, 4(1994): 579–88.

Waterman, A. M. C. *Revolution, Economics, and Religion: Christian Political Economy, 1798–1833*. Cambridge: Cambridge University Press, 1991.

Watson, Nicola. *Revolution and the Form of the British Novel, 1790–1825: Intercepted Letters, Interrupted Seductions*. Oxford: Clarendon, 1994.

Watts, Michael R. *The Dissenters*. Oxford: Clarendon, 1978.

Welsh, Alexander. *George Eliot and Blackmail*. Cambridge: Harvard University Press, 1985.

———. *The Hero of the Waverley Novels with New Essays on Scott*. 1963. Princeton: Princeton University Press, 1992.

———. *Strong Representations*. Baltimore: Johns Hopkins University Press, 1992.

West, Shearer. *The Image of the Actor: Verbal and Visual Representation in the Age of Garrick and Kemble*. London: Pinter, 1991.

Whale, John. *Imagination Under Pressure*. Cambridge: Cambridge University Press, 2000.

Whelan, Frederick. *Order and Artifice in Hume's Political Philosophy*. Princeton: Princeton University Press, 1985.

Whelan, Kevin. *The Tree of Liberty: Radicalism, Catholicism, and the Construction of Irish Identity, 1760–1830*. Notre Dame: University of Notre Dame Press, 1996.

White, Hayden. *Metahistory: The Historical Imagination in Nineteenth-Century Europe*. Baltimore: Johns Hopkins University Press, 1973.

———. *Tropics of Discourse*. Baltimore: Johns Hopkins University Press, 1978.

White, James Boyd. *When Words Lose Their Meaning*. Chicago: University of Chicago Press, 1984.

White, R. J. *Waterloo to Peterloo*. London: Heinemann, 1957.

Williams, Bernard. *Problems of the Self*. Cambridge: Cambridge University Press, 1973.

Williams, David. *Lessons to a Young Prince by an Old Statesman on the Present Disposition in Europe to a General Revolution*. In *Select Pamphlets*. Philadelphia: Mathew Carey, 1796.

Williams, Raymond. *Culture and Society*. 1958. Reprint, New York: Columbia University Press, 1973.

———. *Keywords*. New York: Oxford University Press, 1983.

———. *Writing in Society*. London: Verso, 1983.

Wilt, Judith. *Secret Leaves: The Novels of Sir Walter Scott*. Chicago: University of Chicago Press, 1985.

Winch, Donald. "The Burke-Smith Problem and Late Eighteenth-Century Political and Economic Thought." *The Historical Journal* 28 (1985): 231–47.

Wolin, Sheldon. "Hume and Conservatism." In *Hume: A Re-Evaluation*, ed. Donald W. Livingston and James T. King. New York: Fordham University Press, 1976. 239–56.

Wollstonecraft, Mary. *A Vindication of the Rights of Men; and, A Vindication of the Rights of Woman*. Ed. D. L. Macdonald and Kathleen Scherf. Ontario, Canada: Broadview, 1997.

Wood, Neal. "The Aesthetic Dimension of Burke's Political Thought." *Journal of British Studies* 4,1 (1964): 41–64.

Wordsworth, William. *Wordsworth: Poetical Works*. Ed. Thomas Hutchinson, rev. Ernest de Selincourt. Oxford: Oxford University Press, 1988.

Worthen, William. *The Idea of the Actor*. Princeton: Princeton University Press, 1984.

Wright, Julia M. "'I am ill fitted': Conflicts of Genre in Eliza Fenwick's *Secresy*." In *Romanticism, History, and the Possibilities of Genre: Re-forming Literature, 1789–1837*, ed. Tilottama Rajan and Julia Wright. Cambridge: Cambridge University Press, 1998. 149–75.

Young, Arthur. *Travels in France During the Years 1787, 88, and 89*. Ed. Constantia Maxwell. Cambridge: Cambridge University Press, 1950.

Zerilli, Linda. *Signifying Woman: Culture and Chaos in Rousseau, Burke, and Mill*. Ithaca: Cornell University Press, 1994.

Žižek, Slavoj. *Mapping Ideology*. London: Verso, 1994.

———. *The Sublime Object of Ideology*. London: Verso, 1989.

Index

Adams, James Eli, 180n.3, 184n.39
Addison, Joseph, 171n.118
Agamben, Giorgio, 183n.30
agency, radical ideas of, 47–51, 166n.49
Agnew, Jean-Christophe, 174n.20, 176n.47
allegory, 60–61, 72–73, 139–40, 163n.6, 171n.118
Althusser, Louis, 167n.59
Anderson, Benedict, 8, 149n.21
Anti-Jacobin, 11, 77
antiquarianism
    attitude of professional historians toward, 101
    and the marketplace, 78–79, 83–84, 87–88, 89–90, 178n.62
    and national unity, 75–76, 173n.10, 174n.18
    object of, 135
    and patriotic traditionalism, 76–79, 80–82, 104, 174n.24
    See also Scott, Sir Walter
Apter, Emily, 183n.24
Arendt, Hannah, 49, 109, 177n.51, 187n.75
artifice, 42–46, 61–63
authority, 35, 110–11, 127–28. *See also* Carlyle, Thomas; fetishism

Baillie, Joanna, 72, 171n.120
Baker, Keith Michael, 161n.147
Bakhtin, Mikhail, 9, 122, 151n.28
Banks, P. W., 162n.157
Barrell, John, 148n.6, 161n.151, 175n.33
Benhabib, Seyla, 51, 183n.25, 188n.89

Bernard, John, 118
Bhabha, Homi, 8, 179n.76
Blair, Hugh, 40, 73, 163nn.8–9
Blakemore, Steven, 163n.2
Bolton, Betsy, 148n.6
Boulton, J.T., 162n.2
Bourdieu, Pierre, 156nn.92, 94
Brantlinger, Patrick, 160n.143, 181n.10
Britain
    class divisions in, 114, 116–18, 134
    and empire, 31–32, 126, 128, 131–32, 143
    industrialization, 32, 110, 115–16
    theatrical public sphere, 133–34
Bromwich, David, 160n.136, 165n.33, 183n.31
Bull, John, 81, 175n.27
Bulwer-Lytton, Edward, 118
Burgess, Miranda, 148n.6, 155n.84, 150n.132
Burke, Edmund, 113, 125, 127, 168n.68, 172n.123, 183n.29
    as conservative ideologist, 8, 46, 162n.159, 174n.24
    and Dissenters, 47
    on habit, 4, 114, 142, 183n.31
    on inheritance, 98, 144
    and Ireland, 25–28, 172n.127
    and irony, 6, 9, 11, 24, 29, 111, 112, 115, 145
    Letter to a Noble Lord, 28, 117
    Letter on a Regicide Peace, *IV*, 62
    Observations on a Late State of the Nation, 59
    Philosophical Enquiry, 41, 52, 66–67, 68, 168n.69

217